To Lee Prussia,

who was first to extend me the opportunity to employ my Fed watching talents, and to whom I am forever grateful — Bob Jones

POWER OF COINAGE

HINDSIGHT OF FED WATCHER

By Robert A. Jones

Educational Dynamic Systems, publisher

Educational Dynamic Systems,
Incline Village, NV 89450-7498

Printed in the United States of America
Library of Congress Catalog Card Number 87-82380

ISBN 0-9619135-0-9

Contents

Introduction

There is always the risk that this book was created by ego instead of need. There has been a long-standing need, however, for either financial market participants or market economists to accurately record the structure and functioning of various financial markets. These potential authors lack the required time because of the press of professional demands. There seems to be an unmet need among students, market trainees, members of Congress, and academicians for descriptive material which this book hopefully fulfills.

Information about Federal Reserve structuring and operations has been in abundant supply. Such information is included throughout this book with the belief that its depth will be its distinguishing feature. Anticipating varied readership acquaintance with principles of monetary theory, a "building block" approach toward theoretical understanding was used in the context of historical narratives. No attempt was made to write a history book, and historical references were therefore general.

Historical narratives do not readily facilitate an organization of descriptive material which is neatly isolated by subject matter. Many structural changes of the past were interrelated, the understanding of which is best facilitated by following more of an historical outline than a topical one. Yet chapter headings in this book use a subject outline in order to give a general emphasis on the different subject matter contemporaneously evolving from the past.

The building block approach used means that the introduction to basic concepts is gradually expanded in latter chapters to include all relevant sophistication of today's monetary theory. The progressive path starts with Congressional delegation of its power of coinage to the Federal Reserve. The second chapter emphasizes that controlling monetary growth is no easy matter, which leads to the constant question of whether controlling monetary growth is an important national objective. This book subsequently makes a detailed examination of the tools of monetary control, concluding that Congress has not adequately monitored Federal Reserve use of these tools.

Apart from a useful educational purpose, this book is dedicated toward (and hopefully distinguished by) new theoretical observations. The most important of these is that the demand for bank credit is inelastic to interest rate changes and, at times, business loan demands defy theory by sloping upward (that is, increase as interest rates rise). Such demand behavior contrasts sharply with the interest elastic demand for domestic non-financial debt (aggregate credit demand). The inelasticity of bank credit demand belies Federal Reserve attempts to control money supply growth by targeting money rate changes as a means of regulating the demand for money (bank credit).

When Federal Reserve officials use the term "demand for money," they usually are referring to the demand for checkable deposits, or more specifically, the demand to *hold* money. When interest rates rise, the demand for non-checkable deposits is supposed to rise because interest rates payable on these savings and time deposits rise faster than rates payable on checkable deposits. Such increased opportunity cost of holding highly liquid checkable deposit credit reduces the "demand for money" when interest rates rise.

The so-called "demand for money" assumes that non-checkable deposit credit does not represent money even though it serves as a store of value. Though non-checkable deposit credit technically does not serve as a medium of exchange, it is sufficiently liquid for Federal Reserve officials to target their growth as a part of M2 (which, at the time of this writing, commands greater policy emphasis than M1 or M3).

The "demand for money" concept can be expanded, recognizing that yields on such liquid assets as treasury bills often rise relative to rates on non-checkable M2 assets. The opportunity cost of holding time and savings deposits is also increased when interest rates rise. It is therefore deemed appropriate for Federal Reserve officials to attempt regulating M2 growth by controlling the "demand for money" through money rate targeting.

However, the broader the monetary aggregate targeted, the less valid the notion of money rate targeting becomes. Investments in non-bank securities must be paid for with bank deposit credit. A non-checkable M2 asset, which is transferred by its owner to a checkable account for purposes of buying a treasury bill, will not disappear as deposit credit in the banking system. The seller of the treasury bill will deposit proceeds of the bill sale, perhaps in a non-checkable M2 account. The dollar deposit base of the banking system is not affected by financial transactions motivated by interest rate spreads, though these spreads impact deposit composition. Accordingly, the greater the proportion of total deposits (bank credit) included in a monetary aggregate, the less responsive "money demand" will be to money rate targeting. However, there is a substantial difference between the demand to *hold* money as opposed to the demand for *additional* money.

There are a few economists (including some at the Federal Reserve) who view the "demand for money" as the demand for bank credit. Almost all money supply growth occurs when a bank (or thrift) creates new checkable deposit credit through loans or investments. This book will emphasize that such bank credit extended through loans and investments is influenced more over the short run by the demand for bank credit than by the availability of reserve credit. Money supply growth is thus determined, in this view, by the supply of reserves and the demand for bank credit. The demand for bank credit and the demand for additional money are the same. This is a traditionalist view of bank credit which monetarists have long disavowed, but is the viewpoint supported by detailed analyses in the beginning chapters.

In addition, some traditionalists advocate Fed targeting of bank credit rather than a monetary aggregate. The latter involves circulating currency which is irrelevant to money supply growth. More importantly, if deposit shifts are as fluid as M2 advocates claim, then the entirety of the dollar deposit base (bank credit) should be the focus of controlling monetary expansion (as opposed to any volatile subcomponent). This book supports the bank credit emphasis of traditionalists.

Federal Reserve targeting of money rates to limit the demand for money (bank credit), and hence money supply growth, has not been successful. Monetary growth has, in fact, exceeded targeted growth rates much more often under money rate targeting than under reserve targeting. This failure is caused mainly by the interest rate inelasticity of demand for bank credit (money).

Admittedly, interest rates which are quite high, relative to an underlying rate of inflation, will eventually weaken the growth of gross national product and national income. There is no known theoretical debate about the *income* elasticities of various types of credit demands. Hence, the demand for new money (deposit credit extended through bank loans and investments) can be influenced by interest rates, but only after the restraining effects of higher rates are transmitted through weakened income flows impacting the demand for bank credit.

This book also distinguishes non-cost from cost methods of restraining monetary growth. Conventional theory implicitly assumes that the cost of money (money rates such as the Fed funds rate) accurately reflects the amount of reserve restraint administered by officials of the Federal Reserve System. A high 14 percent discount rate, however, can be accompanied by an accommodative reserve policy to create a 14 percent Fed funds rate. Conversely, a 4 percent discount rate can be accompanied by appreciable reserve restraint to create a 7 percent Fed funds rate. Though reserve restraint increases the spread of the Fed funds rate over the discount rate, such reserve restraint nonetheless has far less interest rate effect than increases in the discount rate.

Whereas discount rate policy can be used as the principal means to raise the cost of money, reserve restraint is treated in this book as a non-cost focus on limiting the availability of reserve credit, and thus limiting the growth of deposit credit. If there is a cost approach used to restrain monetary growth, such outcome will occur after weakening the economy.

A non-cost approach is presented as a means of more readily influencing the behavior of monetary aggregates, with significantly less economic impact. Accordingly, non-cost strategies inherent in reserve targeting by the Federal Reserve address the dual objectives of full employment and price stability better than the cost emphasis of funds rate targeting. Rate targeting in the past has helped to reduce monetary growth and price inflation, but at the expense of significantly higher unemployment rates. Reserve targeting during the 1960s, in contrast, was accompanied by less volatile economic conditions and more moderate money growth and prices.

Structural weakening of the Federal Reserve System by Congress is closely examined, and helps explain why Federal Reserve officials have retreated from using reserve management as a primary tool of monetary control. An attempt is made to convince the reader that there are both room and reason for improving the Federal Reserve's efficiency in controlling the growth of the nation's money supply.

Other new theoretical observations define the enormous economic risks of the recent replacement of monetary objectives with economic objectives of monetary policy. The income velocity of money is theoretically removed from financial sector influences to arrive at an exclusive real sector picture; and velocities of money and credit aggregates are differentiated by cyclical and secular patterns.

Behind today's rather confusing picture of money velocities are substantial problems of accurately defining and measuring money. The inventory of problems presented is quite detailed as well as demoralizing. Yet, money does matter, and any policy neglect of monetary growth cannot be justified merely by the challenge of definitional and measurement problems.

There seems to be a language barrier impeding Congressional exercise of its responsibility to properly delegate its power of coinage to the Federal Reserve. To overcome barriers to understanding, the beginning definitional steps taken in Chapter One are quite basic, yet sufficiently comprehensive to permit the stripping away of a number of widely-held mis-impressions supporting the language barriers. In this connection, a long-overdue theoretical emphasis is placed on liability management as one of the key links between reserve management and bank asset management. Even the latter has been badly misrepresented in print by those who lack the experience of bank management.

One of the shortcomings of this manuscript is an occasional lack of empirical evidence to fully support theoretical conclusions. Detailed data were often not available. Hopefully, the logical support given will encourage gifted econometricians to attack or defend some of the new theory advanced. Pride of authorship is not particularly strong because suggested structural re-definitions and theoretical conclusions proposed in this book were obtained from contacts with the more than one hundred leading financial and monetary economists throughout the world, with whom Money Market Services conducts weekly surveys of market opinion. Because Money Market Services is the only entity conducting extensive market opinion surveys (since 1977), its economists are regarded as experts in the field of market opinion (as well as in other fields of professional endeavor). While much of this manuscript reflects structural and theoretical perceptions collected from other economists, I must fully accept responsibility for its editorial criticism of the U.S. Congress and the Federal Reserve System.

I believe that financial structures and relationships are more accurately defined in this text than in academic and government forecasting models, partly because these definitions formed the basis for the accurate forecasting of major interest rate swings of the past 15 years.

If this manuscript has value-added for the economics profession, then credit the author and editors for good intermediation, and credit the collective genius of market participants for good thoughts.

This book is intended to be a call for Congressional action. New information may be interesting, yet of minimal value unless it leads to corrective policy actions. I believe that sufficient knowledge has been developed in economics to promote maximum growth of global living standards; this knowledge can soon replace military solutions to economic problems. This is the economic objective toward which the collective effort of many to publish this book has been dedicated.

Robert A. Jones
Lake Tahoe
May, 1987

CHAPTER 1

Delegating the Power of Coinage

THE MEDIUMS OF EXCHANGE

Coins

Money is traditionally defined as a medium of exchange and a store of value. As a medium of exchange, money must be easily carried and readily accepted in exchange for goods and services. Metal coin was the most common medium of exchange prior to this century, in contrast to the personal and business checking accounts so widely used today.

The historical acceptance and use of coins as a medium of exchange depended on their ability to serve as a store of value. Coins were usually made of scarce metal, such as gold or silver, to ensure that a limited supply would preserve their purchasing power in the marketplace. As an additional supply constraint, national governments generally were granted exclusive powers of coinage.

Currency

The United States Constitution grants the power of coinage exclusively to the federal government. During the Civil War years, legislation broadened this power to include the issuance of paper currency. A shortage of Treasury holdings of gold and silver necessitated the payment of Union Army wages in promissory notes rather than coin. Congress subsequently enacted the Legal Tender Act, which required merchants to accept the new notes as payment on all debts, or else the debts could be declared null and void.

Since enactment of the Legal Tender Act, all Treasury currency has declared: "This note is legal tender for all debts, public and private." With this statement, the government forces its currency to be accepted as a medium of exchange, even though the currency's supply may not be sufficiently restricted to maintain its purchasing power in the marketplace.

Few people realize that the issuance of currency and coin in the United States no longer represents a source of money supply growth. Today, the federal government is not allowed to issue newly-printed currency to pay for its purchases of goods and services. The government must make payments from specified deposit balances which are credited with tax revenues. Any shortfall of revenues to government expenses must be made up through borrowings by the government from the private sector.

The circulation of currency in the private sector arises only from a private depositor's "cashing of a check." Such withdrawal of currency from bank vaults represents a substitution of one form of money (demand deposits) for another (currency). Between Civil War issuance of greenbacks by the government and today's sophisticated monetary system lay major changes from which today's monetary structure emerged.

Significant changes began after the Civil War with Congressional action to reduce the national debt through fiscal surpluses. Because much of the national debt was held in promissory notes that had become legal tender, reductions in the debt lowered the amount of legal tender in circulation. The shortage of money led to price deflation and prompted the creation of a new medium of exchange.

To offset currency shortages, Congress established a Comptroller of Currency to charter and regulate a new group of banks having the authority to issue legal tender. These nationally chartered banks were to be permitted to issue their own notes as legal tender which state chartered banks were not permitted to do. A ten-dollar bill issued by a nationally chartered bank, for example, carried the bank's name on the face of the bill, but was otherwise identical to a ten-dollar bill issued by the Treasury. Nationally chartered bank note issuance was limited by the amount of Treasury notes and bonds each bank held in portfolio, and thus did not completely fill the currency void. But large banks were anxious to obtain Federal charters from the Comptroller of Currency, and they advertized their new charters by using names such as First National Bank of Chicago ... St. Louis ... etc.

Checking Accounts

New York bankers introduced the checking account to supplement scarce currency prior to the turn of the century. In contrast to savings and time deposits in banks, the checking account guaranteed its depositor the right to withdraw funds on demand. Checks were accepted as a medium of exchange because of both this "demand" feature and the establishment of the New York Clearing House Association. Bank members of the Association agreed to "cash" checks drawn on other member banks, and to remit payment on their depositors' checks that other member banks presented for collection through the Clearing House. Personal and business checks could thus be "honored" at any one of many banks in New York City. The popularity of New York checking accounts encouraged the establishment of other clearing houses throughout the country.

Bankers refer to checking accounts as demand deposits because of the depositor's right to withdraw funds on demand. Demand deposits, currency, and coin were the accepted mediums of exchange from 1900 to 1980. The aggregate amount of these types of money in circulation was termed M1 by the Federal Reserve. This was the narrowest definition of "money" in use. A broader money supply aggregate, M2, included savings and small time deposits and other highly liquid but low-denomination assets in addition to Ml. Since the savings component of M2 does not serve as a medium of exchange, the Ml aggregate has, until recently, generally been used to gauge the growth of the nation's money supply.

HOW MONEY GROWS

Structure of the Federal Reserve

To understand how money is created, and how it is not, a brief examination of the structure and functions of the Federal Reserve System ("the Fed") is necessary. Founded in 1913, the Fed is composed of 12 Federal Reserve Banks in various financial centers of the nation, and a seven-member Board of Governors in Washington, D.C. Board members are appointed by the President of the United States and confirmed by the Senate.

Member banks of the Federal Reserve System hold the capital stock of their district Reserve Bank, thereby becoming stockholders. However, their dividends are set by statute and most of the profits of the Reserve Banks are returned to the U.S. Treasury. The member banks elect six of the nine members of the board of directors for their district Reserve Bank, of whom no more than three may be bankers. The remaining three directors are chosen by the Board of Governors in Washington D.C. The directors appoint district Bank presidents subject to the approval of the Board of Governors. Directors establish policies governing local operations, but cannot set reserve requirements or enact other policies that infringe on the national policies set by the Board of Governors. In this context, member banks do not truly ''own'' their district Reserve Banks, because they cannot fully control the Banks' assets.

Membership in the Federal Reserve System is voluntary for state-chartered banks but compulsory for nationally-chartered banks. Before 1980, member banks were required to deposit sufficient reserves in district Reserve Banks to meet reserve requirements stipulated by the Board. When system operations began, member Banks deposited gold, silver, and currency with district Banks to establish their reserve accounts. Vault cash held by Banks later qualified as reserve credit. Since 1980, all depository institutions that issue fully checkable deposits have been required to hold reserves at Reserve Banks and also have had access to Reserve Banks' ''discount window.'' This change has greatly reduced the significance of the distinction between member and non-member institutions.

Currency Issuance

Since the establishment of the Fed, it has been unlawful for the federal government to issue currency from the Treasury's Bureau of Printing and Engraving to pay for goods and services. All newly-printed currency is shipped to Federal Reserve district banks who, in turn, ship the currency to member banks on request with a corresponding debit to the member banks' reserve accounts. If federal tax revenues do not meet government expenditures, the Treasury must borrow funds in the bond market. Proceeds from taxes and security issues are held in both private banks and Federal Reserve Banks. However, all Treasury disbursements are made exclusively from the Treasury's deposits held in Federal Reserve Banks. When these are depleted the Treasury replenishes them by drawing on its accounts at private commercial banks.

Currency flows from member bank vaults into public circulation when depositors withdraw cash from a bank. Withdrawals are accomplished by cashing a check at a bank. Such transactions substitute one form of money for another, because both currency and demand deposit credit are components of money supply. Thus, currency issuance does not represent a source of money supply growth because the process of issuing currency to the public requires corresponding reductions in demand deposits. Money supply growth is instead accomplished through expansion of bank loans and investments.

Bank Loans

It is said that goldsmiths invented bank loan practices centuries ago by storing gold for their clients. These goldsmiths made a profit by lending much of the gold deposited with them for safekeeping, retaining only sufficient reserves of deposited gold to meet anticipated withdrawals. Similar to today's banker, goldsmiths were constantly tempted to increase loan volume, and minimize reserves needed to meet withdrawals.

During the 1800s, many American banks failed to keep adequate reserves of gold and silver to meet withdrawal demands. These state chartered banks made loans by issuing their own notes promising redemption in gold or silver on "demand" by presenting the note at the issuing bank. Without adequate state or federal stipulation of minimum reserve requirements, banks were tempted to issue an excess of bank notes through this loan process. As a result, American banking history of the past century was marked by waves of bankruptcies caused by inadequate reserves.

The introduction of demand deposits nationwide enabled banks to make loans by crediting the demand deposit of the borrower. Accounting entries for loans produce an increase in loans on the asset side of bank balance sheets with a corresponding increase in demand deposit credit on the liability side (depicted in the illustration). Growth in demand deposit credit (money supply) is thereby produced by mere bookkeeping entries, and is dependent on borrowing and lending decisions made in the private sector.

BANK BALANCE SHEET[1]

Assets[2]	*Liabilities*[2]
Cash and Cash Items in	Due To Banks
Process of Collection	Wages Payable[3]
Due From Banks	Depositor Liabilities
Investments (Marketable)	Demand Deposits
Maturing in One Year	Other Checkable Deposits
Maturing after One Year	Savings Deposits
Accrued Interest and	Time Deposits
Receivables	Accounts Payable
Loans	Notes Payable
Business	
Consumer	
Mortgage	
(less reserves for bad debt)	
Reserves Held[4]	Capital Structure:
Buildings and Equipment	Long Term Debt
	Stockholders Equity

NOTES:
1. The balance sheet depicts what is owned (assets), and who owns it (liabilities and capital structure). Bank balance sheets, also known as bank statements of condition, issued to regulatory authorities, must contain more detail than shown. Statements issued to the public vary in detail and arrangement.
2. Listed in descending order of liquidity
3. Payables are often aggregated for public disclosure purposes, and listed after depositor liabilities even though wages payable legally have a preferred claim to depositors in the event of bankruptcy.
4. Reserve balances are always considered to be a highly liquid asset, and thus listed after cash. From a practical point of view, however, reserve levels cannot be reduced below required reserve levels to fund unexpected illiquidity arising from loan losses, security trading losses, or unexpected depositor withdrawal volumes.

The above balance sheet is shown in a general form partly to introduce so-called "T-Account" analyses to be used by the author. In terms of aggregate value, deposits followed by loans and investments are the dominant entries on bank balance sheets. In subsequent T-Account analyses, the following entries will be important:

Cash Items	Due To Accounts
Due From Accounts	Deposits
Investments	
Loans	
Reserves	

When making a loan, a demand deposit is increased (+) along with total loans (+):

Loans	+	Demand Deposits	+
Total Assets	+	Total Liabilities	+

Bank loan customers or borrowers incur the expense and burden of additional indebtedness in order to purchase goods and services, rather than to create idle cash balances. Borrowers pay merchants by writing checks against newly-created demand deposit credit. Because there are approximately 14,000 banks in the United States, the average bank's share of its local deposit market is low—normally less than 20 percent. As a result, there is a more than 80 percent probability that a loan customer's check will be payable to a depositor's account in a different bank. Thus the increase in deposits which results from a bank loan generally does not remain on the books of the lending bank.

When a bank receives a check for deposit drawn on another bank, it presents the check to the issuing bank for payment. In making that payment, this issuing bank's reserve account at the Fed is debited and that of the receiving bank is increased. Thus, when a bank makes a loan to a customer, there is a high probability that it will sustain a loss of reserves. When bank loans are made, total demand deposits and the money supply increase, and there is likely to be a redistribution of reserve credit held among banks as well. But the *total* amount of bank reserves does not change, as shown in the following T-Account illustration.

CREATION OF DEPOSIT CREDIT AND
ITS DISTRIBUTION AND RESERVE EFFECT

Step 1, a loan creates deposit credit:

Bank 1

1. Loans +	1. Demand Deposits +

Step 2, depositor of first bank makes check payable to merchant having a demand deposit in Bank 2, which is cleared through a Fed District Bank:

Bank 2 (momentary)

	2. Demand Deposits + (sends check to Fed for collection)

Fed

	Bank 1 Reserve Account −
	Bank 2 Reserve Account +

Bank 1

1. Loans +	1. Demand Deposits +
2. Reserves −	2. Demand Deposits −
Asset Change = 0	Liability Change = 0

Bank 2

	2. Demand Deposits +
2. Reserves +	
Assets = +	Liabilities = +

BANK RESERVES

The willingness of an individual bank to make a loan partly depends on the bank's ability to withstand a loss of reserves. When banks receive new deposits, the corresponding increase in reserve credit might allow for additional loan extensions. For the entire banking system, however, the aggregate volume of new loans and the subsequent creation of new demand deposit credit primarily are determined by the amount of reserve credit outstanding relative to the existing level of required reserves. If more reserves are available than are required, banks can increase their loans and, as a result, the volume of bank deposits grows.

The reserve requirement is the percentage of deposit liabilities banks must hold in reserve to meet deposit withdrawals. This percentage varies with type of deposit. Today, the reserve requirement on most checkable deposits is twelve percent, while non-personal time and savings accounts (those not held by individuals) have a requirement of three percent. These requirements may, within certain limits set by statute, be altered by the Board of Governors and apply to all depository institutions, whether or not they are members of the Federal Reserve System.

THE 1907 BANKING COLLAPSE

Prior to the establishment of the Federal Reserve System in 1913, reserve requirements were set by the Comptroller of Currency, the regulator of nationally-chartered banks, and by state governments who regulate state-chartered banks. These authorities permitted bank demand deposits in other banks (officially classified as "cash due from other banks") to qualify as reserve credit. These authorities did not fully consider the fact that interbank demand deposits were subject to the same fractional reserve requirements levied against regular demand deposits. The "due from" assets claimed by a given bank as reserves were, in fact, only deposits in another bank fractionally backed by its own reserves.

This meant that the growth of reserve credit was not dependent upon increases in actual bank holdings of gold and Treasury currency. If a particular bank experienced a shortage of reserve credit, it could borrow reserve credit from another bank and continue to expand loans and deposits. These funding practices did not represent a transfer of existing reserve credit from one bank to another. Instead, interbank borrowings manufactured new reserve credit without interference from government authorities. As a result, the ratio of bank holding of Treasury currency to total demand deposits declined significantly. In a broad sense, the federal government's constitutional power of coinage had been fully delegated to the private sector.

A bank needing more reserve credit prior to 1907 could increase "due from" accounts (demand deposits) at another bank which qualified as reserve credit by merely borrowing from another bank.

Borrowing Bank		*Lending Bank*	
due from +	due to +	loans +	demand deposits +

As interbank demand deposits became an important source of reserve growth shortly after the turn of the century, the entire banking system became vulnerable to an unexpected public demand for Treasury currency. When the public's demand for cash increased in 1907 (for a variety of documented reasons), banks were unable to obtain sufficient currency from other banks to meet depositor demands. Within days, the interbank borrowing rate shot up to 125 percent and a depositor run on banks forced a temporary shutdown of the entire banking system.

The 1907 banking collapse was primarily caused by pyramiding of reserves. Small banks held reserve credit in the form of demand deposits in larger, regional banks who as correspondents processed deposit and reserve transfers for them. These regional banks, however, were required to hold reserves equal to only about 15 percent of their demand deposits, including the deposits which actually represented the reserves of the smaller banks. Moreover, regional banks in turn held their reserves as demand deposits in larger money center banks. An important factor contributing to this unstable pyramiding was that prior to the 1930s, banks were permitted to pay interest on demand deposits. Bankers thus tried to minimize non-interest bearing forms of reserves (cash and gold) in favor of interest bearing instruments such as demand deposits. The bulk of bank reserve credit in 1907 was held in the form of interbank demand deposits.

Assuming a 20 percent reserve requirement, for every $100 of demand deposits, a small bank might keep $20 on deposit with a larger regional bank. The regional bank might then keep $4 (20 percent of $20) on deposit in a money center bank to meet reserve requirements on the smaller bank's demand deposit. The regional bank's "due from" a money center bank would then increase the money center bank's reserve requirement by a mere 80 cents (20 percent of $4). Such pyramiding of bank reserves meant that the ratio of available bank reserve credit to total deposits of the banking system was far less than the 20 percent minimum stipulated by banking authorities. In 1907, when deposit withdrawals from small banks prompted widespread demand on regional and money center banks for reserve credit, there was insufficient reserve credit available to keep the banking system liquid.

CREATION OF THE FEDERAL RESERVE

A Presidential commission was established in 1908 to investigate the causes of the 1907 banking collapse. The commission concluded that there should be a central depository for all reserve credit in the United States. A central reserve bank could ensure that the financial assets held as reserves for bank deposits would not be diluted.

The proposed Federal Reserve System faced stiff political opposition in Congress, as had previous central banking proposals. A compromise was reached between free market advocates and central banking proponents (who also considered themselves supporters of free enterprise). The compromise called for nationally-chartered banks to become members of the Federal Reserve System, leaving membership for state-chartered banks voluntary. Although reserve requirements imposed by the Federal Reserve on member banks were generally stiffer than those imposed by state governments, many state-chartered banks opted for System membership to take advantage of free check-clearing services (involving interdistrict transfers of funds) offered by the Fed.

THE RE-DISCOUNT FACILITY

The 1908 Presidential commission also recognized the need for an elastic supply of currency, to avoid repetition of the 1907 crash. The commission recommended that a re-discount facility be established for the new Fed. According to the proposal, member banks could borrow cash reserves from the Fed to meet unexpected cash demands of the public by re-discounting commercial paper at the Fed's re-discount window. This also made membership attractive to state-chartered institutions.

Bank investment portfolios at the turn of the century consisted primarily of commercial paper: short-term (generally 30-day) promissory notes issued by large manufacturing corporations. Most notes were unsecured but traditionally financed inventories that investors regarded as highly liquid. Instead of paying interest, the promissory notes were sold at a discount from their stated par value. At maturity the investor would receive the note's par value, equalling the amount of original investment plus an additional amount representing interest earned.

When banks re-discounted commercial paper at a Federal Reserve Bank, they sold it at an interest rate which discounted its future redemption value to its present value. Because the paper had originally been purchased at a discount, its subsequent sale to the Fed at a discount was said to be a "re-discount," and the rate set by the Federal Reserve for these transactions was described as the "re-discount rate". When member banks re-discounted commercial paper at the Fed, bank reserve balances at the Fed were credited on the liability side of the Fed's balance sheet and commercial paper held by the Fed increased on the asset side.

RE-DISCOUNTING AT (BORROWING FROM)
THE FED BY A MEMBER BANK:

Bank		*Fed*	
Investments: Comm. Paper −		Comm. Paper held +	Bank Reserve Acct. +
Reserves +			

Today, banks continue to hold short term commercial paper as well as Treasury bills which are essentially government promissory notes. An old expression states that bankers are in the business to make loans and not investments. Because commercial paper and bill yields in the open market are generally less than bank lending rates, yields on bank investment portfolios have always been less than those on bank loan portfolios. It is therefore important to examine briefly why banks make investments, and how the Fed once funded these investments through the re-discount facility.

Bankers prefer to minimize reserve assets, such as cash and balances at the Fed, because these assets do not earn interest. Although reserve requirements originally were imposed to ensure that banks would always be able to meet depositors' demands for cash, reserve assets are actually among the most illiquid of bank assets, because reserves cannot be reduced below minimum requirements. Hence, in addition to the minimum required reserve credit, bankers hold interest bearing and highly liquid investments that can be sold quickly to meet unexpected cash withdrawals or reserve shortages. These have frequently been referred to as secondary reserves, which provides an added motive for holding highly liquid paper.

In drafting the Federal Reserve Act, members of Congress realized that a single bank could quickly obtain additional reserves by selling commercial paper in the open market. The financial crash of 1907, however, demonstrated that liquidity demands can arise unexpectedly on a broad front. If many U.S. banks suddenly were forced to sell commercial paper holdings in the open market, there could be insufficient funds to enable all of the reserve-deficient banks to continue operations. In particular, it is worth reiterating that asset sales do not add to the total reserve base of the whole banking system, but only redistribute reserves among banks. It was thus considered essential that the new Fed be able to provide additional reserve balances to banks during times of temporary stress.

During World War I Treasury officials began to fund war expenditures by issuing Treasury bills. These new instruments were identical to commercial paper, except that bills were backed by the government's taxing authority. Bills had greater credit-worthiness than commercial paper, and were thus sold at a lower discount rate than commercial paper. To make bills a more attractive investment for commercial banks, Treasury officials persuaded Fed officials to institute several changes at the re-discount window.

Fed officials permitted member banks to *borrow* reserve credit, using Treasury bills as loan collateral, rather than selling bills outright to the Fed. The re-discount rate became a simple interest rate applied against reserve borrowings. Under the new borrowing procedure, Fed accountants credited reserve accounts of borrowing banks, and showed an increase in "loans to member banks," on the asset side of the balance sheet. The re-discount window became known as the discount window, and the re-discount rate was referred to as the discount rate (even though it was a simple rate of interest on a loan).[1]

MEMBER BANKS BORROWING THROUGH
THE DISCOUNT FACILITY OF THE FED:

Member Bank		*Fed*	
Reserves +	Due to (Fed) +	Loans to Member Banks +	Reserve Accts. +

To further encourage bank funding of the war effort through Treasury bill purchases, Fed officials kept the discount rate relatively low and, at times, lowered the discount rate below prevailing Treasury bill rates. Banks could therefore borrow funds from the Fed to purchase bills, which were yielding more than the cost of borrowed reserve funds. Bankers increased profits without use of stockholder funds. Bankers thus expanded their investments during the war for reasons other than their need for secondary reserves or to offset weak loan demand.

[1]To understand the difference between discounted rates and yields (interest rates), assume a Treasury bill has a par value of $100, matures in one year, and may be purchased for $90. The discount rate is determined by taking the interest earned ($10) and dividing it by the par value ($100) thus: 10/100 = 10% (the discount rate). The actual yield on the investment is determined by taking the interest earned ($10) and dividing it by the purchase price ($90) thus: 10/90 = 11% (the actual yield).

Federal, state, and local governments do not fund capital improvements through long-term bank loans. These governments instead borrow funds by issuing debt securities on a competitive bid basis (with some local government exceptions). Because the Constitution does not allow the federal government to directly tax state and local governments, the interest earned from state and municipal debt securities is exempt from federal income taxes. These securities are therefore known as tax-exempt securities. Taxable debt issues of the federal government have higher yields than tax-exempt state and municipal issues. Some analysts believe these create a tax loophole for rich investors. As personal income tax rates increased, however, the tax-exempt yields declined relative to taxable yields. Tax-exempt investors thus receive lower yields, and thus in a sense pay taxes to local governments instead of the federal government. With the increase of corporate tax rate, bank investment in tax-exempt securities increased in order to limit federal tax liabilities.

State and local government deposits in commercial banks require full collateralization with qualifying securities such as Treasuries. These security pledging requirements are frequently as high as 125 percent of the deposit levels. Bank investment portfolios must therefore be large enough to collateralize government deposits.

Credit demands of the public sector are funded through the issuance of marketable debt securities that, if purchased by banks, create new demand deposit credit. For example, when a bank purchases Treasury securities from a member of the public, the bank's payment will be in the form of a check drawn on itself. When this check clears, the seller's holding of demand deposits increases. Such creation of new demand deposit credit (money) is identical to the creation of new money through bank loans.

BANK PURCHASES A MARKETABLE SECURITY FROM ONE OF ITS DEPOSITORS:

Investments +	
	Demand Deposits +

SECURITIES MARKETS

Most purchases of securities are made in money and bond markets. Money markets are distinguished from bond markets by the trading of debt instruments having maturities of less than one year (such as commercial paper and Treasury bills). Bonds are issued when maturities exceed one year.

THE BOND MARKET

Corporate, municipal, and Treasury bond markets are each composed of primary and secondary markets. Security transactions in primary markets are distinguished by bond dealers serving as intermediaries between issuing entities and investors. These dealers temporarily hold debt securities for resale and maintain posted bids and offers on any security. Dealers generally confine their activities to either the corporate, the municipal, or the federal debt market (which includes Treasury and Federal Agency debt securities). The "municipal" bond market includes debt securities issued by both local and state governments.

Primary dealers have sufficient capital to purchase large blocks of new debt securities issued by businesses or governments, and have established contacts with many investors. Bond traders in dealer firms bid on new debt issues for profitable resale to investors. In municipal and corporate bond markets, new-issue bidding by a primary dealer is often done in concert with other primary dealers, who are collectively capable of bidding for the entire new-issue amount. For each new tax-exempt or corporate bond issue, two to six syndications of primary dealers normally bid for the total amount of the issue.

In the Treasury debt market, dealer underwritings of new debt issues do not involve the entire new-issue amount. Treasury debt issues are auctioned nationwide by the Treasury through the twelve Federal Reserve Banks. These competitive-bid auctions are open to any investor, and primary dealers compete with individual investors as well as with each other.

Many large commercial banks operate primary dealerships in municipal and Treasury securities, which they are legally able to underwrite. Securities purchased for bank investment departments, however, are not usually purchased from their ''in-house'' dealership, but are generally bought directly from the issuer, or from other primary dealers. Most banks, particularly smaller ones, acquire Treasury debt in secondary markets, where outstanding marketable debt is traded as opposed to buying and selling of new issues in the primary market. Bank security purchases in secondary markets are almost always handled by dealers. Secondary markets are distinguished from primary markets by dealer purchase of debt securities from investors or other dealers, not from issuers. Such purchases in secondary markets are motivated by potential profit from re-sale to investors or other dealers. Secondary markets create liquidity for investors by increasing the marketability of their security holdings, and thus enhance the value of investments in debt securities having good secondary markets.

MONETIZING MARKETABLE DEBT[2]

When a bank purchases Treasury debt in secondary markets, it makes payment to a dealer. The purchasing bank wires funds to the receiving bank where payment is due on the dealer's demand deposit. The paying bank instructs the Fed to debit its reserve account and to credit the reserve account of the receiving bank. Thus a bank purchase of government debt produces a credit to the demand deposit of the seller and a debit to the reserve account of the purchasing bank. The demand deposit credit, without a corresponding demand deposit debit, creates new demand deposits in the same way as the making of bank loans. The bank's investment increases the demand

[2]Economists prefer to limit application of the word ''monetization'' to the supply of reserves by the Fed because this supply permits the creation of money. Though permitting monetary growth, reserve supplies do not guarantee it. A loan or investment by a bank is the act that creates money, often without much regard for reserve availability. Accordingly, the author prefers to use ''monetization'' as the act of creating money through bank loans and investments, and through Fed security purchases from nonbank reporting dealers.

deposit component of the money supply without changing the total level of bank reserves. In the foregoing example, reserve credit lost by the purchasing bank is merely gained by the bank where the seller's account is to be credited.

BANK 1 PURCHASES MARKETABLE DEBT FROM A DEALER MAINTAINING A DEMAND DEPOSIT ACCOUNT IN BANK 2:

Bank 1

Investments +	
Reserves −	

Bank 2

	Demand Deposits +
Reserves +	

Fed

	Res. Acct. Bk. 1 −
	Res. Acct. Bk. 2 +

NOTE: Demand Deposits rise because of an investment made by Bank 1; total reserve credit remains unchanged.

Another example involves a bank purchase of securities from the dealer operation of another bank. When a bank purchases an outstanding Treasury debt security from a bank dealer, there is no money supply effect because the bank dealer's demand deposit is not included in the demand deposit component of the monetary aggregates. In other words, when a bank buys securities from another bank, there is no change in total investments held by all banks and, as a result, no money supply effect.

As indicated earlier, the Treasury holds demand deposit accounts both at Federal Reserve Banks and at most commercial banks. When banks purchase Treasury securities in the primary market (from the Treasury), there is an equivalent increase in Treasury balances, but these are not included in Federal Reserve measures of the money supply. When the Treasury adds to its balances at Federal Reserve Banks, total reserves in the banking system are reduced. If the Treasury deposits the proceeds of its securities sales in a commercial bank, there is no reserves effect.

However, the Treasury does not incur the expense of borrowing money in the bond market unless its immediate liabilities exceed incoming tax revenues. When the Treasury issues drafts (checks) against its account at the Fed, payable to members of the private sector, most of the drafts will be deposited in checking accounts. Demand deposits and money supply both grow. Receiving banks submit Treasury drafts to the Fed for collection. In turn, the Fed debits the Treasury's deposit account and credits the reserve accounts of the receiving banks. The payment from Treasury balances increases bank reserves, offsetting the reserve loss incurred when banks purchased new debt from the Treasury. Thus the net effect of Treasury borrowing and spending is for total reserves to remain unchanged, but money supply to grow because of the additional bank investments in Treasuries. However, if *nonbank* investors had purchased the new debt, there would have been no demand deposit effect; debits to private demand deposits for the purchase of Treasury debt would be offset by the Treasury payments to the private sector.

TREASURY NEW-ISSUE PROCEEDS DEPOSITED AT THE FED:
(aggregating District Reserve Bank Treasury deposits)

Step 1: Banks purchase marketable debt from Treasury in auction.
Step 2: Treasury pays down on liabilities to private sector (demand deposits).

Banks

(1) Investments	+	(2) Demand Deposits	+
(1) Reserves	−		
(2)	+		
	+		+

Treasury

(1) Cash	+	(2) Payables	−
(2)	−	(1) Debt Outstanding	+
	0		0

Fed

	Reserve Acct. − (1) + (2)
	Treasury Deposit + (1) − (2)
	0 0

State and local governments can be substituted for the Treasury in foregoing examples to produce identical results (allowing for the fact that state and local deposits reside in banks and not the Fed). In every case, bank loans and investments produce deposit expansion in the banking system without changing total bank reserves. Bank loans and investments (representing the bulk of bank assets) create deposit credit (representing the bulk of bank liabilities). Bank loans and investments are called bank credit. Extension of bank credit over the years has produced 96 percent of all deposit credit in existence.

In sum, when bank credit increases the dollar deposit base of the banking system, demand rather than savings or time deposits are initially increased regardless of whether bank credit was extended through loans or investments. In time, newly manufactured credit will be re-deposited in other, non-checkable, accounts included in broader monetary aggregates, such as M2. If the definition of money supply is limited to M1, bank credit extensions may not be associated with sustained M1 growth, depending on deposit composition tendencies within the banking system.

Because of the ease with which non-M1 bank deposits can be converted to checkable deposits for spending purposes, there has been a growing disposition of Fed officials to place greater monetary policy emphasis on the growth of M2. As will be examined later, M2 and M3 (in particular) approximate total bank deposits plus bank vault cash, the latter not having an effect on money supply growth. Accordingly, the growth of bank credit is central to the growth of broader monetary aggregates. Because growth of the dollar deposit base increases reserve requirement levels, the Fed's provision of reserve credit to the banking system is also central to the growth of monetary aggregates.

FEDERAL RESERVE OPEN MARKET OPERATIONS

From the beginning of Fed operations in 1914 through 1921, all deposit growth and money supply growth in the United States was produced through unrestricted extensions of bank credit. During

World War I, this growth was inflationary, and was fueled by an excess of reserve credit supplied through the discount window to encourage bank investments in Treasury bills. By 1921, Fed officials had decided to slow the growth of bank credit by making reserves less available. Less reserve credit available would force bankers to halt the rapid growth of their investments in Treasury securities. If bank lending policies were not subsequently tightened to match the reduced growth of total reserves, some portion of bank investment portfolios would have to be liquidated.

Regulation A

A supplemental Fed regulation, Regulation A, was established in 1921 to reduce the availability of reserves through the discount window. This landmark regulation has survived the test of time, and has not been substantially amended.

Regulation A stated that member bank reserve borrowings were no longer a "right," but a "privilege." Fed officials asserted that the discount facility had never been intended to be a permanent source of bank capital, but should be only a short-term recourse to meet unforeseen liquidity needs. Longer-term liquidity adjustments should be accomplished through a change in bank policies governing the extension of loans and investments.

In passing the Federal Reserve Act of 1913, Congress realized that it had not restricted member bank use of the re-discount facility, except for specifying commercial paper eligible for re-discounting. Congress realized that reserve borrowings would enable banks to increase money supply through extensions of new loans and investments. But it assumed that manufacturing company issuances of commercial paper represented a source of financing for new productive capacity. Because reserve borrowings would be limited to manufacturing paper used to finance additions to productive capacity, it was reasoned that the money supply-induced growth in aggregate product demands would be equal to the increase in product supply capacity. Reserve borrowings, if limited by eligible commercial paper, would therefore not be inflationary. Congressmen believed that they had created a market-controlled means of providing for non-inflationary growth of bank reserves.

Because of encouragement given to member banks to help finance the war effort through continuous borrowings from the Fed, reserve borrowings had come to be regarded as an unrestricted right of member banks. Regulation A thus represented a major change, restricting member bank access to the reserve borrowing facility. This restriction remains in effect today.

From the late fifties until February 1983, the reserve maintenance period was one week, extending from Thursday to Wednesday. The reserve computation period was also one week, but was two weeks prior to the reserve maintenance period. In other words, reserve requirements based on deposit liabilities during the computation period had to be met two weeks later during the reserve maintenance period. There was a two-week lag in required reserve accountability. The reserve maintenance period was also referred to as a ''reserve settlement week.'' During the settlement week, the daily average of reserves held by a bank had to equal or exceed the required reserve daily average determined two weeks earlier. If reserves held exceeded required reserves, then a bank held excess reserves in addition to those required.

Regulation A limited the term of reserve borrowing to one day, except in emergency situations. This limitation was not unreasonable because the reserve maintenance period was only one week prior to 1983. Weekends and holidays are included in daily averages of reserves held and required; reserve balances on Friday automatically carry into Saturday and Sunday. Accordingly, if a bank borrows reserves from the Fed on a Friday, the increase in reserves held by the bank affects three days of the seven-day average of reserves held. Banks anticipating a large borrowing need went to the discount window on Fridays, rather than on other business days, hoping to maximize borrowings without unduly attracting concerned attention of discount officers.

Under Regulation A, banks abusing the borrowing privilege have been subject to disciplinary measures, such as a loan portfolio review by discount officers having the authority to make binding recommendations. If a discount officer forbids a bank to roll over a short-term loan, the bank stands to lose the affected corporation's loan business that took years of marketing effort to acquire.

The Federal Reserve was established as an independent government agency whose operations were intended to be financially self-sustaining. The Fed's interest income from reserve loans had been expected to fully finance Fed operations. The success of Regulation A in reducing member bank reserve borrowings in 1921 lowered Fed interest income, and left the Fed in financial need. A request for congressional aid would probably have been rejected, and might have given Fed critics in Congress the opportunity to gain some control over Fed policies.

Open Market Operations Begin

Fed officials therefore decided to boost sagging income by purchasing Treasury securities in the open market. To pay for securities, Fed officials simply issued the seller a draft (check) against a Reserve Bank. The seller would subsequently deposit the Fed's draft in his or her demand deposit at a bank. The seller's bank would then submit the check directly to the Fed for collection. Fed accountants, presented with Fed drafts from member banks seeking collection, simply credited bank reserve accounts at the Fed for the amount due. Although this accounting procedure clearly manufactured new reserve credit, the effect of Fed Treasury security purchases was not immediately obvious to Fed officials.

RESERVE AND DEPOSIT EFFECTS OF SECURITY
PURCHASES BY THE FED FROM A NON-BANK DEALER:

Dealer		*Dealer's Bank*	
(2) Cash +			(3) Dealer Demand Deposits +
(1) Securities −		(4) Reserves +	
0		+	+

STEPS:

1. Fed buys securities from dealer, and
2. issues draft to seller.
3. Seller deposits draft in bank which
4. is submitted to Fed for collection.

A recent college graduate employed at the Boston Federal Reserve district bank in 1921 noticed that every time System holdings of Treasury bills temporarily increased, there was a corresponding decrease in the total volume of member bank reserve borrowings. Conversely, every time System holdings decreased, there was a corresponding rise in member bank borrowings. This co-variation occurred because any change in Fed security holdings produced an equal change in the volume of available reserve credit. Against a relatively stable level of required reserves, fluctuations in the volume of reserve credit produced either deficient reserve positions among member banks (prompting reserve borrowing), or excess reserves (reducing reserve borrowing).

A given purchase of Treasury bills by the Fed produced an equivalent increase of reserve balances, due to credits made to reserve accounts of banks submitting Fed checks for payment. Conversely, any open market sale of bills by the Fed lowered member bank reserve accounts by an equal amount. In this case, checks written against buyer demand deposits were submitted to the Fed as payment. Fed accountants debited the reserve accounts of member banks against whom the checks were drawn, then sent these checks to the banks for demand deposit debits. The relationship between System holdings of Treasury securities and reserve borrowings led Fed officials to realize they had accidentally discovered a new and powerful tool of monetary control.

Money Supply Growth and Net Borrowed Reserves

Economic literature often refers to bank "demands for excess reserves" to explain why excess reserves are held in varying amounts. This creates a false notion that there are bank demands for excess reserves. While small banks usually have little incentive to manage their reserve positions efficiently because of the small volume of funds involved, bankers generally avoid accumulation of excess reserve balances at the Fed because they do not earn any interest. If a banker discovers that excess reserves are increasing, he might use this credit to purchase interest-bearing marketable debt. Over the past two decades (and prior to 1985 as will be discussed), excess reserves in banks have been minimal. This means that total reserve levels generally reflect changes in required reserve levels, not changes in bank demand for excess reserves.

SUMMARY OF RESERVE AGGREGATES

DATE	TOTAL RESERVES	REQUIRED RESERVES	EXCESS RESERVES
1959	13.6	13.2	0.4
1960	13.5	13.0	0.5
1961	13.9	13.1	0.8
1962	14.2	13.7	0.5
1963	14.5	14.0	0.5
1964	14.9	14.0	0.9
1965	15.4	15.0	0.4
1966	15.8	15.5	0.3
1967	16.5	16.1	0.4
1968	17.5	17.2	0.3
1969	18.1	17.8	0.3
1970	18.7	18.5	0.2
1971	20.1	19.9	0.2
1972	21.5	21.3	0.2
1973	23.2	22.9	0.3
1974	24.4	24.2	0.2
1975	24.8	24.6	0.2
1976	13.6	13.1	0.5
1977	26.1	25.9	0.2
1978	27.7	27.5	0.2
1979	28.1	27.8	0.3
1980	29.7	28.7	1.0
1981	31.7	31.4	0.3
1982	32.9	32.6	0.3
1983	35.6	35.1	0.5
1984	38.1	37.4	0.7
1985	42.7	41.8	0.9
1986	49.9	48.9	1.0

NOTE: Billions of dollars, seasonally adjusted; averages based on monthly data.

When the level of total reserves drops below the level of required reserves, some member banks will have to borrow reserves at the discount window to meet reserve requirements. The difference between total reserves and those borrowed at the Fed is known as nonborrowed reserves. Net borrowed reserves equals reserve borrowings less excess reserves. When the level of nonborrowed reserves drops below the level of required reserves, an increase in net borrowed reserves necessarily results. When liberal reserve policies of the Fed allow nonborrowed reserves to exceed required reserves, net borrowed reserves acquire a negative sign, or are reported as free reserves.

EXAMPLES OF THE RELATIONSHIP
BETWEEN THE DIFFERENT RESERVE AGGREGATES

Net Borrowed Reserves
  equals: Required Reserves less Nonborrowed Reserves
    example*: $34.0 bln. - $33.0 bln. = $1.0 bln.
  equals: Reserve Borrowings less Excess Reserves
    example*: $1.3 bln. - $.3 bln. = $1.0 bln.

Free Reserves
  equals: Nonborrowed Reserves less Required Reserves
    example*: $33.0 bln. - $34.0 bln. = -$1.0 bln.
  equals: Excess Reserves less Reserve Borrowings
    example*: $.3 bln. - $1.3 bln. = -$1.0 bln.

*Example uses representative data of the past decade, in which total reserves held would equal $34.3 bln.

NOTE: Net Borrowed Reserves of -$.5 bln. is the same as $.5 bln. of Free Reserves. The opposite of Net Borrowed Reserves is Free Reserves, not Net Free Reserves (as mistakenly referred to by many financial analysts). "Free" is a net concept so that "Net Free" is redundant.

There are three types of reserve borrowings: seasonal credit, extended credit, and adjustment borrowings. During the 1970s, Dr. Arthur Burns, then Board Chairman, introduced the seasonal borrowing privilege for smaller member banks who demonstrated seasonal needs for reserve credit, but lacked access to the national money market. The Burns plan was somewhat misleading since almost all banks have a demonstrated seasonal need for additional reserve credit. More important, not all small member banks lack access to the money market; many can, and actively do, trade federal funds (that is, lend reserve credit to each other).

The Burns plan sought to stem attrition of System membership among smaller state-chartered banks who found Fed reserve requirements far more onerous than state-imposed requirements. To mitigate this cost discrimination, the Burns plan essentially gave smaller banks continuous access to the discount facility for periods as long as six months. Because the discount rate has almost always been lower than the funds rate (the interbank rate on reserve credit), particularly during the 1970s, smaller banks could obtain low-cost reserve credit for resale at a much higher rate in the funds market. Even though the Monetary Control Act of 1980 provided for a phased-in uniform extension of bank reserve requirements to all depositories, the seasonal borrowing program continues, though without much justification. In 1985 the Fed began to set a separate seasonal borrowing rate close to the prevailing Fed funds rate in order to eliminate arbitrage abuse of the seasonal borrowing privilege. Seasonal borrowings have thus declined to insignificant levels below $100 million. More recent liquidity problems among agricultural banks have been accommodated through extended credit.

Under its legal requirement to be a "lender of last resort," the Fed makes loans to troubled banks on an extended basis. Credit extended on an emergency basis is treated by the Fed as analogous to nonborrowed reserves, because bankers are not under any short-term pressure to repay extended credit borrowings. Although this is also true of seasonal borrowings, the Fed typically lumps seasonal and adjustment borrowing together for reserve management purposes. Typically, however, the volume of seasonal borrowing is small. Adjustment borrowings, which represent loans to banks to permit them to meet their reserve requirements, must be repaid in one day.

So, net borrowed reserves is equal to adjustment and seasonal borrowing less excess reserves, while extended credit is included in nonborrowed reserves. The volume of extended credit borrowing is not affected by open market operations, whereas adjustment borrowings are, as will be explained. For operational purposes, net borrowed reserves are usually defined at the Fed as adjustment borrowings less excess reserves.

The net rather than total reserve borrowing concept underscores the fact that in a sense some reserve borrowings need not have occurred, because reserve-deficient banks could have borrowed excess reserves existing elsewhere in the banking system. Frequently, however, small banks hold excess reserves as "insurance" against unexpected reserve drains late in the reserve maintenance period. An increase in reserve borrowings late in a reserve settlement period frequently creates additional excess reserves among member banks. Under lagged reserve requirements, open market operations could precisely control *net* borrowed reserves (by adjusting nonborrowed reserves to a known level of required reserves); they could not precisely control total reserve borrowing because of the existence of excess reserves. On occasion, additional borrowing leads to more excess reserves, but not net borrowed reserves.

The most relevant definition of net borrowed reserves is required reserves less nonborrowed reserves. The level of required reserves represents the demand for reserve credit, while the level of nonborrowed reserves represents the amount of reserve credit controlled through Fed open market operations. When Fed officials buy significant quantities of bills, the level of nonborrowed reserves can rise above the required reserve level.

In such circumstances, a free reserve position (representing a level of borrowings less than excess reserves) is established for member banks. Free reserves thus indicate that member banks do not need to borrow significantly from the Fed.

The correlation discovered in 1921 between Fed security holdings and the level of reserve borrowings therefore stemmed from the Fed's ability to affect and, if it wished, control the level of nonborrowed reserves through open market operations. With lagged reserve requirements, the Fed could use this ability to vary nonborrowed reserves through open market security transactions, and thus control the level of net borrowed (or free) reserves in the banking system.

If open market operations sustain a high level of net borrowings, a growing number of banks will be forced to the discount window more frequently. This action would, because of the associated threats of administrative discipline, encourage reserve-scarce banks to adopt more restrictive loan and investment policies. In practice, slowing of bank credit extensions generally lag Fed-induced increases in net borrowings by at least six months, as will be explained. The slower growth of bank deposits moderates the growth of required reserves, and thus total reserves. Money supply growth moderates as a result of slower deposit growth.

After Fed officials understood the influence open market operations could have on the growth of bank reserves and money supply, they formed in the early twenties an internal committee to formulate open market policy. This committee evolved by the mid-thirties into today's Federal Open Market Committee, or FOMC. These actions were contrary to original Congressional intentions to prevent the central bank from pursuing specific monetary policies. Concurrent with the formation of the original FOMC, Fed officials also consolidated all open market activities of district banks within one group of open market officers operating out of the New York district bank. Establishment of the Open Market Desk in New York City was chosen because Wall Street housed most of the major dealers in money and bond markets.

Open Market Procedures

Since Fed operations in the open market began, trading procedures have established orderly and equitable buying and selling of securities. The Trading Desk at the New York Federal Reserve Bank limits its dealings to well-capitalized primary dealers who are also willing to submit daily reports to the Fed regarding their positions and transactions. These are known as reporting dealers. The Fed, in turn, pays for direct telephone lines between reporting dealers and the New York Desk. When the Desk enters the market, Desk officers simultaneously contact each reporting dealer, to solicit competitive bids for securities to be sold or offers for securities to be purchased. The number of reporting dealers has varied over the years, but averaged about 25 until the 1980s, when the number rose to approximately 35 to 40.

During the competitive bid solicitations, Desk officials do not reveal the amount of securities they intend to purchase or sell. Dealers have about 15 minutes to phone in bids or offers; the Fed's notification of accepted bids or offers takes an additional 20 to 30 minutes. Bids and offers show rates or prices at which a dealer is willing to buy or sell various quantities of bills or bonds.

OPERATING FACTORS AND THE CONTROL OF NONBORROWED RESERVES

Precisely controlling the volume of nonborrowed reserves through open market operations was not as simple as originally anticipated. Many operating factors that are not easily forecasted also affect the level of bank reserves. Major operating factors that affect nonborrowed reserves include the amount of Treasury deposits at Federal Reserve Banks, Federal Reserve float, and currency in circulation. A number of other operating factors affect reserve levels but they are relatively minor in size and effect.

Levels of Treasury Deposits at the Fed

When tax payments are made to the Treasury by check, the Treasury deposits these funds in its account at the Fed. The Fed debits the reserve account of the bank against whom the check was drawn, and credits the Treasury's account. A similar drain of bank reserves occurs when Treasury accounts at the Fed are credited with proceeds from selling new Treasury debt. Similarly any Treasury payment made to a member of the public by check is processed by debiting the Treasury's account at the Fed with a corresponding credit to the reserve account of the bank whose customer received the check. In other words, any increase or decrease in Treasury deposits at the Fed will produce an equal and opposite effect on bank reserve. If Desk officials want to keep nonborrowed reserves unchanged during a statement week in which Treasury deposits at the Fed increase, the Fed will have to purchase securities as an offsetting supply of reserve credit. Analysts call such an open market operation ''defensive operation.'' Each day, Desk officials forecast the upcoming daily averages of Treasury deposits to calculate the defensive reserve adding (or draining) requirement needed to keep the relationship of nonborrowed reserves to required reserves unchanged. If Desk officials are targeting a specific level of net borrowed reserves, the defensive adding requirement is calculated to change the nonborrowed reserves level by an amount equal to the change in the week's level of required reserves. On any given day, however, it is difficult for either the Treasury or the Fed to predict accurately the net volume of Treasury transactions with the public. Fed forecasters of daily Treasury deposit levels receive daily help directly from Treasury officials in Washington, D.C. Nonetheless, these daily forecasts are often in error due to unexpected inflows of tax receipts, or an unexpected volume of government payments.

Over the years, both Federal spending and tax receipts have increased rapidly. The April 15 (originally March 15) tax deadline, when personal checking account credit is transferred to the Treasury's account at the Fed, has produced successively larger drains on bank reserves. Quarterly corporate income tax payments (due the 15th of March, June, September, and December) have also produced large transfers of demand deposit credit to the Treasury's account at the Fed. On these dates, the Fed's Open Market Desk has had to buy a sizable volume of securities. Reporting dealers could easily project such defensive purchases, and often profited by positioning securities whenever low prices permitted. Dealers could also scale up their offers, knowing that Desk officials would have to accept some of their high priced offers to fulfill the defensive requirement.

To prevent these problems, a Treasury Tax and Loan Account (TT&L) system was developed in the 1960s. The Treasury subsequently deposited tax payments in TT&L accounts within the banking system rather than at the Fed. Any commercial bank could become a depository of the Treasury upon proof of capital adequacy and membership in the Federal Reserve System. The Treasury draws funds from TT&L accounts only when needed to pay down liabilities; Fed officials debit the reserve accounts of affected member banks with corresponding credits to the Treasury's account at the Fed. In effect, large tax payments remain in the banking system in TT&L accounts, not affecting bank reserves. Such use of TT&L accounts enables Treasury officials to maintain a steady level of deposits at the Fed, while reducing the Treasury's effect on daily levels of nonborrowed reserves.

Congress now requires banks to pay interest on Treasury balances at rates comparable to open market rates. The banks, moreover, must fully collateralize TT&L balances by the pledging of government debt. Under these requirements, all Treasury receipts are first deposited at the Fed, then redeposited in TT&L note accounts in the banking system. If a bank's collateral is insufficient, it must kickback funds to the Fed. When collateral in the marketplace is short, these returns frequently push Treasury deposits well above their commonly targeted level of $3.5 billion each day. Nonetheless, the TT&L system continues to house large Treasury receipts within the banking system and reduces daily reserve variations.

Federal Reserve Float and Bank Float

Federal Reserve float is another important factor affecting the level of nonborrowed reserves. When the Fed arranged to clear member bank checks on an interdistrict basis, it also guaranteed funds collection within two business days. Assume, for example, that a demand depositor on the West Coast mails a check to a manufacturer on the East Coast. When the check is received, the manufacturer deposits it in demand deposit at a local Eastern bank. This bank sends the check to the local Fed for collection. The Fed must then send the check to the Fed district bank on the West Coast for collection. The West Coast district bank, upon receipt of the check, debits the reserve account of the bank on which the check is drawn, and sends the check to the paying bank so that it can debit the demand depositor's account.

Meanwhile, the East Coast Fed district bank credits the reserve account of the East Coast member bank after two business days regardless of whether the West Coast member bank's reserve account was concurrently debited. If there is any clerical or transportation delay in submitting the check to the West Coast district bank, chances are that the West Coast member bank's reserve account is debited a day or two after the East Coast member bank's reserve account was credited. In this situation, the East Coast bank's reserve account increased without an immediate and corresponding reduction in the West Coast bank's reserve account, causing a temporary increase in nonborrowed reserves. This increase in reserve credit is called Federal Reserve float.

CREATION AND REDUCTION OF FED FLOAT

Step 1: Eastern bank receives check drawn on Western bank. Check is submitted to local Fed for collection which is made in the form of a reserve account credit after two working days. Fed float is created.

E. Bank

Reserves	+	Demand Deposit	+
	+		+

E. Fed

Fed. Float*	+	Res. Acct.	+
	+		+

Step 2: West Coast Fed receives check four days later, debiting reserve account of Western bank. Float is eliminated.

W. Bank

Reserves	−	Demand Deposit	−
	−		−

W. Fed

Fed. Float*	−	Res. Acct.	−
	−		−

*Fed float is tracked by District Reserve Banks, but calculated at the Board by comparing clearing data of District Banks. Fed float is calculated on a system-wide basis and is not subject to local District accounting (determination) as is implied in the above illustration (demonstrating principle).

Several pronounced seasonal patterns in Fed float ease the open market forecasting task of Fed staffers. Business payments on invoices are typically due between the tenth and fifteenth day of each month. Fed float rises accordingly after about a two-day lag. Recurring clerical problems at Fed check processing centers cause an increase in float credit which is called "holdover float." Bad weather often delays air transportation of checks between Fed District Banks, which as another cause of float credit is referred to as "transportation float." When bad weather descends on money centers, money market traders know that Fed float and nonborrowed reserves will rise, and they can expect offsetting Fed security sales in the open market.

In addition to Fed float, the existence of bank float can make matters even more confusing. When the East Coast bank initially receives the check for deposit, it credits the depositor's demand deposit account for the amount, even though the bank has not yet collected the funds. The liability side of the bank's balance sheet shows an increase in demand deposits. On the asset side of the balance sheet, the bank credits an account called "cash items in process of collection." After two business days, when the Eastern Fed District Bank credits the bank's reserve account, the bank's accountant reduces "cash items" on the asset side of the balance sheet and increases by an equal amount another asset account called "reserves on deposit with the Federal Reserve." During the time between giving credit to the demand deposit and actually collecting from the Fed, bank float existed.

BANK FLOAT AT E. BANK:

E. Bank		*E. Fed*	
(1) Cash Items +			
	Demand Deposit + (1)		
(2) −	(2)	Fed Float* +	Res. Acct. + (2)
(2) Reserves +			
+	+	+	+

Step 1: Bank float is created when demand deposit credit is given without collection from Fed.

Step 2: Bank float is eliminated by Fed extension of float credit.

*Fed float is tracked by District Reserve Banks, but calculated at the Board by comparing clearing data of District Banks. Fed float is calculated on a system-wide basis and is not subject to local District accounting (determination) as is implied in the above illustration (demonstrating principle).

Fed float and bank float are subtracted from money supply totals to avoid double accounting of demand deposits. Bank float, for example, represents a demand deposit increase (through a check transaction) occurring without an immediate debit to another demand deposit. In accounting for money supply, bank float must be subtracted from total demand deposits reported by all banks or it causes double accounting of existing demand deposit credit. In the exfjample, East Coast bank float declined while the Fed was completing its transaction on the West Coast. Accordingly, double deposit accounting could continue to occur after bank float has declined and as Fed float increases. For this reason, Fed float is also deducted from money supply totals.

The demand deposit component of Ml (narrowly defined money supply) is calculated by first subtracting bank float from the gross demand deposits of nonbank businesses, persons, municipalities, and state governments. That difference is called net demand deposits, from which Fed float is further subtracted.

Currency in Circulation

The last major operating factor is the amount of currency in circulation. This factor is not the same "currency in circulation" discussed at the beginning of this chapter. To distinguish between the two currency references, analysts often use the names of the official Federal Reserve reports in which these aggregates appear. The first of these is the Weekly Money Stock Report, officially designated the H.6 report, which presents money supply data and includes all currency outside of bank vaults. A second weekly report, the H.4.1, details all operating factors affecting member bank reserves. The amount of currency in circulation reported on the H.4.1 Report is the total amount of currency shipped by the Fed to member banks. In general terms, the difference between H.4.1 currency and H.6 currency is that the former includes the vault cash of depository institutions that is part of their total reserves.

Earlier in this chapter, it was shown that shipping currency from the Fed to member banks causes an equivalent decrease in reserve balances held at the Fed, and increases vault cash (which also qualifies as reserve credit). The issuance of currency to banks, therefore, does not affect total bank reserves. When depositors withdraw cash from banks, however, both vault cash and total reserves are reduced. Bankers arc experts at predicting minimum vault cash requirements, and closely match currency transactions with the Fed to public currency needs. When cash demands of the public increases, H.4.1. currency rises far more than vault cash, often producing a significant reduction in reserve credit. Therefore, H.4.1 currency increases are associated with corresponding reductions in bank reserves (usually prompting offsetting Fed purchases of securities).

Member Bank

Reserves at Fed	−		
Vault Cash	+		
	0		0

Fed

Currency Held	−	Reserve Acct.	−
	−		−

Member Bank

		Demand Deposit	−
Vault Cash	−		
	−		−

Any increase in the amount of currency reported in H.4.1 reflects an equal reduction in bank reserves, exclusive of vault cash. There is an absorption of reserve credit on deposit at the Fed whenever H.4.1 currency increases. Conversely, any return flow of currency from banks to the Fed, which reduces reported H.4.1 currency outstanding, increases reserves on deposit at the Fed. When banks experience inflows of cash deposits, such as after the Christmas shopping season, they regularly ship the excess vault cash to the Fed for credit to their reserve accounts. The Fed either recirculates the currency or destroys it, depending on its condition, and receives replacement currency from the Treasury's Bureau of Printing and Engraving.

When Desk officials forecast their defensive open market requirements they have to project daily in H.4.1 currency and vault cash. Fortunately, these trends are predictable due to pronounced seasonal patterns. Summer vacations, for example, dramatically increase the public's demand for currency.

The secular long-term increase in circulating currency has been very difficult to explain. At the present, data show amount of currency outside of bank and business vaults at $500 per capita. A typical family of four persons, according to currency data, should have about $2,000 in cash lying somewhere around the house. Of course, this is not the average case. Where, then, is all the excess currency? Probably it has been going primarily into the underground economy, and to increased offshore holdings (also partly related to the underground economy—drug trafficking).

Of all the operating factors affecting bank reserves, only currency in circulation exhibits secular growth. Accordingly, this significant rise in reserve absorption has to be offset routinely by Federal Reserve purchases of securities. Fed balance sheets over the years show that the two fastest growing H.4.1 accounts are currency in circulation and Treasury security holdings.

The purchase of securities by the Fed not only increases bank reserves, as shown earlier in this chapter, but can also increase demand deposit credit. When the Fed buys securities from a nonbank dealer, the payment draft issued is deposited in a nonbank demand deposit, thus boosting this component of the nation's money supply. When the Fed purchases securities from a bank dealer, however, payment is made directly to a bank's reserve account and does not directly affect demand deposit levels. Nearly half of the reporting dealers are nonbank dealers, so about half of Fed security purchases create new demand deposit credits.

CAN THE FED ALWAYS CONTROL MONEY SUPPLY GROWTH?

Conditions during the Depression years proved that reserve supply methods of controlling monetary growth were not as effective as had been hoped. Monetary growth remained very weak during most of the Depression, causing some analysts to accuse the Fed of following tight monetary policies. A superficial investigation might support this criticism, because Fed officials did liquidate most of their security holdings and raised reserve requirement ratios to the highest level permitted by law. An examination of circumstances and motives behind these Fed actions, however, provides a better understanding of the actual posture of monetary policies during the 1930s.

The United States and its major overseas trading partners were still on the gold standard during the Depression. American price deflation dramatically improved the price competitiveness of U.S. goods and services in global markets, and the U.S. trade surplus rose appreciably. International payments made in gold had reserve effects best understood by first contrasting payments in gold with current methods of transacting international trade.

A foreign purchaser of U.S. goods currently remits payment to a U.S. exporter in dollars. To do this, the foreign importer must purchase dollar credit in the foreign exchange market. The importer pays for dollar credit with a check drawn against his deposit account denominated in a foreign currency and maintained in a foreign bank. The importer actually receives a draft check from a seller of dollars. That draft is drawn against the seller's account in an American bank. This draft (in dollars) is then deposited by the importer into his American bank account, against which a check will be made payable to the American exporter. The receiving bank reserve account is credited, with a corresponding debit to the reserve account of the bank against which the dollar draft was drawn.

After the American exporter deposits the check into his demand deposit account, the importer's demand deposit account will be debited, as will be the reserve account of the importer's American bank. The exporter's demand deposit is credited along with the exporter's bank's reserve account. In this illustration, reserve credit was first transferred from the bank holding the deposit account of the seller of dollars in the currency exchange market, to the bank holding the importer's deposit account; subsequently, reserves were transferred from the importer's bank to the exporter's bank. The international transaction thus had no effect on U.S. bank reserves.

Under the gold standard, however, the importer first had to purchase gold abroad and deliver it to his bank for submittal to the exporter's bank in the United States. The gold was not actually shipped to the United States, but sent instead to the central bank of the importer's country, where it was stored in a separate vault area representing American central bank (Fed) ownership. That foreign central bank would then instruct the Fed to credit the Fed's gold account (listed on the asset side of the Fed's balance sheet) and a corresponding credit would be issued to the reserve account of the exporter's bank (included on the liability side of the Fed's balance sheet). Finally, the exporter's bank would credit the exporter's demand deposit by the amount of new reserve credit received by the bank from the Fed. Under the gold standard, then, the American trade surplus produced an increase in the Fed's gold account and an increase in reserve credit.

Such growth of member bank reserves was quite rapid compared to that of required reserves. During the Depression, the demand for credit weakened as product demands in the private sector weakened. Public sector expenditures did not automatically strengthen, as they would under current fiscal policy, to offset private sector weakness through rising transfer payments. Cutbacks in business and personal loan demands were thus accompanied by very low public sector financing requirements. The weakness of aggregate credit demands made it impossible for banks to expand their loans and investments, despite the gold-related rise in total reserve credit.

With the increased supply of reserves and the reduced demand for credit during the Depression, interest rates fell significantly. Treasury bill rates occasionally fell below zero by a quarter of a percentage point. (Treasury bills were considered a much safer method of storing liquidity than bank demand deposits which, at that time, earned no interest.) Other money market rates were close to zero. There was simply not enough marketable debt available for banks to purchase with rising excess reserves. Given weak loan demand in the private sector and weak government credit demands, new deposit credit could not be manufactured and required reserve levels could not rise in response to the growth of total reserves. At times during the Depression, banks sustained daily averages of excess reserves near or above $6 billion.

Such excessive bank liquidity risked an explosion of deposit credit and money supply had the demand for credit suddenly strengthened. In hindsight, it may seem ridiculous to have been concerned about a resurgence of product and credit demands during the Depression. At the beginning of the Depression, however, economists constantly warned against renewal of inflationary pressures. Washington officials repeatedly assured the public that recovery prospects were in sight throughout the Depression. Concern about excessive bank liquidity, therefore, was not taken lightly.

The growth of reserve credit led Fed officials to reduce their holdings of Treasury securities. Reserve requirement ratios were raised to their maximum limits in order to absorb some of the excess reserve credit. These were not tightening moves. Excess reserves continued to average above $5 billion. Yet such excess reserve availability could not stimulate the growth of money supply during Depression years.

THE DEPOSIT MULTIPLIER[3]

Banking students are taught the principle of multiple deposit expansion and contraction with an implicit assumption of strong demand for bank credit. In classroom examples, the student is often asked to assume a 20 percent reserve requirement on demand deposits. It is supposed that the Fed creates $10 million of new reserve credit through an equivalent purchase of Treasury bills. Then it is assumed that there is only one bank in the U.S., which is credited with the increase in reserve credit. That bank now has $10 million of excess reserves. The bank increases loans or investments by $50 million with an equal increase in new demand deposit credit, and the bank's reserve requirement accordingly increases by $10 million. Excess reserves are absorbed by increased required reserves, while demand deposits and money supply increase by $50 million (Deposits grow by a multiple of five in response to new reserve credit, since 5 x 20 percent equals 100 percent. Had the reserve requirement on demand deposits been 10 percent, the deposit multiplier would have been 10.)

---

[3]A comparison of the money and deposit multipliers might be of further help to understanding the reduced policy importance of currency in circulation. The money multiplier is: Monetary aggregate = Monetary Base times multiplier; or multiplier = MA ÷ MB, where MB = reserve balances plus currency in circulation and MA = deposit aggregate plus currency. Thus multiplier $= \frac{\text{dep.} + \text{cur}}{\text{res.} + \text{cur}}$ which is similar to the deposit multiplier, which $= \frac{\text{dep.}}{\text{res.}}$. In fact, the deposit multiplier determines first order changes in the money multiplier.

The foregoing is subsequently made more realistic for the student by including many competing banks. A given bank receiving additional reserve credit makes new loans only up to the amount of new reserve credit obtained. This lending restraint stems from the likelihood that borrowers will write checks on their new demand deposit credit that become payable to depositors in another bank. The receiving bank experiences an increase in required reserves from the new deposit, as well as an increase in its reserve account after check collection through the Fed. The increase in the receiving bank's reserve account, however, is greater than the increase in its required reserve level, which is a fraction of the deposit increase. The receiving bank can thus make new loans in the amount of its increase in excess reserves.

This example can be repeated for other banks in the check collecting and lending stream, involving successively lower loan amounts and excess reserves transferred to other banks, until the original increase in excess reserves is fully absorbed by higher required reserve levels. The student sees, after measuring total deposit expansion through multiple bank transactions, that the deposit multiplier can be calculated using the reserve requirement ratio. The higher the reserve requirement, the lower the multiplier. This deposit multiplier principle illustrates the "high power money" characteristic of reserve credit in a fractional reserve system.

Step 1: Fed buys $100 million of Treasury bills in the open market from a depositor in Bank A.

Fed		*Bank A*	
Securities Held +100	Reserve Accts. +100	Reserves +100	Demand Dep. +100

Step 2: Bank A has excess reserves of $80 million, assuming that demand deposit reserve requirements are 20 percent, and assuming no previous existence of excess reserves at the Bank. Bank A thus decides to loan $80 million to a depositor, which is subsequently deposited in Bank B.

Bank A

(2) Loans	Demand Deposits
+80	+100 (1)
	+80 (2)
(1) Reserves	−80 (2)
+100	
− 80	(2)
+100	+100

Bank B

	Demand Deposits
	+80 (2)
Reserves +80	
+80	+80

Step 3: Using assumptions in Step 2, Bank B makes a loan of $64 million to a depositor, which is subsequently deposited in Bank C.

Bank B

(3) Loans	Demand Deposits
+64	+80 (2)
	+64 (3)
(2) Reserves	−64 (3)
+80	
(3) − 64	
+80	+80

Bank C

	Demand Deposits
	+64 (3)
Reserves +64	
+64	+64

Step 4: Compare final data of Bank A with Bank B, and extend to other Banks.

BANK	*DEMAND DEPOSITS*	*LOANS*	*RESERVES*
A	+100	+ 80	+ 20
B	+ 80	+ 64	+ 16
C	+ 64	+ 51	+ 13
D	+ 51	+ 41	+ 10
E	+ 41	+ 33	+ 8
F	+ 33	+ 26	+ 7
G	+ 26	+ 21	+ 5
etc.	–	–	–
TOTAL	+500	+400	+100

NOTE: The sum of reserves distributed among banks is equal to reserve balances at the Fed. So, when the Fed adds $100 million of reserves to the System, the sum of additional reserves among all banks equals $100 million. There are no excess reserves because deposits increased by $500 million. The 20 percent reserve requirement on $500 million equals $100 million (increase in required reserves). Had the reserve requirement been 10 percent instead of 20 percent, the deposit multiplier would have been 10 times instead of 5 times, as shown below.

BANK	*DEMAND DEPOSITS*	*LOANS*	*RESERVES*
A	+100	+ 90	+ 10
B	+90	+ 81	+ 9
C	+81	+ 73	+ 8
D	+74	+ 67	+ 7
etc.	–	–	–
TOTAL	+1,000	+900	+100

The student is often left with the impression that the Fed can control the growth of deposits and money simply by controlling the growth of total reserves through open market operations. Rarely is the student asked to consider the reserve effect on deposit expansion if there is no loan demand (while investment opportunities are constricted by reduced supplies of new marketable debt). Of course, new reserve credit under these circumstances would represent unusable excess reserve credits, as was the case during the Depression. Admittedly, the Depression example is extreme. Nonetheless, constant variations in the demand for credit always impart some limitation other than reserve requirement ratios on the deposit multiplier.

The most vivid example of demand-constrained deposit multipliers is constantly displayed in small town banks. Loan demands in rural banks have rarely been sufficient to absorb deposit-related excess reserves, and have always been lower than in money center banks. Country bankers are therefore motivated to sell (lend) excess reserve credit regularly to money center banks, whereas corporate loan demand from corporations is generally intense.

	RESERVE POSITION OF 8 MAJOR NYC BANKS			ASSETS OF 10 MAJOR NYC BANKS*	
	Excess Reserves or Deficit	Net Purchases of Funds	Basic Reserve Surplus or Deficit	Commercial and Industrial Loans	Total Loans and Securities
81 June 19	− 54	10441	−10919	51729	129038
81 Dec. 18	− 9	8676	− 8680	55126	133801
82 June 18	− 15	11835	−11870	59212	135906
82 Dec. 18	− 41	12849	−13022	61316	147898
83 June 17	−144	11303	−11581	56875	143459
83 Dec. 16	− 6	11405	−11406	58252	148742
84 June 14	−140	9075	− 9272	64118	163799
84 Dec. 20	−106	8162	− 8401	63334	170117
85 June 20	− 63	9133	− 9343	61277	179732

* Comparable data for the first three columns on bank assets are not available.

The wide disparity between small banks with excess reserves and large banks with constant reserve deficiencies divides the U.S. banking system into two distinct segments. The distinction arises only from differences in credit demand faced by each class of bank. These differences gave rise to bank liability management options that, in recent decades, have further weakened the Fed's ability to influence bank loan and investment policies and also its ability to control monetary growth.

This chapter has presented a broad picture of U.S. financial history to show how the course of monetary events forced a reticent Congress to delegate its Constitutional power of coinage to a central bank, the Federal Reserve. The Fed gradually developed sophisticated methods of controlling the creation of new money. The power to control "coinage," however, was compromised by limiting the growth of money supply to the manufacture of new deposit credit through bank credit extensions, which were generally affected more by credit demand changes than by Fed control of reserves supplied to the banking system. The delegated power of coinage has also been compromised by the growing dynamics of bank liability management, to which our attention now turns.

CHAPTER 2

The Federal Reserve Versus Liability Management

INTRODUCTION

Federal and state laws prescribe the percentage of various deposit liabilities that commercial banks must hold in the form of reserves. As we saw earlier, these regulations do not ensure that reserves always will be sufficient to meet depositors' demands. The reason is that a $100 cash withdrawal reduces a bank's reserves by $100 but its required reserves by only $10. Rather, reserve requirements serve as a tool of monetary control. Conventional economic theory ascribes the rate of deposit and monetary growth in the banking system to the amount of reserve credit supplied by the Federal Reserve System. According to this theory, when the Fed moderates the supply of bank reserves, bankers are forced to slow deposit liability growth by reducing their loans and investments; thus, the Federal Reserve can control the growth of total bank deposits (and hence the growth of money supply) by targeting its supply of reserve credit to the banking system.

However, throughout most of the 1970s, the rate of monetary growth exceeded the target rate set by the Fed and reviewed by Congress. Some economists blamed the Fed's apparent unwillingness to control money growth and combat inflation by slowing the rate at which reserve credit is supplied to the banking system.

Graph 2.1

M1 Versus Targeted Growth

(monthly data of daily averages)

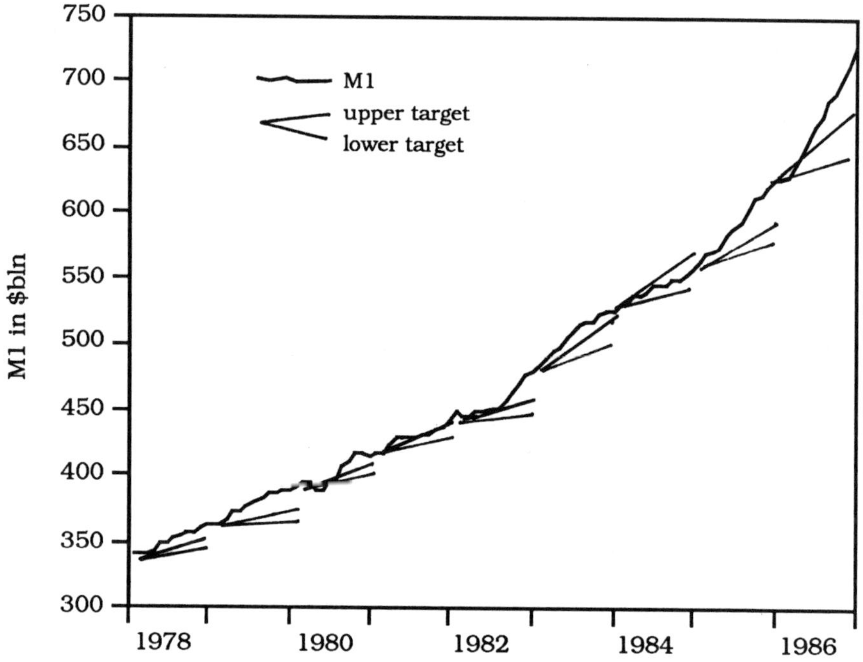

Source: Federal Reserve Bulletin.

Economists tend to overlook the fact that loan demands and reserves are unevenly distributed within the banking system. Many small banks are flooded with excess reserve credit because the communities they serve have little demand for bank loans. If the Fed reduces the availability of reserve credit within the banking system, however, many large banks can be caught lacking reserve credit. Large corporate loan demands are focussed on the large money center banks, which usually leaves large banks in need of more reserve credit to accommodate loan demands.

To meet reserve requirements, these banks could reduce their loan and investment activity (thus reducing deposit growth). Alternatively, they may secure reserve credit from smaller banks with excess reserve credit, either by borrowing in the Fed funds market or by raising the interest paid on certain time deposits to induce an inflow of deposits and reserves from other banks. These options fall within the scope of liability management, while adjustments in loan and investment policies constitute asset management.

Because of liability management, restrictive reserve policies may fail to slow the growth of bank loans and investments during the initial six to nine months of firmer policy. Banks needing reserve credit respond to policy tightening by utilizing more aggressively the pools of excess reserve credit available throughout the country, and the expansion of total deposits continues relative to the slower growth in total reserves. The resultant increase in deposit and money multipliers represents the more efficient use of existing reserve credit through liability management. Related evidence is presented and discussed at the end of this chapter.

The dynamics of liability management limit the Fed's influence over money supply growth. Most monetary theory, however, fails to consider bank liability management options, thereby fostering academic misconceptions.

ACADEMIC MISCONCEPTIONS

Textbooks incorrectly define trading in the federal funds market as the borrowing and lending of *excess* reserve credit among member banks. Fed funds trading, however, involves all reserve credit, not just excess reserves. Motivated by arbitrage opportunities in the Fed funds market, many banks regularly lend some of their existing reserve credit to other banks on an overnight basis, even if they lack excess reserves. They are able to do this because reserve requirements must be met only on average over the reserve maintenance period.

Textbooks also inaccurately state that banks cannot make new loans or investments unless they have excess reserve credit or a reserve surplus with which to fund these loans and investments. The eight weekly reporting New York City banks, however, have aggressively booked new loans in recent decades without ever posting a weekly surplus in their "basic reserve position" (defined as total reserves less net funds borrowed in the Fed funds market). At present, these banks must often borrow more than $10 billion of reserve funds in the Fed funds market each day to meet reserve requirements. Deficits in basic reserve positions have not deterred these banks from rapidly expanding their loan portfolios.

Moreover, textbook portrayals of banking behavior oversimplify the Fed's role in controlling deposit and monetary growth. Typically, textbooks refer to bank Treasury bill holdings as "secondary reserves" to show that a reduction in reserve credit by the Fed can force banks to sell their highly liquid bills. These bill sales in turn reduce deposit credit and money supply growth. At the present time, however, the banker's first line of defense against illiquidity is not an asset management decision such as the liquidation of bills, but liability management.

Suppose for example that a bank is seriously short of reserve credit, perhaps due to restrictive Federal Reserve policy. Reduced availability of reserve credit has forced bill rates and other money market rates to rise significantly since the bills held in the bank's investment portfolio were purchased. Since this means that the market prices of bills of comparable maturity have declined, a sale of bills from the portfolio could produce a trading loss or, at a minimum, reduce significantly the rate of return on the bill investment.

A banker faced with losing money from a liquidation of bills may consider raising needed reserve credit by issuing a certificate of deposit (CD). Purchase of a CD by a depositor at another bank transfers deposit credit and reserve credit from that bank to the CD-issuing bank. Moreover, if the purchaser of the CD pays for it by drawing down his checking account, the total required reserves of the banking system will decline because the reserve requirement on CDs is lower than on checkable deposits. In this case the textbook discussion is correct in concluding that the Fed policy of reducing the supply of reserves leads to a decrease in the stock of demand deposits (and M1), but is incorrect in inferring that the availability of bank loans is reduced. Acquiring this deposit liability could cost the bank more in interest than it is earning on its bill holdings, but it could prevent the bank from having to liquidate those bill holdings at a loss. The banker in these circumstances might be wise to expand deposit liabilities, rather than liquidate investments, especially if he expects the increase in interest rates to continue. Indeed, market expectations (measured by Money Market Services, Inc.) typically project continuation of an existing cyclical trend in interest rates. The extension of deposit liabilities, at a time of rising interest rates, "locks in" today's CD rate over future months when CD rates are likely to be higher. The bill investment can be allowed to mature without replacement (if liquidity is subsequently needed), or rolled-over into higher yielding bill investments in the near future.

Liability management options can be exercised through various deposit markets, including the CD, Eurodollar and Fed funds markets. Bear in mind that bank liability managers do not merely take advantage of existing markets; they created these markets, which are described in the following sections.

THE NEGOTIABLE CD MARKET

Large banks began issuing certificates of deposit during the 1960s. Although CD maturities are often set to meet specific needs of large investors, standard maturities range from 30 days to one year. The minimum denomination has been $100,000; round lots of $1 million are sold at slightly higher interest rates. Unlike Treasury bills or commercial paper, the CD carries a stated rate of interest payable at maturity and is issued at a stated par value that, along with accrued interest, is paid to the investor at maturity. CDs are negotiable instruments, which means that they can be traded in money markets after issuance and prior to maturity. Although a CD can be sold in secondary markets prior to maturity, secondary market activity has not been sufficient to sustain narrow margins between bids and offers. CD liquidations in the secondary market can, therefore, slightly reduce the investor's return (even if CD rates remain stable).

The Federal Deposit Insurance Corporation (FDIC), to which nearly all U.S. banks belong, limits the amount of deposit insurance per depositor account to $100,000 at any given bank. Consequently, a CD investment, which may be ten times this amount, is essentially a commercial bank's unsecured promissory note. Investors mitigate credit risk by purchasing only CDs issued by the largest commercial banks in the United States, reasoning that the size of a large bank reflects its solvency, by virtue of good management and asset diversification.

In general, investors will not accept CD paper issued by smaller banks. Conceivably, collectives of small banks could be formed to issue CD liabilities under a mutual name, collectively achieving asset diversification and size commensurate with that of large banks. But small banks have no need to issue CDs; these banks regularly supply excess reserve credit to the Fed funds market. Small banks could purchase CD funds for resale in the funds market, but the loss from paying CD rates that are generally higher than the Fed funds rate renders this option unattractive.

The CD market therefore exists primarily to transfer excess liquidity from smaller banks to accommodate the greater loan demands of reserve-deficient large banks. An increase in the number of CDs outstanding usually reflects an increase in the transfer of demand deposit credit and reserve credit from non-CD-issuers (small banks) to CD-issuers (approximately two dozen large banks). Of course, a given bank may purchase funds from (issue CDs to) one of its depositors, thereby preventing loss of deposit and reserve credit to another bank. Some of the past growth in CDs has thus produced a shift in the composition of deposits at the large banks; the growth in CDs was partly associated with a reduction in other time and savings deposits. For the most part, however, CD expansion reflected the large banks' acquisition of depositor funds and related reserve credit from small banks.

The cost of buying reserve credit through the CD market is slightly higher than the prevailing CD rate, due to the current 3 percent reserve requirement imposed by the Fed on CD deposit liabilities to non-personal holders. However, the downtrend in the number of outstanding CDs since 1983 is due not to this requirement but rather to the establishment of new Money Market Deposit Accounts (MMDAs).

In December 1982, banks were permitted to introduce MMDAs to compete with money market mutual funds administered and marketed by nonbank financial companies. Although MMDAs offer some features of checking accounts, no reserve requirements are imposed on deposits by individuals; business accounts have a 3 percent reserve requirement. To date, large bank MMDA rates have been competitive with money market fund rates and other bank MMDA rates, and have attracted substantial depositor funds into MMDA accounts.

MMDA funds are less expensive to banks than CD funds, primarily because a larger proportion of the total are personal accounts, which are not subject to reserve requirements. But CDs are more effective than MMDAs in tapping the large pool of liquidity among non-money center banks. Unlike MMDAs, CDs are issued in large denominations that enable bank liability managers to effect large and sudden changes in the funding of assets.

The CD market encourages the efficient utilization of total reserves of the banking system by enabling reserve credit to flow from areas of weak demand for bank credit to areas of strong demand. This flow of funds is controlled not by the Fed but by bank depositors and managers of large banks.

THE EURODOLLAR MARKET

Large banks regularly tap the Eurodollar market for additional reserve credit. The mechanics of the Eurodollar market, however, have confused many economists who, during the 1960s, incorrectly predicted that a runaway expansion of Eurodollar credit would reduce the credit-worthiness of international money markets.

Eurodollars are dollar-denominated deposits in banks outside the United States; thus the Eurodollar market is beyond the jurisdiction of the U.S. government or, indeed, that of any single government. The rate ceilings imposed on some deposit accounts in the United States are therefore not enforceable at foreign branches of American banks. By paying higher interest on offshore dollar deposits than on domestic deposits, American banks began to lure large deposits from domestic banks to offshore markets. Large American banks with overseas branches could bid deposit and reserve credit away from smaller banks not capable of financing overseas operations.

For example, suppose that a London branch of an American bank receives a dollar denominated check drawn on another American bank, and this check is to be deposited in a Eurodollar account. Because of its parent bank's membership in the Fed, the receiving branch can submit the check directly to a Fed district bank for collection (normally the San Francisco or the New York Fed). The Fed debits the reserve account of the paying bank and credits the reserve account of the receiving branch's parent bank.

The parent bank's balance sheet will then show an increase (on the asset side) in reserve balances held at the Fed, with an equal increase (on the liability side) in a deposit account called "due to foreign branches." This "due to" account is essentially a demand deposit account held by the parent bank for its foreign branch. This transaction is called a "Eurodollar borrowing" by the parent. The foreign branch's balance sheet shows an increase in an asset account called "due from parent bank," with an equal increase in the Eurodollar deposit liability account.

Thus, simply by having its foreign branch acquire Eurodollar deposits, the parent bank can acquire new reserve credit from another American bank. American bankers promoted the Eurodollar market as a source of deposit and reserve credit to finance their domestic lending operations. As such, the Eurodollar market is basically a "depo," or deposit, market.

The offshore dollar-deposit market originated shortly after World War II, when the U.S.S.R. decided to avoid risking U.S. nationalization of Russian dollar deposits in American banks. These deposits

EURODOLLAR BORROWINGS

Offshore branch of an American bank (parent) purchases (borrows) deposit credit from a depositor of another American bank:

Parent Bank

Reserves +	Due to +

Offshore Branch

Due from +	Due to +

Fed

	Reserve Accts. Parent Bank + Small Bank −

Small Bank

Reserves −	Demand Deposit −

were thus transferred to banks in London. American banks slowly developed an interest for dollar deposit credit in London, commensurate with the very gradual firming of U.S. reserve conditions in the sixties. When reserve conditions became much tighter in 1967 and again in 1969, U.S. banks expanded their offshore branch bidding for dollar deposits to other European financial centers, and to Asia. The latter offshore expansion was heralded as the beginnings of the Asiadollar market, a term which did not long endure because of the aggressive expansion of the dollar depo market to all corners of the world (particularly where liberal reporting requirements created so-called "tax-havens"). For a long time, the term "Euro" prefaced the offshore dollar market regardless of location. At present, there is a growing tendency to refer to the offshore dollar deposit market simply as the depo market.

Dollar deposits flowed abundantly into various world trade and financial centers commensurate with previous U.S. balance of payment deficits and trade deficits. Such outflow of deposit credit from the U.S. did not have much restraint on money and product flows within the U.S., partly because the growth of bank credit and monetary aggregates was often excessive during postwar years. The abundance of offshore dollar deposit credit facilitated the exchange of many foreign currencies through use of dollar trades as an intermediate step. The dollar was thus referred to as a "vehicle currency" in currency exchange markets.

The dollar also became a vehicle currency in commodity markets. Most commodities in world markets are quoted and transacted in dollar prices. Accordingly, when the dollar depreciates against most currencies abroad, there is a need for foreign suppliers to adjust dollar prices upward to maintain their local purchasing power. Such inflationary implications for U.S. imports can be mitigated through restricted monetary growth (to discourage passing on higher dollar costs to consumers).

EURODOLLAR LENDING TO INDUSTRY

Large banks also lose reserve credit through the lending of Eurodollar credit. Multinational corporations based in the U.S. increasingly borrow Eurodollar credit to finance their overseas operations, in addition to borrowing directly from domestic large banks.

To a large bank, the difference between a loan originating in a domestic parent bank and a loan originating in its foreign branch is not significant. Both loans entail the creation of new deposit credit through loan extension. Checks issued by the borrower against a deposit account will most likely be payable to depositors in other banks and will therefore cost the lending bank a loss of reserve credit. Whether a loan originates in a foreign branch or in its U.S. parent, the bank must replace the reserves lost by bidding for more reserve credit in either domestic markets (such as the CD market) or offshore markets. These liability management actions merely transfer the ownership of existing reserve credit among member banks.

EURODOLLAR TRADING AMONG BANKS

When a large bank unexpectedly acquires excess reserve credit through the CD market or Fed funds market at prevailing or lower rates of interest, the liability manager may want to reduce temporarily the amount of reserve credit already acquired in the Eurodollar market by "selling" (lending) Eurodollar deposits to other banks bidding for deposit credit. Rates paid on Eurodollar deposits vary according to the deposit's maturity, which is specified in days or months. These deposits may not be withdrawn prior to maturity, so the deposit credit can be given a second maturity matching its first, then "sold" to another bank. In offshore deposit markets, continuous bidding and offering activity enables the liability manager to adjust Eurodollar positions quickly to meet fluctuating needs for reserves.

In addition to reserve considerations, trades in depo markets depend on changes in rate spreads between various deposit maturities and between offshore deposits and domestic deposits. Unusual rate spreads prompt arbitrage trading. Whether motivated by rate spreads or by reserve needs, inter-bank trading of Eurodollars does not exist as a means to market new loans. The Eurodollar market is essentially a deposit market through which large banks can adjust their reserve positions as needed to sustain domestic and overseas loan growth.

THREAT OF EURODOLLAR EXPANSION

Economists have expressed concern about the lack of reserve requirements on Eurodollar deposits, even though they recognize that no governmental jurisdiction can impose such requirements on an international market. They often conclude that Eurodollar loans, not limited by deposit reserve requirements, could infinitely expand Eurodollar deposit credit. This expansion could in turn create an upsurge in dollar credit with inflationary consequences should the credit flow back to the U.S.

In reality, Eurodollar borrowings by American banks are effectively subject to reserve requirements. When a foreign branch acquires a Eurodollar deposit and submits the related check to the Fed for collection and credit to the reserve account of its U.S. parent bank, the parent bank records an increase to its reserve account and a corresponding increase in the "due to" account (demand deposit) of its foreign branch. The "due-to" account, as a U.S. demand deposit, is subject to the same Fed-imposed reserve requirements as other domestic demand deposits. As long as the offshore branch holds the Eurodollar deposit, the parent bank's reserve requirement remains at a higher level.

When a foreign branch acquires a Eurodollar deposit but does not lend it (at a higher rate) to another bank, the increase in the "due to" liability of the parent bank is permanent. At times, in the past, the Fed has imposed a supplemental reserve requirement on these Eurodollar borrowings (due-to accounts) to discourage large banks from tapping the Eurodollar market when reserve policies are tight. The due-to account, as an inter-bank demand deposit, is subject to demand deposit reserve requirements as well as to any supplemental (additional) requirement. A supplemental three percent requirement on Eurodollar borrowings currently exists to discourage their use because of associated higher costs.

Depo trading does not present unlimited opportunities to expand deposit credit. In essence, Eurodollar deposit trading redistributes existing reserve credit and is identical to trading in the Fed funds market, where trades are exempt from reserve requirements. The amount of Eurodollar credit outstanding is limited by the amount of reserves supplied by the Fed, by reserve requirements imposed on Eurodollar borrowings, and by private, rate-related decisions to deposit dollar-denominated checks in offshore banks.

THE FED FUNDS MARKET

Fed funds trading is limited to banks that hold reserve accounts at the Fed. Such trading requires the Fed to transfer reserve accounts between banks for reserves borrowed and lent overnight. The borrowing bank's reserve account is credited one day and debited the next business day. A credit, including the predetermined amount of interest, is made at maturity to the reserve account of the lending bank.

The balance sheets of these banks show changes, not to "due from" or "due to" accounts, but to accounts entitled "Fed funds purchased" and "Fed funds sold." This reference denotes change in ownership rather than change in liabilities and was initially hoped to discourage Fed officials from imposing reserve requirements on purchased Fed funds. Fed officials prefer not to impose such reserve requirements because they would create a cost constraint that would reduce the desired flow of reserve credit among banks. Open market operations directly affect the reserve accounts of bank-reporting dealers and of large money center banks holding deposits for non-bank-reporting dealers. Without an active funds market the influence of Fed open market operations would be limited to fewer than two dozen large banks. With Fed funds trading, however, the restraining influence of restrictive monetary policy is immediately transmitted throughout the nation.

As the funds rate varies in response to changing reserve conditions through each business day, traders attempt to profit from these rate swings. In contrast to most small member banks who sell anticipated excess reserves each day in the funds market, large banks employ traders who continuously buy and sell reserve credit for arbitrage purposes. Traders having to finance reserve deficiencies will nonetheless sell funds if they believe that these funds can later be repurchased at a reduced rate. Conversely, if the funds rate is expected to rise, traders may buy (i.e borrow) fed funds and create an excess reserve position, hoping to sell (lend) such reserve credit later at a higher rate. This speculation and arbitrage produces a highly liquid market through which some $130 billion of daily trades accommodate the desires of liability managers.

THE FED'S POLICIES FOR SUPPLYING RESERVES

The Federal Open Market Committee (FOMC) meets eight times a year in Washington, D.C. to assess economic and financial situations and to formulate an open market policy posture that will foster full employment and stable prices. The Committee has twelve voting members. Permanent voting members of the Committee include the seven members of the Board of Governors and the president of the New York Fed. Presidents of the other eleven Reserve Banks fill the remaining four voting memberships on a rotating basis. However, the non-voting Presidents also attend and take part in the discussion. After each meeting, the FOMC issues a Directive to the Manager of the New York Trading Desk.

FOMC meetings are closed to the public, since immediate public knowledge of changes in reserve policy could potentially disrupt financial markets. Bond dealers possessing immediate knowledge of policy changes, for example, might profit immensely at the expense of other debt market participants. Fed operations and policy deliberations are thus conducted behind a veil of secrecy. Policy changes gradually become visible, enabling financial markets to make needed adjustments in an orderly fashion.

To meet the terms of the Freedom of Information Act, minutes of each FOMC meeting must be made available to the public within a month of that meeting. Analysts in search of clues scrutinize each sentence of the released minutes. However, in recent years, the minutes have reported only general, rather than specific, policy concepts and actions.

Changes in open market policy are sometimes made between formal FOMC meetings, during phone conferences initiated by the Chairman of the FOMC, who is also the Chairman of the Board of Governors. In addition, a conference call is held each business day between Desk officials in New York and FOMC staff members in Washington. One FOMC member, typically a Reserve Bank President, also takes part to ensure that day to day operations are following the policy directive established at the most recent FOMC meeting. During these conferences, the daily reserve situation and proposed open market activity are discussed. If these officials decide that incoming economic or financial data (including monetary data) might warrant a policy change, the FOMC chairman will schedule a separate phone conference to further discuss and vote on a change in open market policy.

The general aims and posture of open market policy decided at FOMC meetings must be translated into specific levels of borrowed and nonborrowed reserves for Desk officials to target. For example, under a completely *accommodative* open market policy, Desk officials would regularly supply banks with all the nonborrowed reserve credit they needed to meet reserve requirements. As banks raised their deposit liabilities and reserve requirement levels through additional loans and investments, Desk officials would finance all additional reserve credit needed. Such a policy posture is accommodative in the sense that no reserve restraint is imposed, though not truly stimulative.

In a truly stimulative open market stance, Desk officials would supply more nonborrowed reserve credit than banks needed to meet reserve requirements. Liberal supplies of reserve credit tend to produce a high level of excess reserve credit and so cause the Fed funds rate to drop, perhaps by more than is required to keep the economy on a non-inflationary growth path.

Prior to 1986, fears of inflation persuaded Fed officials to avoid policies that produced large free reserve positions in which excess reserves exceeded the level of adjustment borrowings. As will be explained in chapter 7, structural changes in recent years appear to have increased the average level of excess reserves so that a situation in which there are substantial free reserves no longer indicates a highly stimulative posture.

TARGETING TOTAL RESERVES

A number of economists believe that the Fed should target a steady growth in total reserves, instead of targeting either borrowed or nonborrowed reserves. Graphs of either weekly or monthly money multipliers hint of a relatively stable trend. If the money multiplier remained stable in the future, as these economists apparently assume it would, then steady and moderate growth in total reserves would result in steady and moderate money supply growth.

This argument for targeting total reserves is appealing, but overlooks two major problems encountered when trying to control money supply growth. First, while the graph of the money multiplier may seem to exhibit stability, quite small changes in the money multiplier produce large dollar changes in M1. Multiplying the historical changes in the money multiplier by a constant (not the actual) level of total reserves produces rather large calculated changes in the money supply. Since irregular and large changes in the money multiplier are difficult to predict, it is difficult to project the level of total reserves that would produce a desired money supply level.

Second, it is impossible to control precisely the growth of total reserves. Banks are authorized to increase their reserve credit by borrowing from the Fed. Bankers try to accommodate strong credit demands by extending new loan and investment credit. This increase in deposit liabilities raises reserve requirements, which banks must meet even if the Fed reduces its supply of nonborrowed reserves. Faced with a shortage of nonborrowed reserves, individual bankers tap the Fed funds, CD, and Eurodollar markets, but these cannot provide added reserves to the banking system as a whole. A system-wide reserve shortage can be met only by added borrowing from the Fed. Of course, discount officers at the Fed threaten heavy borrowers with disciplinary action unless they restore liquidity by reducing extensions of new credit. Realistically, however, the Fed must supply, in any reserve maintenance period, at least enough total reserves (either borrowed or nonborrowed) to meet the requirements of the banking system as a whole. A shortage of nonborrowed reserves affects bank behavior by raising the marginal *cost* of reserves (because they must be obtained at the discount window), not by making reserves unobtainable.

There are limits to the amount of reserve credit that can be transferred from banks with reserve excesses to banks with reserve deficiencies through liability markets. As these limits are approached, short-term interest rates rise, banks have more difficulty staying away from the discount window, and banks must begin rationing their loans and investments. A shortage of nonborrowed reserve credit will therefore not immediately reduce the growth of total reserves (or the level of reserve requirements). Only after a lag does the shortage of nonborrowed reserve credit begin to slow the growth of loans and investments. This slowing, in turn, tempers the growth of deposit liabilities, required reserve levels, and total reserves. Such an indirect relationship between open market operations of the Fed and the level of total reserves makes targeting total reserves impractical.

TARGETING NONBORROWED RESERVES

Due to the problems associated with targeting total reserves, some economists advocate targeting nonborrowed reserves, which can be controlled by the Fed's open market desk. Steady growth in nonborrowed reserves, however, will not yield steady or predictable money supply growth. Again, liability management actions constantly change the degree of efficiency with which existing nonborrowed reserve credit is utilized, thus altering the reserve multiplier and making it difficult to predict the short-term relationship between nonborrowed reserves and money supply. Between October 1979 and mid-1982, the Fed attempted to follow (with wide variations in degree of effort) an operating procedure of targeting nonborrowed reserves as a means of controlling (and slowing) the growth of M1. During this period, the FOMC staff tried to predict changes in the reserve multiplier resulting from liability management and to offset them by varying the supply of nonborrowed reserves. Nonetheless, "multiplier errors" occurred. In addition, targeting nonborrowed reserves created more volatile funds rates and raised the danger of serious financial dislocations. This problem will be discussed further in chapter 5.

THE NET BORROWED TARGET: MUSICAL CHAIRS

Of all operational targets considered by the FOMC, the net borrowed reserve target has given the Fed the most control of money supply growth, a conclusion subject to close examination in chapter 5. The effectiveness of targeting net borrowed reserves and the associated activity of the Fed funds market can be compared to the well-known game of musical chairs. In this game, there are fewer chairs (nonborrowed reserves) than players (reserve requirements). Players walk around the limited numbers of chairs until the music stops, and they each try to sit down. In the funds market, traders pass reserve credit around member banks until the end of the statement period on Wednesday.

In musical chairs, there are not enough chairs to seat all players, so some players will be left standing when the music stops. In the funds market, there are insufficient nonborrowed reserves to accommodate all banks, so a certain amount of reserves will have to be borrowed from the Fed before the end of the statement period. The greater the shortage of nonborrowed reserves relative to required reserves, the higher the level of net borrowed reserves. As the level of net borrowed reserves increases, the number of frequent borrowers exposed to disciplinary action is likely to increase. As a result, short term interest rates tend to rise as banks seek to avoid borrowing through the discount facility.

Open market operations represent the leading edge of restrictive monetary policy by creating a shortage of nonborrowed reserves that forces bankers to the discount window. Discount administration represents the cutting edge of restrictive policy by threatening disciplinary action unless bankers reduce extensions of loans and investments. The greater the discipline at the discount window, the greater the effectiveness of a given net borrowed target. Fed officials do not want to impose too much restraint at the window, because banks need time to make orderly adjustments to loan and investment policies in response to tighter Fed policy.

Liability managers do not become concerned about a one-week or two-week increase in net borrowed reserves. If higher net borrowed reserve pressures persist, however, the liability manager can expect more difficulty funding loan and investment expansion. In making needed adjustments to tighter reserve conditions, bankers must rely more heavily on deposit markets than on the Fed funds market. The latter, having daily and average trading volumes of $100 billion-plus and $10 million-plus (respectively), is suitable for short term adjustments. Intermediate term adjustments (up to one year) must rely on intermediate maturities of debt available in deposit markets.

When bankers secure reserve credit on an intermediate term basis from Eurodollar and CD markets, they produce a change in the composition of bank deposits from highly liquid demand and savings accounts to time deposits. Narrowly defined money supply growth can thus exhibit a relatively quick slowdown response to tighter reserve conditions. Such response, however, is often temporary because the associated change in reserve flows through depo markets enables bankers to continue the growth of bank credit, which represents an expansion in the dollar deposit base that often (and quickly) restores demand deposit growth. The associated increase in reserve requirements can be financed, over the short run, by the liability management-sponsored improved utilization of existing reserve credit, in lieu of accommodative reserve supplies by the Fed. Equivalent first order increases in CDs and demand deposits will nonetheless reflect a reduced proportion of demand to total deposits (bank credit); and M1 growth may persist at relatively high rates in spite of accelerated time deposit growth. As chapter 4 will illustrate in detail, monetary aggregates are quite inferior to the bank credit aggregate insofar as controlling the power of coinage is concerned. It is important to note, for the moment, that liability manager use of depo markets delays the slowdown in bank credit growth (deposit base growth), which must ultimately occur as a result of sustained net borrowed reserve pressures.

OTHER LIABILITY MANAGEMENT MARKETS

Banks are prohibited by law from issuing commercial paper. However, during the 1960s, bankers formed bank holding companies (often one-bank holding companies), which may issue commercial paper. In general, only the holding companies of large banks enjoy sufficient credibility to succeed in issuing unsecured commercial paper. With the proceeds, a holding company can purchase loans from its subsidiary bank(s), unless its commercial paper was purchased by depositors of its own bank who merely rearranged their assets. The commercial paper market provides bank liability managers with a more limited volume of reserve funds than the CD or Eurodollar market.

The importance of the bankers acceptance (BA) market to the liability manager has diminished over the years. BAs originate from loans to international exporters wishing to sell receivables from importers in anticipation of payment. The loan maturity is generally

90 days, roughly the time required to ship goods to the importer. Importer payments to the exporter are used to retire the exporter's indebtedness to banks. The bank loan is secured by the goods in shipment and by insurance on the shipment. Bankers then pool these loans to issue BAs to investors, taking a small portion of the interest revenue in the process. Acceptance pooling enables bankers to issue BAs in amounts desired by investors, rather than in the actual loan amounts. BAs enable large banks to secure more reserve funds from small bank depositors, but the supply is limited by the amount of exporter goods in transit financed by acceptances.

The Federal Reserve used to encourage foreign trade through purchases and sales of BAs in the open market, along with Treasury securities and federal agency securities. However, with the decline in their prominence, the Fed has ceased dealing in BAs.

ASSET MANAGEMENT

Liability management actions may prevent rising net borrowed pressures from causing an immediate slowdown in personal and business loan growth, but the reserve pressure will eventually affect some asset management policies. The first sign of tighter open market policy signals the investment portfolio manager that only rates and bond yields will increase, thereby decreasing the market value of any currently held fixed-income investments. The manager responds by limiting current bond investment expansion. Any initial tightening within a business cycle produces market expectations of further tightening. Thus, policy firming not only causes rates to increase directly, but also triggers an ongoing rise in rates due to market perceptions. Armed with this knowledge, the portfolio manager halts any rapid expansion of bank investments, further slowing overall deposit expansion and money supply growth.

Bankers tend to avoid drastic changes in their lending policies, due to a well-founded fear of losing loan business to other banks. Business and personal loyalties are important determinants of a bank's ability to maintain its market share of existing loan business. The mortgage loan is the exception to consistent lending policies. Because the mortgage contract has such a long term, a small mortgage rate change produces a significant change in monthly interest payments, so bankers assign less importance to customer loyalty. Bankers can attract mortgage loan customers by lowering the mortgage rate or turn them away by raising it.

Since bankers do not want to commit their assets to a fixed, long-term yield when interest rates are increasing, managers will adjust mortgage rates upward when they perceive that policy is firming. As a result the housing sector tends to be an early victim of tight monetary policies.

A FINAL NOTE ON LIABILITY MANAGEMENT

A loose statistical relationship (with a six-month lag) has existed between net borrowed reserve pressures in the banking system and the growth of bank credit, expressed as a ratio of bank credit to aggregate credit demands. Historically, when the Fed has supplied banks with adequate reserve credit to meet required reserves, banks provided about a third of total credit demands by extending new loans and investments. For every $100 million of reserve shortage that forces banks to borrow reserve credit from the Fed, the percentage of credit demands monetized through the extension of bank credit falls by .2 percentage points. In other words, for every $100 million increase in net borrowed reserves, a .2 percent decline in the ratio of bank credit to total GNP (GNP is used here as a proxy for total credit demands) generally occurs six months later. Hence, although liability managers cannot control the volume of reserve credit, they can affect the efficiency with which existing reserve credit is utilized to weaken the linkage between open market operations and growth of the U.S. dollar deposit base (bank credit).

THE RELATIONSHIP BETWEEN RESERVE RESTRAINT
AND MONETIZATION BY COMMERCIAL BANKS

Equation: $BC/GNP = .37 - .000016 * NB + .0017 * T + E$
$(.0032)\ (.000004)\ \ \ \ (.0001)$

BC	= Bank Credit
GNP	= GNP, used here as a proxy for total credit
NB	= Net Borrowed Reserves
T	= Time Trend: T = 1 in 60Q1, T = 40 in 69Q4.
E	= Error
R^2	= .82
DW	= 1.92

NOTES:
1. Quarterly data from the first quarter of 1960 to the fourth quarter of 1969.
2. Numbers in parenthesis are the standard error for the coefficients.
3. GNP is used as a proxy for total credit because of difficulties in incorporating offshore lending activity in available credit aggregates.
4. Quarterly data gives little indication of lags, so no lag is used in the regression.
5. The 1960s were chosen because this was a period of net borrowed targeting, unlike the 1970s or much of the 1980s. The equation is only estimated to reveal the relationship in the 1960s and not to be used for predicting credit flows in the 1980s, as the coefficient values are likely to have changed.
6. The estimated equation suggests that a $300 mln increase in the net borrowed target would have reduced bank credit growth by approximately one percent in the 1960s.

The dynamics of liability management have convinced some economists and Fed officials that the control of monetary growth cannot be achieved through reserve management. They therefore advocate Fed reliance on controlling short-term interest rates as a means of controlling the demand for money, and hence monetary growth. The thesis presented here is that reserve management, while not capable of controlling monetary growth, can significantly influence such growth, and much more so than interest rate targeting. But before examining the issue of targeting interest rates, it is necessary to define the influence of Fed operations and policy actions on various interest rates.

CHAPTER 3

Interest Rates

INTRODUCTION

The relationship between monetary policy and interest rates has long been the subject of debate. During the 1970s, Fed Chairman Arthur Burns so frequently asserted that the money supply (as opposed to Fed actions) determined interest rates that Congress and the public came to agree. Debt market participants held the converse view, namely, that the Fed controlled the level of money rates in order to influence the demand for money and, hence, money supply growth. These two views may seem similar but there are important differences. As for the similarity, if the demand to *hold* money balances is not accommodated by the Fed because of restricted reserve supplies, money rates will increase. Or, if the Fed targets the funds rate to limit the public's demand to hold money balances, this too will raise interest rates.

Thus far in this book, the focus on money creation has rightfully pinpointed bank credit extensions through loans and investments. If there is a demand for new bank credit extensions, then over the short run new money (deposit credit) is likely to be created by banks without much concern about reserve availability. It might be helpful to recall that when you applied for a loan, the banker looked at your ability to repay, and did not look at the bank's reserve position. Of course, in the longer run, trends in reserve availability impact bank loan policies.

In later chapters it will be shown that the demand for bank credit exhibits an inelasticity to interest rate changes, which over the short run means that Fed-induced interest rate changes will not impact the growth of the dollar deposit base—that is, will not affect the pace of money creation. To monetarists, however, such argument is not relevant because the demand to hold M1 balances must decline as interest rate increases push upward the rates payable on non-checkable deposits included in M2. In other words, the opportunity cost of holding M1 balances can be driven up by Fed control of money rates, thereby limiting M1 growth. Some of the economists holding this view seem to lack consistency when, in recent times, they advocated placing more policy emphasis on M2 growth than on M1 growth. Because M2 includes most of the dollar deposit base, in contrast to M1, the related demand for money is more closely aligned with the demand for bank credit than with the demand for holding liquid M1 balances.

The counter-argument notes that M2 assets are easily convertible into checkable M1 balances, and thus partly represent a medium of exchange, and certainly represent a better (and more active) store of value than M1 assets. This is one reason for placing policy emphasis on M2 growth. The demand for money balances is claimed to be applicable to M2 assets because their opportunity costs also rise when higher money rates lift the spread of bill yields over those on M2 accounts.

However, deposit credit used to purchase money market instruments merely transfers the ownership of such credit from the buyer to the seller. Variable interest rate spreads may affect the composition of bank deposits, but do not directly affect the quantity of such credit outstanding. This principle supports the observation that the greater the inclusion of various bank deposits in a monetary aggregate, the less meaningful will be the interest rate effect on the composition of bank deposits. Instead of thinking of money demand as a demand to hold liquid balances, the growth of the broader monetary aggregate is more closely linked with bank credit demands.

To the financial market participant, Dr. Burns' claim that interest rates were determined by the intersection of money supply with money demand was simply not observable from available evidence.

Because M1 growth generally grew well above its targeted range during the Burns years, it was widely suspected that the control of money supply was beyond Fed understanding or capabilities. Fed-induced increases in money rates failed to moderate bank credit demand, and higher rates did not appreciably impact deposit composition.

The more stable composition of bank deposits (between M1 and M2 accounts) was ascribed to unreasonable limits placed on maximum rates payable on M2 accounts, which have since been relaxed in the wake of financial deregulation policies of the 1980s. Yet even today, changing rates and rate spreads cannot be closely linked with changes in deposit composition. The latter, apart from being heavily impacted by financial deregulation, seems to be much more related to national income growth and related spending propensities. Accordingly, the thesis that the Fed can control demands for holding M1 balances does not withstand empirical testing as well as advocates would desire. But more importantly, if the Fed ever hopes to get some grip on money supply growth it must focus on demand for bank credit instead of demand for money balances.

Because Fed control of interest rates has not, and will not, control M1, or M2, or M3 growth, such control will fail to be associated with corresponding changes in money supply growth rates to invalidate the claim of Dr. Burns. In other words, the Fed can control interest rates independent of the short term intersection of money demand and money supply. As subsequent chapters will examine in greater detail, bank credit extensions respond to reserve availability over the long run, but not to interest rate changes over the short run. Reserve restraint which affects monetary growth also affects interest rate behavior (to be investigated in this chapter). However, Fed targeting of interest rates can sever the relationship of reserve availability to money rates, as happened in the 1970s. Under such circumstances, interest rate and monetary behavior can be divergent, whereas they tend to display similar behavior under reserve targeting. This chapter will hopefully make the foregoing point unmistakably clear.

There is also a widely-held notion that the Fed cannot precisely control money rates, or significantly influence the behavior of long term bond yields. Fed chairmen have frequently warned Congress that fiscal deficits have a greater effect on interest rates than the Fed. In the long run, this claim has some validity, but in the short run, it is hard to validate. For example, during his 1984 campaign, presidential candidate Walter Mondale charged that growing fiscal deficits during the Reagan Administration kept interest rates unacceptably high. Fed Chairman Paul Volcker agreed that the Federal government's increased demands on a constant supply of credit forced interest rates too far above the inflation rate. President Reagan countered by citing the record decline in interest rates in 1982, at a time of rising deficits.

To understand the relationship of interest rates to monetary policy, one must first understand the determinants of various interest rates. The following discussion is ordered according to the degree of influence monetary policy exerts on a given interest rate.

THE DISCOUNT RATE

The discount rate is the interest rate the Federal Reserve charges on its loans to member depository institutions. The Board of Governors sets the level of the discount rate on the advice of the Boards of Directors of the Reserve Banks. This rate is the principal determinant of the funds rate, and other money rate levels, as we shall soon see.

THE FUNDS RATE

The funds rate is the interest one bank charges another bank on short term loans of reserve credit. Because the net borrowed reserve level is the difference between the demand for funds (required reserves) and the supply of funds (nonborrowed reserves), changes in net borrowed reserves lead to changes in the spread of the funds rate over the discount rate. When the Fed supplies all of the nonborrowed reserve credit needed to fund required reserves, the spread of the funds rate over the discount rate is minimized, usually within 25 basis points. Because banks prefer not to use the discount window if there is no pecuniary advantage to doing so, adjustment borrowings decline to fractional levels (of about $200 million). As the supply of nonborrowed reserves is restrained relative to required reserve levels, the funds rate spread over the discount rate will rise. If the Desk holds the level of net borrowed reserves constant, a change in the discount rate is associated with an equal change in the funds rate. The discount rate and supply and demand levels in the funds market explain almost all of weekly changes in the funds rate average, whenever Desk officials target net borrowed reserves.

In measuring the supply and demand effects of reserves on the funds rate, a rule-of-thumb that worked well until recently was as follows: When the Fed supplies all the credit that member banks need to meet reserve requirements, so that the level of net borrowed reserves is zero, the funds rate will average 25 basis points (.25%) above the discount rate. For every $100 million of net borrowed reserves sustained through three settlement periods, the Fed funds rate will increase 25 basis points above the discount rate.[1] Structural changes since 1980 have slightly altered this relationship, as will be explained in later chapters.

EQUATION RELATING THE FEDERAL FUNDS RATE TO RESERVES

Equation: $FFR - DR = -1.05 + \underset{(.02)}{.25*B} + \underset{(.25)}{.52*Dummy\ 1} + \underset{(.35)}{1.14*Dummy\ 2} + E$

FFR	= Fed Funds Rate
DR	= Discount Rate
B	= Borrowings
E	= Error
Dummy 1	= 1st week of Quarter
Dummy 2	= 1st week of Year
R^2	= .69
DW	= .72

NOTES:

1. Weekly data from: 46th week of 1981 (removal of the surcharge)
   to: 4th week of 1984 (introduction of CRA)
2. Numbers in parentheses are the standard error for the coefficient

---

[1]For example, if the discount rate is 6 percent while Desk officials are targeting $1 billion in net borrowed reserves, the funds rate average will be 8¾ percent. If the discount rate is 10 percent with a net borrowed target of $2 billion, the funds rate will average 15¼ percent. Or, if the discount rate is 14 percent with no reserve restraint, the funds rate will be near 14¼ percent.

The funds rate spread estimating equation worked well under the system of lagged reserve requirements under which the Fed operated until 1984. Because of an increase in the fractional level of excess reserves, which has been associated with the switch to Contemporaneous reserve requirements (to be discussed in chapter 7), a zero net borrowed reserve level was no longer equated to a 25 basis point spread of the funds rate over the discount rate. Such a spread more recently appears to be consistent with free reserves of approximately $450 million, though there is, as yet, insufficient data available in the wake of the structural change to permit a more specific determination of this ''Y-intercept.'' However, the slope of 25 basis points in the funds rate for every $100 million in net borrowed reserves is expected to remain unchanged.

The important linkage of the funds rate spread to reserve conditions was evident in 1982 when the Fed eased monetary policy in two phases. First, net borrowed reserves were gradually reduced to zero, and the funds rate gradually declined and approached the discount rate level. Next, the discount rate was lowered eleven times by half a percentage point and, on each occasion, the funds rate declined by an equal amount. In effect, the discount rate acts as a floor for the funds rate. According to the formula linking net borrowed reserves to the funds rate, zero net borrowed reserve pressure causes the funds rate to slightly exceed the discount rate even while the discount rate is being lowered.

The relationship between the discount rate and the funds rate arises because to an individual bank the federal funds market and the discount window are alternate sources of reserve funds. If a bank has not abused its borrowing privilege, it has legitimate recourse to the discount window and will have an incentive to go there when the funds rate exceeds the discount rate. However, banks generally prefer to avoid use of the window as much as possible in order to ''keep their powder dry'' for occasions when they really need it. This is because over-use of the discount facility is frowned upon by the Federal Reserve banks. As the funds rate rises above the discount rate because of rising net borrowed reserve pressures, some banks will not be able to resist arbitrage abuse of the discount facility, while most banks will cautiously maintain a safe distance from the discount window. Rising reserve shortages at money center banks soon prompt funds traders and liability managers at large banks to bid more aggressively for reserve credit, thereby putting upward pressure on the funds rate, in order to properly manage their risk exposure to discipline from discount officers. The funds rate rarely falls below the discount rate because there are always some banks needing to borrow reserves, and so willing to pay the discount rate for funds. Given their inhibition against borrowing from the Fed, very few banks will come to the window when funds are available in the private market at lower cost.

In sum, the discount rate acts as a floor for the funds rate, from which funds rate levels will rise in response to a tightening of reserve supply relative to reserve demands.

CALL MONEY AND THE BROKER LOAN RATE

Bond dealers must finance security positions they intend to sell to investors. In early bond market history, stock brokerage firms frequently handled bond dealer operations. Loans required temporarily to finance bond dealer positions within a stock brokerage were considered broker loans rather than dealer loans, since the bond dealership was incidental to the principal business of the borrower.

Bond brokers, on the other hand, do not take positions in debt markets and have no major external financing requirements. Brokers merely bring large sellers and buyers (often dealer firms) together to transact bonds at an agreed price, plus a small commission to the broker. The broker loan rate a bank charges to a borrowing dealer firm does not apply to brokers in fixed-income markets.

The broker loan is often referred to as call money, because the bank's loan to finance dealer positions is callable in one day. If the dealer loan is called the next day, the dealer must find new financing or liquidate the security position, potentially at a loss. Consequently, though dealers continue to rely on broker loans from banks, most of their external financing requirements since World War II have been financed through repurchase agreements.

THE REPO RATE

During the 1950s, dealers introduced the repurchase agreement (repo) as a relatively inexpensive means to finance security positions. Under a repurchase agreement, a corporate treasurer or other investor purchases a specified amount of securities from the dealer, with the agreement that the dealer will purchase those securities back on the next business day or on some predetermined day in the future. In essence, the investor finances the dealer's position through a loan which is collateralized by marketable securities. The difference between the investor's purchase price and its selling price, specified in the agreement, represents the "repo rate," the interest earned on the repo.

Repos are attractive to corporate treasurers because maturities and amounts can be tailored to fit the investment needs of individual corporations. As daily repo and other money rates have become more volatile in recent years, the typical term of corporate repos with dealers has declined to overnight. Thus, the dealer and the corporation can negotiate both repo rates and repo amounts daily, based on specific needs and market conditions. Longer maturity term repos continue to be employed, although most maturities are less than ten days.

Since banks were not allowed to pay interest on demand deposit accounts, repos provided corporate treasurers with an alternative cash management tool which served to reduce corporate demand deposits. Banks responded by offering their own repos to corporate treasurers, competing with repos offered by dealers. In this way, bankers were able to secure reserve credit from other banks. Executed on an overnight basis, the corporate repo became nothing more than a demand deposit that could legally earn interest. To the large banks, the corporate repo also represented another liability management option, enabling them to purchase deposit and reserve credit from smaller banks.

A bank's funds trader purchases corporate repo money when the bank needs additional reserve credit or when the reserve credit can be sold at a higher rate in the Fed funds market. A funds trader will not pay more for corporate repo money than the cost of purchasing reserve credit directly from another bank; that is, more than the funds rate. When the repo rate is lower than the funds rate, large banks with temporary reserve surpluses can profitably arbitrage repo money in the funds market. If the repo rate drops too low relative to the funds rate, Fed funds traders will actively seek and bid for available repo money, thus forcing the repo rate up and more in line with the funds rate.

Aggressive bank entry into the corporate repo market increased the repo rate's dependence on the funds rate rather than on dealer financing needs. The broker loan rate, or call money rate, also became more closely linked with the funds rate. If the broker loan rate was too high or too low relative to repo rates, dealer use of bank financing varied accordingly.

TREASURY BILL RATES

The Treasury auctions 3-month and 6-month bills every Monday and one-year bills at the end of each month. Bids for new bills auctioned must be physically submitted to any Federal Reserve bank (or its branch) by 1:30 p.m. EST. The Treasury then ranks all bids received from the lowest rate (the highest price) to the highest.

The stop rate is the highest (rate) bid the Treasury must accept in order to sell the preannounced amount of bills. The stop rate and the average rate at which bills were awarded are quickly announced, as is the total amount of bids received at each auction. The ratio of total bids to the actual amount of bills issued is called the "bid-cover"; a bid-cover of two is generally considered satisfactory. A smaller bid-cover indicates reduced investor demand for new bill purchases at current rates; a higher bid-cover suggests increased investor demand.

Analysts also look at the difference between the stop rate and the average rate, known as the "bid-tail." A bid-tail of only a basis point (.01%) suggests little uncertainty about where bill rates should be. A bid-tail of five basis points, on the other hand, suggests rate uncertainties that contributed to sloppy bidding.

When dealers are reluctant to buy new bills at current rates, they may scale their bids, offering to take small amounts at lower rates and much larger amounts at higher rates. These high-rate bids, called "throw-away bids," are rarely awarded bills unless investor demand is unexpectedly soft. Dealers can buy bills in secondary markets as well as in primary markets (auctions), but large volume purchases are more readily transacted in primary markets, with far less impact on prevailing rates.

A dealer's decision to increase or decrease bill positions depends in part on the relationship of current bill rates to dealer financing costs. If the repo rate is lower than the current bill rate (adjusted to reflect yield to maturity), then dealers can obtain a "positive carry" from the bill position; they can earn more than the cost to finance their bill holdings. The larger the positive carry, the more aggressive the bidding at bill auctions (and in secondary markets), and the higher bill prices become, pushing bill rates back down toward the repo rate.[2]

The spread between bill rates and repo rates also depends on dealer expectations about future bill rates. If Fed policy is expected to ease, the funds rate and repo rates may decline; dealers may even bid for new bills at rates lower than repo rates. Resultant negative carries on bill positions could quickly become positive after the funds rate declines. More important, declines in the funds rate and repo rates force bill rates downward, thereby increasing the market value of bills held in dealer positions.

TREASURY COUPON YIELDS

Marketable debt issued with maturities of one year or longer generally provides for semi-annual interest payments until maturity, when principal repayment is due. Long-term borrowers' obligations

---

[2]Seasonal exceptions to this cycle exist. Following the April tax deadline, for example, the flow of tax receipts into Treasury Tax & Loan accounts encumbers bank bill collateral (as previously explained), hindering Fed funds traders' bids for corporate repo money. With competition from banks in the repo market temporarily stalled, dealers can significantly reduce their own bid-rates. Under these conditions (when the repo rate is depressed relative to the funds rate), dealers do not attempt to profit from positive carries by more aggressive bidding; they know that collateral shortages are temporary, and that repo rates will soon increase relative to the funds rate.

to investors can be "bonded" through an indenture (contract) that is printed on all bonded debt sold in the open market. On corporate bonds, the indenture spells out how and when the debtor company will repay principal, sometimes specifying a sinking fund to ensure repayment. However, Treasury bonds are backed by the taxing authority of the U.S. government, which is assumed to remove risks associated with repayment and interest payment.

The Treasury issues two types of coupons: notes and bonds. Large-scale issuances of notes began shortly after Congress, in an effort to halt escalating interest rates in the mid-1960s, prohibited the Treasury from issuing bonds at coupon rates exceeding 4¼ percent. The Treasury also is prohibited from issuing new notes and bonds at a discount exceeding 1 percent of par value. These twin limitations essentially made it impossible for the Treasury to issue long term bonds if bond yields in secondary markets were above 5 percent. For example, a 20-year bond carrying a 4¼ percent coupon and priced at 99/100 of par will yield approximately 5 percent.

When the funds rate continued to increase and bond yields increasingly exceeded the 4¼ percent limitation, Treasury officials were faced with the prospect of financing the national debt exclusively with short-term bills, thus requiring complete refinancing several times a year. Because temporary market strains could easily disrupt this process, the Treasury instead began issuing notes, which differ legally from bonds in having maturities of ten years or less. Congress had not considered applying the 4¼ percent coupon rate limitation to notes because note financing by the Treasury had not occurred since the post-Civil War period, and Congressmen were unaware of note financing. Note financing caused the average life of the national debt to decline within two years, prompting Congress to give the Treasury exemptions from the bond financing restriction. The bond exemption, initially only $10 billion, has increased significantly over the years. But the need for note financing persists, due to high deficits and attendant needs to attract investors from all maturity areas of the debt market.

Note and bond auctions follow the basic procedure described for bills, with bids quoted in terms of yields to maturity. Unlike bills, however, once new coupons trade in secondary markets, their bids and offers are stated in terms of price, not rate. The longer the maturity of a fixed-income obligation, the more its market price changes in response to any given change in market yield; a five basis point change in a bill maturing next week has almost no effect on the bill's market price, whereas the same change in 30-year bond yields has a substantial effect on the bond's market price. Therefore, it is logical to trade bills (maturing within one year) on the basis of rates, and coupons on the basis of price.[3]

HISTORY OF RESULTS ON 5-YEAR
TREASURY NOTE AUCTIONS

AUCTIONED	COUPON	AMOUNT[1]	NONCOMPS[2]	COVER[3]	AVG YLD[4]	TAIL[5]
05/27/87	8.250%	$8.00 B	$0.352 B	2.92	8.27%	0
02/25/87	6.625	8.25	.266	3.24	6.73	1
11/25/86	6.625	8.25	.255	3.02	6.66	1
08/27/86	6.500	8.00	.256	2.82	6.51	1
05/28/86	7.750	7.75	.337	2.33	6.53	2
02/26/86	8.125	7.50	.450	2.55	8.12	1
11/27/85	9.125	7.50	.820	3.34	9.13	0
08/28/85	9.625	7.25	.638	3.22	9.62	1
05/29/85	9.875	7.00	.610	2.17	9.95	1
02/26/85	11.375	7.00	.577	2.75	11.43	0
11/28/84	11.00	6.75	.479	2.81	11.02	1
08/29/84	12.75	6.50	.522	2.56	12.78	0
05/30/84	13.875	6.25	.720	2.35	13.93	3
02/28/84	11.75	6.00	.482	2.34	11.84	1

1. AMOUNT: The total size of the issue announced by the Treasury. Additional amounts are issued to the Federal Reserve and Government accounts after allotments to the public.
2. NONCOMPS: Noncompetitive tenders in a Treasury auction are bids for a specific amount of securities at the price, whatever that may turn out to be, equal to the average auction price of the accepted competitive bids.
3. COVER: The ratio of total tenders to accepted tenders in a Treasury auction.
4. AVERAGE YIELD: The yield equivalent of the average price derived from the total of the competitive bids.
5. TAIL: The difference between the high yield and the average yield at auction.

Bill rates and coupon prices must be converted to yields for comparison of investor returns. Analysts graph yield levels (on the vertical axis) against maturity (on the horizontal axis) to obtain a

[3]For current discussion purposes, assume a half percentage point increase in both a one-month bill and a 30-year bond; the bill rate in secondary markets increased 50 basis points from 5½ percent to 6 percent, and the bond yield from 6½ percent to 7 percent. The market value of $1 million par value of the bill declined $416.67 and $7,060.00, respectively.

yield curve. The slope of the yield curve depends on market conditions. If all yields are the same regardless of years or months to maturity, the yield curve is flat. If money rates are higher than bond yields (as when market participants expect the Fed to ease policy and so discount future policy effects on bond prices), the yield curve is downward sloping. If money rates are lower than bond yields, the yield curve slopes upward to the right. This situation can occur when inflation rates are expected to increase, when Fed policy is expected to tighten substantially over the intermediate-term, or when new coupon supplies are at high levels, such as those arising over the past several years from the growing fiscal deficit. Increasing new coupon supplies can also occur when credit demands among businesses are growing, thus making the yield curve even more positively sloped.

Growth in bank loans to businesses and rising supplies of new corporate bond issuances can reflect increased demand for business credit. Rising business loans deplete the ability of banks to purchase new Treasury coupons. New corporate bond issuance requires higher rates so that individual investors will save more money and advance more funds. In either case, rising business credit demands lift Treasury coupon yields farther above Treasury bill and other money market rates. Higher deficits do push up coupon yields, but, if the Fed lowers the funds rate significantly, coupon yields can come down even when fiscal deficits are high. In this case, the entire yield curve moves downward, but its slope remains the same in the absence of easier monetary policy.

CORPORATE BOND YIELDS

Most corporate bonds are issued with a long maturity, such as 30 years, although there are occasionally some 10-year issues. The secondary market for (seasoned) corporate bond issues lacks the depth, breadth, and resiliency of the secondary market for Treasury coupons. Bids and offers quoted for seasoned corporates are relatively wide and do not always reflect market conditions.

Graph 3.1

Positive Sloping and Negative Sloping Treasury Yield Curves

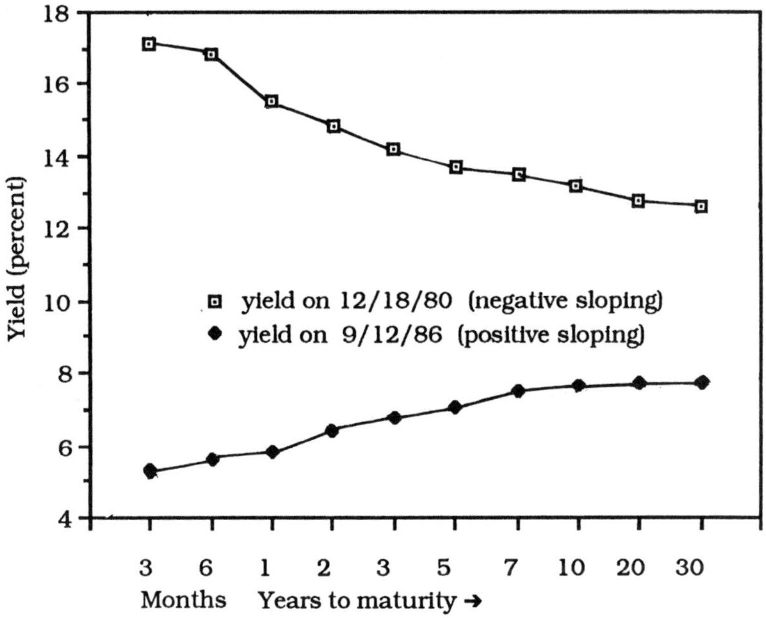

When yields are highest for long-term investments and progressively lower for shorter-term instruments, the yield curve is positive sloping as in the data plotted for September 12, 1986. In the atypical instance of a negative sloping yield curve, yields are highest for short-term instruments and progressively lower for longer-term maturities, as the data for December 18, 1980 illustrate.

Source: Federal Reserve release H.15.

These features preclude construction of a corporate yield curve strictly analogous to the Treasury yield curve, but a hypothetical yield curve may be constructed. Corporate bond prices, converted to yields, can be compared with commercial paper rates paid by corporations, converted to yields. The hypothetical corporate yield curve shows the same slope as, but is higher than, the Treasury yield curve, reflecting investor perceptions of differences in quality between Treasury and private debt obligations.

If the Fed eases policy to bring the Treasury yield curve down, a hypothetical corporate yield curve would decline by approximately the same amount. However, corporate bond yields are influenced not only by monetary policy and perceptions of inflation, but also by market risks associated with length of maturity or with creditworthiness. Nonetheless, monetary policy is historically the most influential factor affecting corporate bond yields and commercial paper rates.

BANK RATES

Bank rates are tied closely to the funds rate and to Fed policy. Rates related to the deposit side of bank balance sheets include the CD rate and the Eurodollar rate. These depo rates track the funds rate, because both rates are bidding for reserve credit. However, the depo rates are usually slightly higher than the funds rate due to their slightly higher degree of risk and smaller trading volumes.

Rates applicable to the asset side of bank balance sheets must relate to the cost of bank funds (deposits) on the liability side. The prime rate is often quoted because it is assumed to be applied uniformly by banks to their most creditworthy customers. In recent years, however, many banks' small business loan customers have demanded lending rates as low as prime rates and obtained credit lines specifying a prime rate. In response, bankers have let their prime rates gradually become high relative to depo rates, secretly negotiating more favorable rates with prime customers. Therefore, the prime rate is no longer the lowest rate charged on business loans. Nevertheless, it does track major changes in the funds rate.

Bankers use mortgage rates to turn on or turn off mortgage credit demands, consistent with the outlook for bank liquidity and interest rates. If bankers anticipate Fed policy tightening, they will raise mortgage rates slightly in advance of a funds rate increase, and well in advance of liquidity constraints (similar to a bond dealer lightening positions in advance of expected Fed tightening). When bankers perceive slowing business loan demands coupled with possible Fed policy easing, they will tend to drop the mortgage rate.

The spread between bank lending rates and bank deposit rates is theoretically held to a minimum by intense competition from other bank intermediaries. When non-performing loans held by banks are increasing, the actual cost of funds available to lend rises relative to quoted depo rates. As a result, the spread of lending rates over depo rates also rises.

FED POLICY AND INTEREST RATES

The behavior of various interest rates and market yield shows that they are significantly affected by the Fed's discount rate and reserve policies. The degree to which interest rates and yields are linked to monetary policy depends on the maturity of their respective debt obligations. Monetary policy is the most important determinant of short rates but is somewhat less influential to longer rates (although it remains a major determinant).

Were there no central bank in the U.S. and no monetary policy, the rate of inflation would significantly influence interest rates. Over the past century, interest rates have tended to exceed the inflation rate by about two percentage points, depending on the maturity of the instruments.

During the second half of the 1970s, inflation rates increased to double-digit levels, due partly to the substantial increase in energy costs. But Fed policy kept the funds rate and other money market rates, and occasionally even intermediate yields, below the rate of inflation. In following a policy of pegging the funds rate, policymakers allowed accelerating inflation to outpace the rise of the funds rate. In other words, the effect of policy was powerful enough to

Graph 3.2

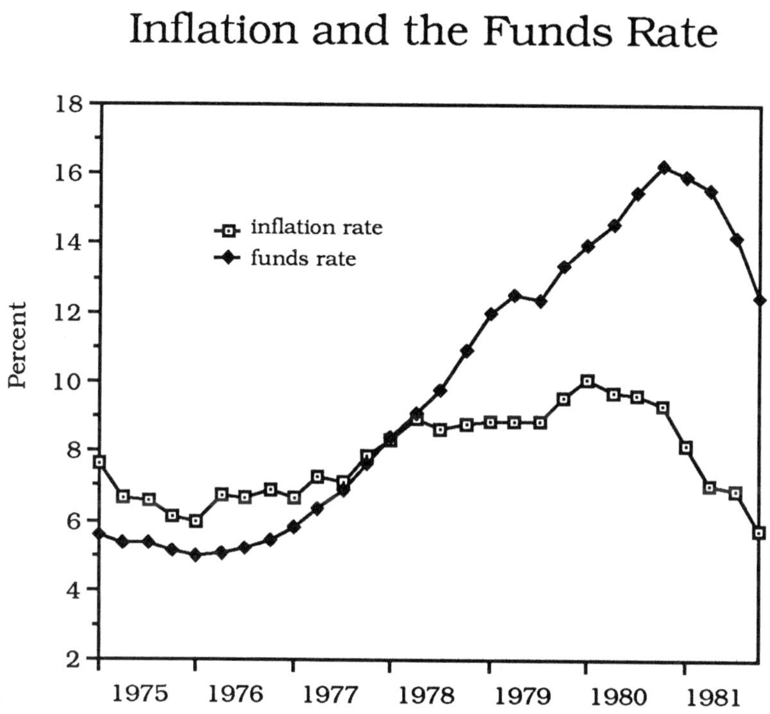

During the seventies, the Federal Reserve attempted to control the money supply with funds rate pegging. The funds rate was inadvertently held below the rate of inflation, which created negative real interest rates. Following the introduction of reserve targeting in October 1979, the funds rate remained above the rate of inflation. The high funds rate averages in 1980 and 1981 were caused partly by significant increases in the discount rate.

Quarterly data were used and smoothed with a five-quarter moving average. Source: National Income and Product Accounts, and Federal Reserve release H.15.

depress nominal interest rates artificially, relative to inflation rates, for an extended period of time. Chapter 5 will cover funds rate pegging in detail.

In the first half of 1982, the interest rate cycle became completely uncoupled from the business cycle. The economy had been in a recession since the preceding year and was nearing a cyclical trough which proved to be deeper than any other since the Great Depression. Nonetheless, interest rates continued to rise as the economy slid further into recession.[4] Despite some weakening of inflationary pressures during the first half of 1982, despite double-digit unemployment rates, money rates remained near record levels. The spread of nominal interest rates over the rate of inflation reached new highs.

Tight Fed policies caused this radical departure from cyclical interest rate behavior. Regrettably, these policies were based on inaccurate money supply data, to be discussed in the next chapter, and on an erroneous belief that a penalty discount rate could strengthen the Fed's control over monetary growth (examined in chapter 6). In short, ill-conceived theory at the Fed produced pro-cyclical monetary policy and led to policy actions which divorced interest rate behavior from economic behavior; interest rate levels became separated from free market forces of supply and demand as never before.

---

[4]Technically speaking, the '81-'82 recession appears to have been a depression; the latter is distinguished from the former by a downturn in personal and business net worth, which available (incomplete) data indicates to have happened in 1982.

CHAPTER 4

Does Money Matter?

THE VELOCITY OF MONEY

The quantity of circulating money (M) multiplied by the number of times each unit turns over (V), equals the level of prices (P) multiplied by the volume of monetary transactions (T). Thus MV = PT. This so-called "equation of exchange" is one of the oldest known relationships linking economic activity and inflation to the quantity of money. The equation has had an appreciable impact on policy thinking at the Fed.

If the transactions measure, T, is defined to include only purchases of domestically produced goods and services, the right-hand side of the equation may be equated to nominal GNP. Changes in "P" (prices) are measured by the GNP price deflator, and changes in the volume of transactions (T) are measured by real GNP. Thus the volume of money in circulation, M, is linked to the nominal value of GNP via V, which economists describe as the "income velocity of money." Velocity is simply the average number of times each dollar in the money supply is used in a transaction that generates income. This relation between MV and PT is a tautology because velocity (V) is *defined* as PT divided by M. Nonetheless the approach is consistent with the Keynesian observation that one person's spending is another's income.

As the U.S. trade deficit surged upward during the eighties, however, U.S. money was increasingly used to buy and sell imported as well as domestically produced goods and services. Nominal GNP (PT) thus grew at a slower pace relative to money supply (M) growth than it had done previously.

This surge in trade deficits has increased the volume of purchases of imported goods—which do not generate income in the US—and hence has reduced the use of the term ''income velocity of money.''

It was convenient for monetary economists to hypothesize that money velocity remains stable. Calculated velocities, plotted on a graph, certainly appeared to be stable. However, if the level of GNP that would have emerged if velocity had remained perfectly constant (or followed a constant upward trend) is compared with actual levels of nominal GNP, substantial discrepancies appear. The velocity of money in fact has been quite unstable and seemingly unpredictable. As a result, the linkage between the quantity of M1 and the economy appears to be quite weak. This led Federal Reserve policy makers to de-emphasize M1 supply growth as a guide to monetary policy during 1984, 1985, and 1986, and to essentially abandon it in 1987.

The behavior of money velocity should not have been the mystery it has been. Using the narrow definition of money supply (M1) to measure ''M'' (which is customary), the upward velocity trend of the sixties and seventies is easy to explain, as is the downward trend of the eighties.

During the sixties, monetary policy gradually became more restrictive, which produced a gradual upward trend in money market interest rates. These trends continued during the seventies, particularly after the OPEC-administered surge in oil prices, which strengthened inflationary pressures in the U.S. The rise in money rates was accompanied by an increase in bank deposit rates, payable on all deposit credit except demand deposits (which were the dominant component of M1). Both individuals and businesses were faced with increasing opportunity costs of holding funds in demand deposits. As a result, they increasingly resorted to methods of minimizing demand balances without restricting their transactions. M1 growth rates were therefore limited in relation to nominal GNP growth, and velocity rose.

Graph 4.1

M1 Velocity Measured by Nominal GNP/M1

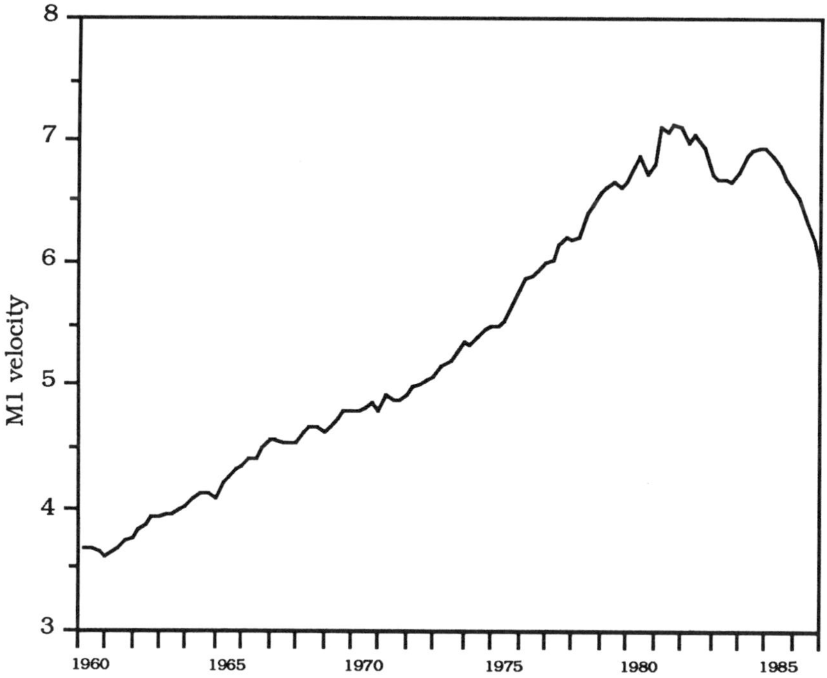

Quarterly data. Source: Department of Commerce, NIPA; Federal Reserve release H.6.

Financial deregulation, which began in 1980, enabled banks and thrifts to pay interest on many types of demand deposits. In addition, savings deposits were allowed to have checkable features, which forced the Fed to include these savings deposits in the definition (and measurement) of M1. Financial deregulation thus encouraged a shift of deposit credit away from less liquid time and savings deposits to highly liquid demand and savings deposits. The decline in interest rates, which began in mid-1982, also reduced the opportunity cost of demand deposits to further spur their growth relative to nominal GNP. Money velocity thus declined significantly.

Fed officials were able to (and did) anticipate some of the trend behavior of M1 velocity. However, a more precise forecast of velocity behavior was not possible, and the resulting uncertainty made it very difficult for Fed officials to establish money supply growth targets as policy objectives. In addition, incoming M1 data became less meaningful to current and prospective economic trends. In 1984, Fed officials began placing more policy emphasis on GNP data than on M1 data as a barometer of current trends and as a determinant of monetary policy. By 1986, Fed officials were content to completely ignore excessive rates of monetary growth during the prior two years, as if money growth had no economic effect whatsoever. This extreme view was exactly opposite to that of monetarism which, six years earlier, persuaded Fed policymakers to make small policy adjustments in response to weekly M1 data.

The $MV = PT$ equation is a useful theoretical tool, and the fact that velocity does not remain completely constant does not warrant a conclusion that money does not matter. The relationship of money to the economy is certainly strong enough to prove that money does indeed matter, and that unchecked monetary growth will eventually produce inflation. The real issue in the money debate is how money and the economy interact during the business cycle, and the related question of what role monetary growth should play in the formulation of monetary policy.

If the velocity of money were better defined, then its behavior would be more stable and predictable, and the importance of money supply growth in monetary policy formulation would be increased. Because the "closed economy assumption" is no longer valid, "PT"

Graph 4.2

Difference Between M1 Velocity Measured by (GNP - Net Exports)/M1, and by GNP/M1

(quarterly data)

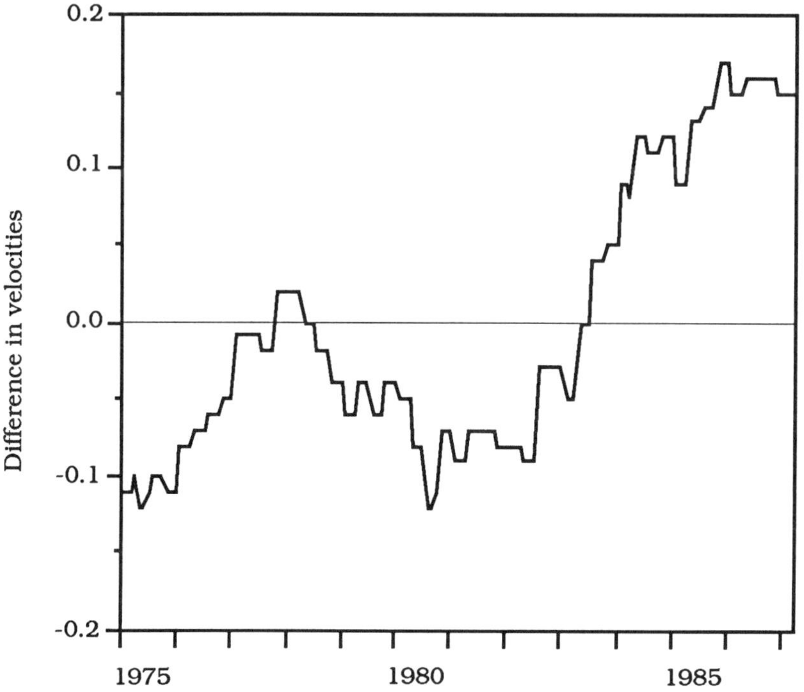

Source: Department of Commerce, NIPA; Federal Reserve release H.6.

(in the money supply equation) should not be defined as nominal GNP, but rather as GNP less net exports or, in the current case of high trade deficits, as GNP plus net imports. When velocity is defined as net imports plus GNP divided by M1, it displays less instability than the current GNP-based measure of velocity. Nonetheless, this adjusted measure of velocity still displays growth prior to 1980 and decline since that time.

The downward trend in M1 velocity since 1980 seems to be partly the result of financial deregulation, which extended checkable features to savings-related deposits. As will be discussed, the Fed included all new checkable deposits in M1 even though their use for transactions purposes was less than conventional demand deposits. One way to avoid the disorienting effects of financial deregulation is to concentrate on currency in circulation. If velocity is defined as net imports plus GNP divided by currency in circulation, it displays on a graph a straight upward trending line over the past three decades. This correlation should confirm suspicions that there is an important link between money and the economy, if only it could be properly defined.

STUDENT IMPRESSIONS

The beginning student in economics is taught to distinguish between effective product demand and the insatiable desire of people to consume. Spendable cash transforms a portion of that insatiable desire into effective demand for goods and services. The following illustration is frequently given to students to demonstrate the effect of spendable cash (money supply) on effective product demand.

Suppose that you are walking on campus and, from a helicopter overhead, a bundle of $10,000 in $20 bills drops to the ground close to you. Because no one claims the cash, you are entitled to keep it. Would such good fortune increase your spending? Most students have very little cash relative to their spending desires, and so they naturally envision a major increase in spending as a result of finding the $10,000. Students thus understand how money supply changes can affect aggregate product demand. Of course, they realize that

Graph 4.3

Velocity

Measured By (Final Sales - Net Exports)/Currency in Circulation

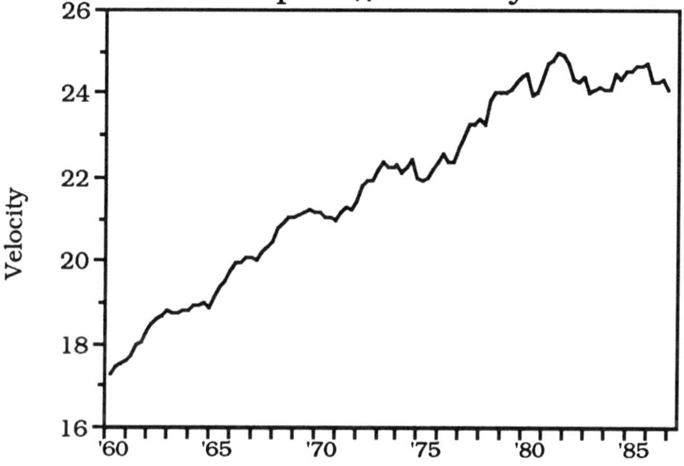

Measured By Nominal GNP/M1

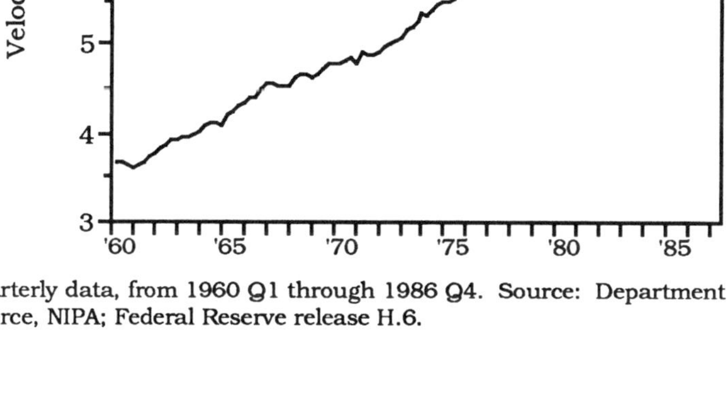

Quarterly data, from 1960 Q1 through 1986 Q4. Source: Department of Commerce, NIPA; Federal Reserve release H.6.

the nation's money supply is not controlled by helicopter pilots, but they quickly believe that some method of controlling money supply growth could control aggregate product demand, and thus prevent damaging cyclical swings in the economy. Because the government operates the money printing presses, some students immediately assume that the Bureau of Printing and Engraving can control the growth of money supply. This assumption was disproven in the first chapter.

The standard college course on money and banking provides the student with the first plausible explanation of how the nation's money supply can be controlled: the Fed can control the volume of reserve credit and, by reducing the availability of bank reserves, can force banks to curtail their lending activity or force them to sell securities. By controlling the volume of reserve credit available, the Fed is supposed to have a substantial effect on the growth of bank loans and investments, the growth of total deposit credit, and the growth of money supply. This power of monetary policy, as a counter cyclical force, is usually over-emphasized.

Having been convinced that the Fed's control over money supply significantly affects the behavior of aggregate product demand, the student's subsequent research on the relationship between money supply and GNP tends to be biased. In comparing the changes of money supply growth with those of GNP, the student can see that both sets of data exhibit cyclical fluctuations. These cyclical patterns, however, are not precisely coincidental. If it is assumed that the co-variance between money supply and GNP depicts a cause and effect relationship, then it must also be determined whether money supply changes subsequently produce corresponding changes in GNP, or whether GNP changes subsequently cause changes in money supply. The latter possibility is never considered by the student because he has been taught to look for evidence of the former. The student observes the statistical evidence and immediately concludes that changes in the economy lag corresponding changes in money supply growth.

Students are led to believe that there is a close statistical relationship between monetary growth and GNP behavior. Partly because of inaccuracies in measurement, however, no one has been able to find a predictable or reasonably precise relationship between money and the economy. No one doubts that money and economic changes are related. At issue is the precise relationship between them, which is critical in assessing the appropriateness of monetary policy. To appreciate the importance of monetary accounting problems, one must first consider the evidence that directly counters the student's impression of the world.

DO CHANGES IN MONEY SUPPLY GROWTH LAG ECONOMIC CHANGES?

The growth of money supply depends on the existence of rising credit demands, and the availability of reserve credit to meet those demands. As previously explained, government credit demands are fulfilled by issuing marketable debt that banks can purchase. Such bank investment creates deposit credit and money supply growth. Private credit demands can be accommodated by existing savings or by bank loans which create new deposit credit. If total credit demands decrease, it is likely that the dollar deposit base and money supply will decrease or remain flat, despite an ample availability of reserve credit. This unusual situation developed during the Depression.

As previously discussed, bank loans and investments accommodate slightly less than one-third of total credit demands. This amount of accommodation can be reduced through applying reserve restraint which causes net borrowed reserves to increase, and also causes the spread of the funds rate over the discount rate to widen. The effect of reserve restraint on money supply growth, however, also depends on how rapidly total credit demands increase during a given cyclical upswing.

Statistics show that almost all major credit sectors exhibit a lagged response to changes in the business cycle. Cyclical changes affect consumer and business liquidity, and these effects account for the lagged response of consumer and business loan demands. History shows that shortly after cyclical peaks in GNP growth, consumer and business liquidity fall to cyclical lows; the personal saving rate reaches cyclical lows, and corporate working capital positions are also low.

Graph 4.4

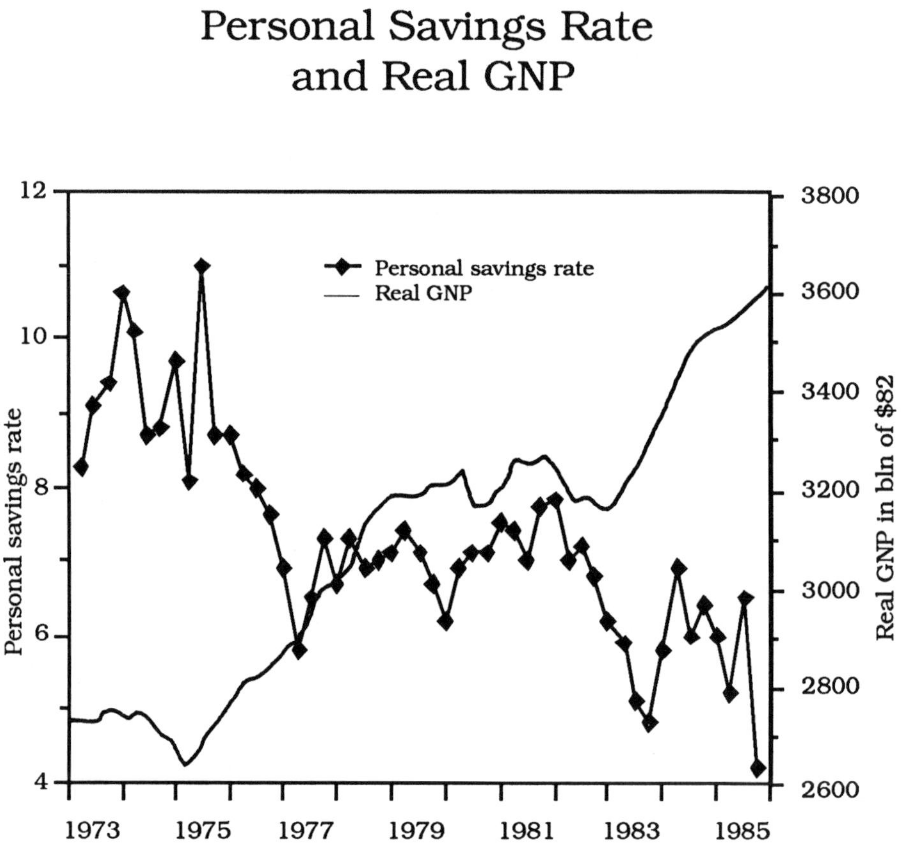

Quarterly data, from 1973 Q1 through 1985 Q3. Source: Department of Commerce, NIPA.

The deterioration in working capital might seem ironic, in view of the rise in internal cash flows associated with cyclical peaks. Cyclical peaks, however, are associated with rising interest rates and relatively high bond yields. Such high bond yields not only discourage long-term bond financing, but also suppress price/earnings ratios in the stock market, to discourage new equity financing. Capital outlays of businesses surrounding cyclical peaks are therefore financed increasingly through short term bank loans. The incurrence of such short-term debt, however, increases current liabilities relative to current assets; working capital is thus reduced.

After interest rates and bond yields decline in response to a cyclical downswing in the economy, corporate treasurers typically paydown bank loans with the proceeds of long-term bond sales, thus locking in lower financing costs over the long run. Working capital positions increase because of the decline in current liabilities. Consumer liquidity also peaks just after the cyclical trough, as evidenced by the personal saving rate.

Because the private sector's liquidity is generally at a high level during the initial phases of an economic recovery, increases in personal and business spending are financed proportionately more from existing liquidity than from new debt. Slightly past the cyclical peak in GNP growth, when liquidity levels are low, spending is financed proportionately more through bank loans.

The demand for new credit is not focussed exclusively on the banking system. The pool of existing savings is constantly tapped through such markets as the commercial paper market, which is used to finance business inventories and consumer installment credit extended by nonbank businesses. Commercial banks compete with various money and bond markets for new credit business, and they usually suffer from a reduced share of the credit market during initial phases of economic recoveries.

The lagged nature of business loan demands is partly caused by inventory management as well as by liquidity changes. The ratio of business inventories to sales usually rises beyond the cyclical peak in total output. Though cyclical downturns are no longer reinforced or caused by excessive inventory levels (thanks to improved inventory management), there continues to be a manufacturing bias against curbing production levels immediately at the first sign of sales weakness. This bias stems from the difficulty in distinguishing an initial cyclical downturn from normal short-term aberrations in monthly sales patterns, and from a reluctance to lay off workers, due to the high cost of rehiring and retraining.

During the initial phase of a cyclical slowdown, a rise in inventories is typically followed by a reduction in output which is not immediately accompanied by a cut in the workforce. Because business inventories are financed primarily through bank loans and issuances of commercial paper, short-term business credit demands in money markets and the banking system continue to rise after the cyclical peak has passed. Also, the easing in output and lagged cut in the workforce reduce national productivity (output divided by employment hours). Such a drop in productivity increases unit labor costs (and causes cost-push inflation). The rise in unit labor costs increases the cost of rising inventory levels, adding to the lagged increase of business credit demands.

In recent business cycles, both consumer credit demands and business credit demands have displayed growth trends which lag cyclical changes in the economy by about two quarters (six months). If the availability of reserve credit were to remain unchanged during the business cycle (but it does not), then bank accommodation (monetization)[1] of business and consumer credit demands would lag the business cycle by about six months. Money supply growth would also lag the cycle by about six months.

The mortgage sector is a significant component of total credit. As previously discussed, the demand for mortgage credit is sensitive to changes in mortgage rates. Because mortgage rates respond quickly to countercyclical policies of the Fed, mortgage credit demands do not lag the business cycle. Overshadowing the mortgage sector, however, is the Treasury: its demand for credit has become the largest

---

[1]Economists prefer to limit application of the word ''monetization'' to the supply of reserves by the Fed because this supply permits the creation of money. Though permitting monetary growth, reserve supplies do not guarantee it. A loan or investment by a bank is the act that creates money, often without much regard for reserve availability. Accordingly, the author prefers to use ''monetization'' as the act of creating money through bank loans and investments, and through Fed security purchases from nonbank reporting dealers.

Graph 4.5

Short Term Business Borrowing and Business Cycles

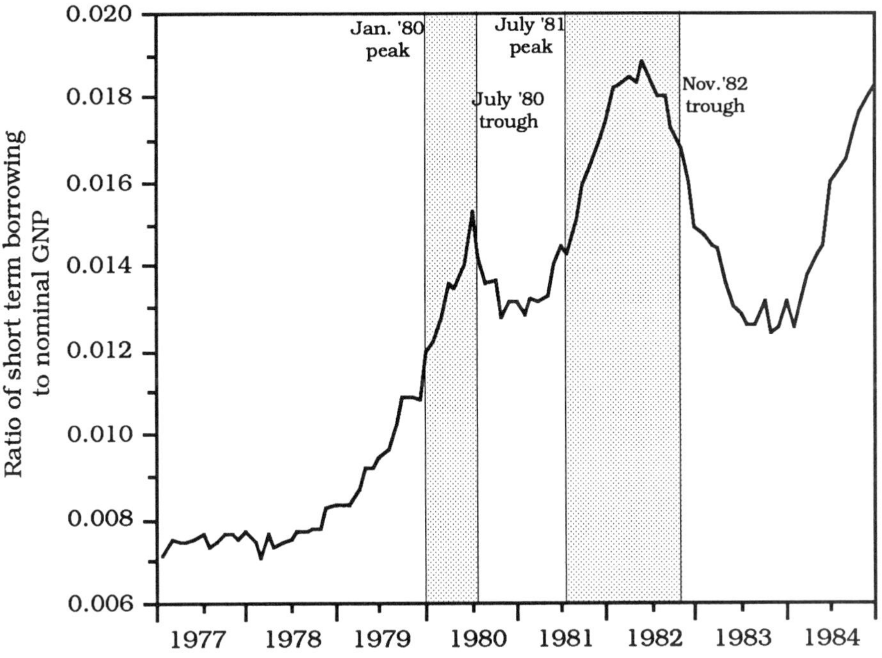

Shaded areas show business cycle peaks and troughs. Short term borrowing by business is defined as nonfinancial commercial paper extensions plus commercial and industrial loans from commercial banks. Monthly data, January 1977 through December 1984.

Source: New York Federal Reserve; Federal Reserve release G.7; Department of Commerce, NIPA.

component of the total credit picture. Although historically the Federal deficit has generally increased immediately in a business slowdown, due to increased transfer payments such as welfare assistance and food stamps, budget deficits can lag the cycle by as much as one year because of lagged tax revenue response to the business cycle.

The total of all credit demands currently exhibits about a three- to six-month lag to the business cycle. Over the years, this lag may have increased slightly because mortgage rates have shown a continuous rise (which apart from demographic factors has decreased the proportion of mortgage credit to other components in total credit), and because fiscal deficits have also increased.

If the Federal Reserve based its policies of supplying reserves solely on reported trends of money supply growth, then restraint against reserve expansion would presumably not occur during the initial phases of a recovery, and would be delayed until credit demands started to increase at a relatively fast pace. Because tightening of reserve policies does not exert a restraining influence on the growth of bank credit without a lag of about six months, excessive rates of monetary growth can easily develop during and after the mature stage of a recovery. This sequence has typically occurred.

When monetary growth remains excessive, frustrated Fed officials apply further restraint. Because of the lags with which such reserve restraint exerts its influence on the banking system, it may happen that restraint begins to moderate monetary growth only after evidence of a recession has already emerged. Fed officials then ease policy, but the full impact of this change in reserve policy is delayed because of weakened credit demands.

The purpose of this section has been to show why money supply growth rates tend to lag the business cycle. Previous cycles of business activity have often been accompanied by a similar pattern of growth in money supply, though the two cycles of money and production are not contemporaneous. The question is which cycle leads the other, and because the presence of money is such an important determinant of effective product demand, the prevailing view is that money cycles influence and lead the business cycle.

The contrary view presented here is that the creation of new money is governed more by the demand for new money (bank credit demand) than by reserve availability. This demand for new money lags the business cycle due to such factors as liquidity. Furthermore, the availability of reserve credit, governed through Fed operations, tends to be influenced by a lagging policy variable (money supply), and its influence on bank credit extensions is also lagged. Unless Fed officials are able to accurately foresee economic trends and the lagged monetary response, it is not possible for them to formulate a forward-looking reserve policy to counteract delayed cyclical behavior of money supply growth.

If the foregoing is correct, then there will be a policy tendency towards pro-cyclical reserve management during initial stages of a recovery and recession. Each expansion becomes laced with monetary risks of inflation during its mature and terminal phase, and each contraction can be prolonged or deepened by policies of excessive reserve restraint past the cyclical turn. Such pro-cyclical accusations have rarely been made by Wall Street economists even though they have often characterized Fed policies as "boom or bust" policies.

The foregoing view contrasts sharply with monetarism, but does not negate monetarist emphasis on controlling the growth of money supply. The monetarist argument could be strengthened if money velocity exhibited more stable behavior. Perhaps such evidence would emerge if the money cycle was *lagged* to nominal GNP before calculating velocity. However, other refinements would first have to occur before the importance of money can be substantiated.

Changes in spending should be closely associated with changes in the amounts of both currency and the transactionable deposit balances used as a medium of exchange. Indeed, the volume of Fed currency shipments to member banks has been used by forecasters as a reliable clue about upcoming retail sales data. But there is no such relationship between retail sales and demand deposits (or other types of checkable deposits). The lack of demand deposit co-variance with consumer spending must mean that they are not always used as a medium of exchange, or that they are not accurately tallied in the accounting for money supply. In fact, abundant evidence indicates that both problems exist.

PROBLEMS IN DEFINING M1

The critical analysis of this section deals only with money as a medium of exchange, not as a store of value. During most of the 1970s, Fed Chairman Burns promoted M1 as a policy objective. To monetarists such as Dr. Milton Friedman, however, the necessity of controlling the growth of money supply should not be limited to the narrowly-defined M1 aggregate. Because money serves as a store of value as well as a medium of exchange, deposit credit serving as a store of value (such as savings accounts) also constitutes a supply of money which can affect economic activity. Indeed, during selected periods of time in the past, M2 and M3 aggregates have correlated more closely with nominal GNP trends than M1. In other words, M2 and M3 velocities seemed to be more stable and predictable than that of M1. Of course, there have also been time periods in which M1 velocity was more stable.

Velocity behavior, however, is not the criterion to be used in judging the appropriateness of particular monetary aggregates, because structural changes have had such a dramatic impact on velocities. These impacts will be defined in more detail in this chapter. The issue of appropriate monetary focus must, in the absence of conclusive data, be based on theory and feasibility of measurement.

The author's bias will be increasingly exposed with detailed examination of monetary measurement problems. To summarize the bias, bank credit is the most appropriate policy focus. Bank credit accurately measures increases in dollar deposit credit which are manufactured by depository institutions other than the Fed. The latter accounts for only two percent of the growth in the dollar deposit base. Bank credit is the broadest monetary aggregate, essentially representing total dollar deposit credit; it is similar in concept to M2, except that it excludes currency in circulation and large CDs. The currency exclusion, however, is beneficial because as already discussed, the currency component is not a source of monetary growth, and is therefore not particularly useful in the pursuit of controlling money supply *growth*.

In this section, M1 definitions become blurred as the effects of structural change are examined. These effects include changes in the composition of deposit credit, which are not relevant to broader monetary aggregates (particularly bank credit); they are relevant only to the measurement of money as a medium of exchange. Though the Burns policy focus on narrowly-defined money has been criticized by a number of monetarists, the availability (amount) of transactionable deposit credit is more closely associated with changes in some economic variables, such as retail sales, than broader monetary aggregates (which include money as a store of value).

It is premature for this narrative to attempt convincing the reader about the appropriateness of various monetary aggregates for monetary policy-making purposes. For those inclined to place significant emphasis on money as a medium of exchange (M1), the examination of measurement problems in this section could be disheartening. Yet, bear in mind, no one aggregate is without theoretical or measurement problems. But, if money does matter, from a national policy point of view, then we must come to know just what kind of money we are talking about.

The currency component of M1 is easy to define: it is the total amount of currency circulating outside of banks and thrifts. It is easily measured by subtracting the total amount of vault cash reported by banks and thrifts from the total amount of currency issued by the Federal Reserve Bank to its depository institutions. This is the only easily identifiable and measurable component of money supply. There are, however, minor problems such as unknown amounts of currency lost or held abroad. The checkable deposit component of M1 is significantly impacted by a number of definition and measurement problems.

Money Balances Held by the Government

In theory, the growth of money supply has an important impact on the growth of spending and incomes in the private sector. Making the assumption that fiscal policy is an exogenous element and countercyclical in business cycles, or at least that government spending is not closely related to government holdings of money, money balances held by the federal government are supposed to be excluded from all money supply measurements. Although most Treasury balances are excluded, the balances held by state and local governments are included in the M1 definition of money. The reason for including state and local government money holdings in the monetary aggregates is that it is assumed that these holdings respond to the same variables (income and interest rates) as does private money demand. Federal holdings are excluded because they are not systematically related to interest rates and income variables.

The above assumption is, however, suspect because, under the established federated system of welfare liabilities, state and county fiscal policies have, in a de-facto sense, been closely linked with counter-cyclical fiscal policy of the federal government. State and local credit demands now parallel federal demands (though by less magnitude), and not private credit demands. In addition, fiscal management of money balances by state and local governments mimic those of federal agencies and, to a slightly lesser extent, the Treasury. Accordingly, it would be safer to assume the behavior of *all* government money balances to be distinctly different from private balances, and exclude all (as opposed to just Treasury) money balances of government from the M1 aggregate.

It should also be noted that government money balances are relatively stable and not influenced by fiscal surpluses or deficits. The level of government balances is determined on the basis of transactional requirements. A surplus of tax revenues over spending would not be used to increase balances, but to reduce the outstanding debt; outstanding debt would be allowed to mature without replacement. Though a strong theoretical case can be made for excluding all government money balances from M1, an even stronger technical case can be made for including all government transaction deposit accounts in the M1 aggregate.

One of the biggest monthly federal liabilities is Social Security. Benefit payments are made at the beginning of each month; the actual payout date varies from month to month, depending on when the first weekend occurs within each month. Each payout transfers a large amount of Treasury funds to checking accounts in the private sector, and, because these payouts recur many times within each year, they create seasonal increases in M1. However, because these seasonal boosts to private checking accounts can vary a day or two at the beginning of each month, it is difficult to adjust M1 accurately for seasonal variations. Although the Federal Reserve attempts to adjust the monetary aggregates for such special seasonal effects, seasonally adjusted weekly M1 data sometimes display large swings at the beginning of each month.

If federal and other government balances were included in the M1 definition, however, this seasonal adjustment problem could be avoided, and weekly M1 data would be far more meaningful. The exclusion of those balances from M1 is a major problem in measuring money supply.

Compensating Balances

The biggest problem in defining the demand deposit component of M1 is not the exclusion of Treasury balances, but the inclusion of compensating balances. It used to be a common practice among bankers to insist that business loan customers leave a small portion of their loan proceeds on deposit (in a demand deposit). This compensating requirement was usually set at 10 percent of the total amount of a business loan, but gradually declined to 5 percent under the threat of competition, before becoming less of a general practice.

As the use of compensating balance requirements became less pronounced in the business loan sector, it grew in the state and local government sector. State and local governments increasingly asked commercial banks for assistance in the computerized processing of tax receipts and expenditures. Government officials were unwilling to budget funds for these banking services, but found compensating balance requirements to be a politically acceptable means of paying for banking services.

A compensating balance requirement is a daily average balance that must be kept in a demand deposit as a quid pro quo for receiving specified banking services. By definition, a compensating balance is not a medium of exchange because it cannot be used to paydown liabilities. The related money supply measurement problem is, at times, most serious in the state and local government sector.

If governments maintained their minimum balance requirements at a constant level throughout each year, the compensating balance requirement would not represent a serious problem in defining money supply. However, because the compensating balance requirement is stipulated in terms of a daily average computed over the life of the agreement, treasurers of local governments need not maintain a minimum balance on any given day as long as the deficiency of a given day is made up by depositing more than the minimum requirement on another day. If interest rates do not change, bankers do not care on which day the compensating balance requirement is met, because such interest-free deposit credit can be immediately sold in the funds market for a profit. If bankers could accurately forecast daily rate changes, they might attempt to control the maintenance of compensating balances, but would not succeed because of competitive pressures.

Because the funds rate has risen so much over the past two decades, the profit on Fed funds sales has become quite large for a relatively small volume of funds. As a result, the compensating balance requirement imposed on local governments has become relatively smaller, as bank competition for the government deposit increased. These less burdensome requirements allow government treasurers to keep their demand deposit balances at minimal (transactional) levels most of the time; they can occasionally dump funds into these deposit accounts for a short period of time, in order to meet the daily average minimum deposit requirement.

The unevenness of deposit management is due to the unevenness of interest rate spreads and levels throughout the year. Proper investment of temporarily idle funds has increasingly become an important source of (interest) income for state and local governments. Temporary investments in Treasury bills or repos have been popular. These investments afford reasonable returns with minimal risk. At times during each year, bill rates and repo rates decline relative to other money market rates. The easing of bill and repo rates relative to the funds rate, as an example, occurs sometime after mid-April, when a large inflow of Treasury tax receipts prompts Treasury officials to paydown maturing bills, and the supply of bills in the bill market is reduced. In turn, such scarcity of bill collateral pushes the repo rate down along with the bill rate. During these times of reduced bill and repo rates, local treasurers liquidate repo and bill investments (often with a corresponding trading gain in bills) and substantially build up their demand deposits in order to re-establish the minimum daily average deposit. If these periods of government demand deposit padding occurred regularly within each year, there would be no major problem: such padding effects could be adjusted for predictable seasonal variation. Unfortunately, it generally occurs at unpredictable times because the market spreads also vary unpredictably.

It is not unusual for a county treasurer to pad demand deposits by $100 million (at times by $400 million) for a one-week period, four to six times each year. Such activity among thousands of county treasurers (not to mention city and state treasurers) can produce very significant intermittent gains in weekly M1 levels. Yet these gains represent funds that, by agreement (contract), cannot be used as a medium of exchange. Weekly M1 gyrations can therefore be rather meaningless as long as compensating balances are not excluded from monetary measurements, such as theory would dictate.

It may be argued that an aberrant upward surge in M1 caused by local government padding has little importance to the growth trend of M1 because it will be offset by an aberrant decline in M1 after treasurers re-invest balances in bills and repos. However, it will shortly be demonstrated that the averaging of weekly and monthly data permits aberrant data to heavily skew calculated trends, and is thus a key problem in monetary accounting.

Other Checkable Deposit Problems

Prior to 1980, thrift institutions in several New England states were permitted to offer savers an interest-paying account with negotiable orders of withdrawal. These so-called "NOW" accounts were basically savings accounts against which a limited volume of checks (negotiable orders of withdrawal) could be written. NOW drafts were readily accepted among merchants, and NOW accounts came to be fairly popular. Congress thus permitted a nationwide extension of NOW accounts in 1980. When banks and thrifts were first authorized to offer NOW accounts on a nationwide basis in

1981, there was a predictable shift of consumer savings from ordinary savings deposits into the new NOW account. There was also a sizable shift of consumer funds from non-interest bearing demand deposits into NOW accounts, which offer both interest payments and a checkable feature.

Because of the checkable feature of the new NOW account, Fed officials decided that it would have to be included in the narrowly defined money supply (M1) instead of being included as a savings account in M2. The shift of savings account funds into NOW accounts thus caused an upward impact on the newly defined M1 aggregate. M2 was unaffected because NOW account funds were included as an M1 component of M2. The shift of funds from savings and time accounts in M2 into M1 created a meaningless surge in the reported growth rate of M1 and brought into question the appropriateness of defining NOW accounts as a medium of exchange rather than a medium of savings.

To make monetary accounting even more difficult, Congress also permitted banks to offer their clients an automatic transfer of savings account, known as ATS. With this account, a depositor's overdraft of a checking account is funded by an automatic transfer from the depositor's savings account to his checking account. The ATS account, then, is basically a savings account, but Fed officials also felt it appropriate to include it in the M1 definition of money supply. ATS and NOW accounts together are what Fed officials term "other checkable deposits" (OCDs) included in M1.

The extent to which OCD balances reflect money as a store of value, as opposed to a medium of exchange, could be partly resolved if deposit turnover surveys produced consistent and non-debatable results. To avoid distracting arguments on this point, it will hopefully suffice to state that a number of deposit surveys all indicate that turnover rates on transaction accounts (check volumes relative to average balances held) are lower for consumer OCDs than they are for consumer demand deposits; but the extent to which OCDs contain relatively more savings funds than transaction funds is subject to rather wide debate.

Consumers' use of OCDs as savings accounts varies in accordance with the spread between money market rates and maximum rates paid on OCDs. Fed officials have stated that a reduction in this spread lowers consumers' opportunity cost of holding savings in OCDs as opposed to investing these savings in money market instruments. Fed officials have thus concluded that declining money market rates can boost OCD totals and increase M1 growth. Accordingly, a policy-related easing of money market rates can create M1 growth, which is precisely the objective of policy easing. But how meaningful is such rate-sponsored growth in OCDs?

The inseparability of transactional balances from savings funds in OCDs means that it is no longer possible to accurately measure money as a medium of exchange, ignoring for the moment money as a store of value.

Overnight Repos

A major manufacturer in the Midwest has just issued payroll checks to its employees. These check credits represent clearing house funds: banks accepting these payroll checks as deposits must submit them to a local clearinghouse for collection from the bank against which the checks were drawn. Because this clearing process requires one day, the manufacturer knows that its demand deposit will not be debited until the next business day. Yet, the manufacturer has funds in its demand deposit, available for overnight investment. Such funds could easily exceed $50 million.

The corporate treasurer of the manufacturing firm is regularly contacted each day by several dealer firms and will probably execute an overnight repurchase agreement with one of these dealer firms. The repo specifies that the manufacturer will purchase securities from a dealer, who agrees to repurchase the securities from the manufacturer (usually) on the next business day, at a repurchase price which is slightly higher than the purchase price. If the repo is executed with a bank dealer, the manufacturer instructs its bank to wire funds to the dealer bank, which thus obtains reserve credit on an overnight basis. Utilizing the Fed's inter-district wire service, the bank dealer wires the securities, purchased on an overnight basis, to the manufacturer.

On the next business day, the dealer buys back the securities at a slightly higher price than the previous day's selling price; this difference represents interest earned by the manufacturer. The manufacturer instructs its bank to wire the securities back to the dealer, who then wires funds back to the manufacturer.

In using the overnight repo, the corporate treasurer was able to earn interest on demand deposit funds that were temporarily idle, awaiting the clearing of payroll checks. When the payroll is issued on a Friday, the treasurer executing an overnight repo is able to collect three days' interest (over the weekend).

In a repo transaction with a bank dealer such as that described above, the seller's (the manufacturer's) demand deposit was reduced overnight, but there was no offsetting increase to a demand deposit elsewhere in the banking system. The dealer's bank received a credit to its reserve account for the amount of the repo, and the manufacturer's bank's reserve account was debited. Accordingly, because of the repo, total demand deposit credit in the banking system was reduced for one business day, with no change in total reserves.

The corporate repo executed with a bank is identical in all relevant respects to a corporate demand deposit against which interest is payable, and thus circumvents the prohibition of interest payments on corporate demand deposits. Corporate treasurers regularly roll over daily repo agreements, in the amount of funds not needed until the next business day. Because the clearing of a demand deposit check requires a minimum of one day (clearinghouse funds), and because repo agreements are executed through the Fed's wire system and represent "good funds" immediately payable (cleared), the daily corporate repo volume can be based on the current day's volume of checks written against the corporate demand deposit. The corporate repo thus serves as a demand deposit, but not all corporate repos should be included in the M1 aggregate.

To the corporate treasurer, it makes no difference whether daily repo requirements are accommodated by bank dealers or by nonbank dealers. In the accounting for demand deposit credit, however, there

CORPORATE REPO TRANSACTION WITH A BANK:
(buying bank)

Corporation	
(1) Cash −	
(3) Investments +	

Bank of Corporation (BC)	
	Demand Deposits − (1)
(2) Reserves −	

Fed	
	Reserve Accts (2)
	BC −
	BB +

Buying Bank (BB)	
(3) Investments −	
(2) Reserves +	

NOTES:

1. Cash account of corporation is reduced when it instructs its bank (BC) to wire funds to the buying bank (BB) through the Fed. Payroll checks have been distributed, but will not clear (affect cash balance held at BC) on this business day.
2. BC wires BB funds through the Fed, as instructed by the corporation.
3. Though analysts refer to this example of a corporate repo clearing, accounting involves two Treasury bill transactions; first day bill purchase by corporation from BB is reversed on second day.[2]

---

[2] To compare repo entries with Fed funds entries, bank Fed funds purchases are not booked on the liability side of the balance sheet as a ''due to'' account, which represents an interbank demand deposit (or a short-term liability). Such accounting would artificially build the deposit base which banks often highlight in their consumer advertising. Most banks are net sellers of Fed funds (reserve balances). Funds sold represent a ''due-from,'' but are rarely so posted on the asset side of the balance sheet, offsetting the reserve account reduction. Because most banks buy and sell Fed funds each business day, a detailed disclosure is made on the balance sheet showing Fed funds sold, and a contra-account (on the asset side) of Fed funds purchased. On statement dates, almost all banks (particularly reserve deficient money outer banks) prefer to show more Fed funds sold than bought (with a positive rather than negative net Fed funds posted). Such predisposition of banks requires large amounts of excess reserves, obtained either from the Fed's discount window or the Open Market Desk's increased supply of nonborrowed reserves. On important bank statement dates, each of the above three reserve aggregates rises sharply, temporarily distorting reserve statistics because of a one-day excess reserve demand (for ''window-dressing'' purposes).

is a big difference. Under terms of a repo agreement with a nonbank dealer, the corporation wires funds to the dealer's deposit account. (When executing a repo with a bank dealer, the corporation wires funds to the reserve account of the bank.) Because corporate repos executed with nonbank dealers have no net demand deposit effect, these repos should not be included in M1, or else there would be a double accounting of deposit credit.

Some Wall Street economists have been contending corporate repos executed by nonbank dealers should continue to be excluded from any monetary aggregate, but that repos executed by bank dealers should be included in M1.

Several years ago, the Fed decided to include bank repos (executed with corporations) in money supply data; but O/N repos were put in M2, not M1. Term repos were included in M3 only. Apparently Fed officials recognized the bank repo problem, but took half-action to resolve it.

An important reason for including bank dealer overnight repos in M1 emerges from the large changes in daily volumes of such repos. For example, during periods of collateral shortages, repo rates decline (as already noted) and corporate treasurers are likely to pad their demand deposit balances to meet any outstanding compensating balance requirements.

Many of the variations in the volume of repos made with bank dealers recur at the same time each year and are thus seasonal in nature. Seasonal adjustments to demand deposit data can negate these effects, in terms of measuring growth. There are also many non-seasonal, unpredictable variations in repo volumes; these variations often produce meaningless changes in seasonally adjusted weekly and monthly M1 data. Such erratic and nonsensical behavior of reported M1 levels reflects the inappropriateness of defining M1 to exclude bank-executed repos.

Overnight Eurodollars

The U.S. money supply is basically defined as domestic money, but the dollar deposit base has expanded offshore, boosted in recent years by the spectacular upsurge of the U.S. trade deficit. Transaction deposits in domestic banks are included in monetary aggregates, while many dollar-denominated deposits in offshore banks are excluded. Accordingly, depositors' preferences for offshore banking can create variations in the reported levels of money supply. The Fed is constantly trying to expand its reporting coverage of offshore dollar deposits in foreign banks, but constantly falls far short of this noble objective. The partial accounting of these deposits are included in M2 and M3, but not M1.

To the corporate treasurer, an overnight Eurodollar deposit is exactly the same as a repo with a bank dealer, except that the repo is collateralized with Treasury securities whereas the Eurodollar deposit has no such backing. Furthermore, the FDIC insures domestic deposits up to $100,000 for each account, but there is no such deposit insurance for offshore deposits. Nevertheless, the corporate treasurer is generally not concerned about the safety of offshore deposits placed with branches of the nation's largest 15 banks; such concern would force the treasurer to consider severing all relations with those banks.

There is a very small, obvious risk associated with the overnight Eurodollar deposit in comparison with the corporate repo. For this reason, Eurodollar rates are somewhat higher than repo rates. If a large bank deems it necessary to temporarily tap the Eurodollar market for reserve credit, then its offshore bank will increase its aggressiveness in bidding for Eurodollar deposits. Under these circumstances, the corporate treasurer will probably buy more overnight Eurodollar deposits than overnight repos. The overnight Eurodollar deposit obviously results in an increase in offshore deposit credit with a corresponding decrease in domestic demand deposit credit. When the spread of overnight Eurodollar rates over repo rates increases, the demand deposit component of M1 usually displays weaker growth.

The overnight Eurodollar deposit is basically the same as the overnight repo with the bank dealer; it represents a demand deposit on which interest is payable. It is therefore argued that overnight Eurodollar deposits should be included in M1, but they are not. How can anyone justify putting OCDs into M1, while excluding overnight bank repos and overnight Eurodollars?

The exclusion of overnight Eurodollars, like that of overnight repos, creates meaningless gyrations in weekly and monthly levels of reported domestic demand deposit credit. In turn, these variations divorce changes in M1 levels from reported economic activity.

Super-NOW Accounts

Super-NOW accounts were introduced in January 1983 as part of the on-going deregulation of the banking system. These accounts differed from regular NOW accounts by offering unregulated and higher rates of interest, but by requiring substantial minimum balances. Because Super-NOW's have the same transactional features as NOW accounts, they are included along with NOW accounts in the definition of M1. Surveys showed, however, that the average minimum balance requirement was close to $4,000; these funds cannot serve as medium of exchange. True, these balances serve as a store of value, but the M1 focus is on mediums of exchange, which minimum NOW account requirements are not. This failure to exclude minimum requirements may have had significant impacts on reported M1 growth during the first half of 1983, the introduction phase of Super-NOW accounts. Assuming that average minimums required were correctly surveyed at $4,000, and that trade-reported guesstimates of the mid-1983 number of Super-NOW accounts were not far off the mark, then H.6 monetary data released at the time by the Fed suggest that between a quarter to half of M1 growth was caused by transfers of savings and time accounts into Super-NOWs to meet the minimum balance requirements.

In 1986 the regulatory limitation on regular NOW account deposit rates was lifted, thus ending the legal distinction between NOW and Super-NOW accounts. However, many banks continue to impose substantial minimum balance requirements on checkable accounts that yield higher returns.

DISCUSSION OF M2 AND M3 AGGREGATES

It has been traditional to regard M1 as including only financial assets that function as mediums of exchange. M2 is a broader aggregate that adds to M1 by including such liquid stores of value as savings and small time deposits and shares in money market mutual funds. M2 thus serves as a measure of both money and highly liquid assets that can easily (and without much risk) be converted into mediums of exchange. Until recently, Fed officials had assumed that M1 was more closely related to economic activity than M2. In the past several years, however, Fed officials have been gradually placing greater policy emphasis on M2 as the trend of M1 growth has deviated from its historical relationship with general economic activity. In other words, M1 definitional problems and related structural changes contributed to its demise as a policy objective when definitional corrections should have been made instead. Had such changes occurred in a timely fashion (including corrections for the yet-to-be discussed "due from" bias), the author can only guess that a resultant stability in M1 velocity, though not superior to M2 or M3, would have nonetheless discouraged Fed officials from eventually demoting the M1 aggregate to a non-targeted status.

The M2 aggregate has some of the problems of M1, such as the exclusion of Treasury balances. But M2 does include overnight repos and Eurodollars, and thus escapes some of the problems associated with M1. M2 thus correlates somewhat better than M1 to economic activity, perhaps due partly to its broader definition of money to include its function as a store of value.

There is no succinct term applied to M2; it is referred to merely as "one of the broader monetary aggregates." The theoretical distinction between M2 and M3 is rather vague. M3 includes large (more than $100,000) CDs, term repos, and money market funds that are open only to institutions and not available to individuals, in addition to M2 components. Thus M3 merely includes a few additional liquid assets that are not accessible to small savers (because they are available only in large denominations). It is not clear why M3 is supposed to have any greater or less importance than M2.

MMDAs (Money Market Deposit Accounts) were introduced nationwide at the end of 1982. They were developed because money market mutual funds managed by nonbank financial institutions had proven to be very popular. They enabled the small investor to obtain a portfolio of money market instruments as diversified as those of large investors. The minimum denomination of $10,000 on Treasury bills, as an example, had prevented many small investors from participating in the Treasury bill market. It should be noted that this minimum was raised from $1,000 by the Treasury in 1969, at the urging of bankers wanting to discourage disintermediation.

The money market mutual fund allowed small investors not only to participate in the money market, but also to write a limited volume of drafts (checks) against their asset holdings in the fund. This automatic redemption by check feature attracted many small investors. Federal Reserve officials viewed money market mutual funds as essentially checkable deposits on which money market rates of interest were earned. Fed officials argued that Congress should impose reserve requirements on these accounts, because of the checkable feature. But Congress bowed to political pressures and refused to extend reserve requirements to the nonbank institutions offering money market mutual funds. Commercial bankers then pressured the Fed and Congress to enable banks to offer a competing type of deposit.

The Money Market Deposit Account (MMDA) was patterned after money market mutual funds. It permitted limited check writing and provided an unregulated yield. Reserve requirements were imposed at a low three percent, but were limited to non-personal accounts. Household MMDAs were exempted from all reserve requirements.

Some Fed officials, however, still want to extend reserve requirements to all money market mutual funds and MMDAs, because they feel that these accounts are essentially deposits with checkable features. Consistent with such conviction, Fed officials included MMDAs in M2 because they were viewed as substitutes for short-term (liquid) time and savings accounts.

Bank credit, the basic source of deposit credit, is very similar to M3 which, without the currency component, represents a summation of various deposit categories.

M3 consists of M2 plus institution-only money market mutual funds, term repos, and large CDs. The terms of large CDs are generally between 30 and 60 days, so at first sight they appear to be logical candidates for M3 instead of M2. Large CDs, however, are negotiable instruments having an active secondary market: any CD investor can immediately sell a CD at a reasonable market price, so CDs basically have the same liquidity as Treasury bills. One might question, therefore, why large CDs are not also included in M2.

PROBLEMS IN MEASURING MONEY SUPPLY GROWTH

There are four basic problems encountered in trying to accurately measure money supply *growth*. These are found in the "due from" bias, the procedures used in estimating data seasonal adjustments, and the conversion of short-term change into annual rates of growth.

In the correspondent banking relationship, a small bank will utilize the check collection capabilities of a larger clearing bank. Clearing banks establish correspondent banking networks as a means of increasing their demand deposits. On the asset side of the smaller bank's balance sheet, the demand deposit held at a clearing bank is called "due from other banks." This "due from" account is credited when the clearing bank has made collection on a check submitted by the correspondent.

When a small bank credits a customer's deposit for deposited checks drawn on other banks, it should not post an increase to its "due from" account, because collection on these checks has not been made. When the correspondent submits these checks to a clearing bank for collection, the correspondent is supposed to post an increase to an asset account called "cash items in process of collection." At this juncture of the collection process, the small bank's balance sheet should show an increase in the "cash items" account which is equal to an increase in deposit liabilities. After the clearing bank makes collection, the small bank should decrease "cash items" with a corresponding increase in its "due from" account.

The "cash items" account represents bank float. As previously explained, bank float arises because a deposit account in one bank has been credited for a deposited check, while the deposit account in the other bank on which the check was drawn did not simultaneously receive a debit for the amount of the check. In the accounting for M1 deposits, the total level of demand deposits reported by all

ACCOUNTING FOR BANK FLOAT:

The following illustrates accounting entries without imposing either Fed or Clearing House involvement that frequently occurs; the end result would not change, but the illustration would be complicated.

*Correspondent Bank**

(1) Cash items process of collection +	(1) Demand Deposit +
(3) −	
(3)(4) Due from (reserves) +	
+	+

Clearing Bank

	(2) Due to accts Correspondent bank +
	Paying bank −
0	0

Paying Bank

	(3) Demand Deposit −
(3)(4) Due from (reserves) −	
−	−

*Correspondent***

	(1) Demand Deposit +
(1) Due from +	
+	+

*correct version
**incorrect with "due from" bias

NOTES:
1. Demand deposit credit for deposited check on which no collection has been made.
2. Draft forwarded to clearing bank for collection—one day later.
3. Correspondent receives credit advice and paying bank receives check drawn on its account—another day later.
4. "Due froms" qualify as reserves in most state chartered, small banks.

banks will exceed the actual level unless bank float ("cash items") is subtracted from the reported total. Gross demand deposits must be reduced by the amount of "cash items" to arrive at net demand deposits. Net demand deposits must still be further reduced by the amount of Fed float, in order to avoid double accounting of deposit credit included in M1 (as explained in the first chapter). If banks regularly fail to fully report cash items in process (bank float), preferring instead to improperly post bank float in "due from" accounts, such "due from" bias means that an insufficient amount of actual cash items is subtracted from gross demand deposits, causing an overstate of net demand deposits.

Small banks regularly fail to credit their "cash items" accounts for checks submitted to correspondents for collection. Instead, these banks have a "due from" bias because they prefer to immediately credit their "due from" accounts for checks submitted to correspondents. The "due from" bias saves the small banker from the expense of additional accounting entries involving "cash items." Bankers see no harm in circumventing the "cash items" account because it normally takes a few days for the correspondent to collect on checks submitted.

When banks fail to fully account for all cash items in process of collection, the reported total of bank float (cash items) will be understated. If gross demand deposits are reduced by an understated amount of bank float, the resultant net demand deposit calculation will include some double counting of deposit credit. When gross demand deposits rise because of an increase in bank float, the underreporting of bank float in favor of "due from" postings will give the wrong impression that net demand deposits also have risen.

Fed officials have long recognized the existence of the "due from" bias. On reporting forms from which M1 data are compiled, a footnote associated with the "due from" entry asks reporting banks to estimate the amount of cash items included in the "due from" total. Banks regularly overlook the footnoted request partly because it is impossible to reasonably estimate the cash items entries included in "due froms" because of the many other sources of "due from" credits. The "due from" bias, however, probably totals more among non-member depositories where "due froms" often qualify as reserve credit; non-member reporting is infrequent to FDIC officials, and assumed to be incomplete with regard to reporting cash items.

Many economists have dismissed the effects of the "due from" bias on M1 data because interbank deposits ("due froms") are excluded from M1 data; if there are cash items in "due from" accounts, then they have already been excluded from M1 deposits.

The question regarding cash items, however, is whether they are fully subtracted from gross demand deposits. Cash items are not included in M1 deposit data, but they still have to be subtracted from gross demand deposits to avoid double accounting. The "due from" bias in M1 data cannot be resolved by subtracting "due froms" from gross demand, in addition to subtracting cash items, because "due froms" include much more than just cash item entries. The "due from" subtraction would thus understate net demand deposits.

To ensure understanding of this matter, it must be recognized that both cash items and portions of "due from" accounts (improperly containing cash items) have in fact been directly associated with a boost in non-bank gross demand deposits, representing a double accounting of deposit credit (newly deposited credit and yet-to-be debited demand deposit credit). Cash items (bank float), regardless of being correctly posted in the cash items account or incorrectly hidden in "due from" accounts, must be fully subtracted from gross demand deposits in order to fully eliminate double accounting of deposit credit. However, if one cannot account for that portion of "due froms" containing cash items, then this portion of bank float is not, and cannot be, deducted from gross demand deposits. The confusing question is not one of inclusion, but one of exclusion. Neither cash items nor "due froms" are included in gross demand deposits; but all of the former and part of the latter are associated with gross demand deposit gains representing bank float, which must be fully subtracted (excluded), but is not.

Bank float, similar to Fed float, follows seasonal patterns that are predictable except during winter months, when unexpected storms create transportation float and increase holdover float. Unadjusted data on net demand deposit levels exhibit patterns whose regularity stem partly from this seasonal regularity of bank float; so net demand deposit data are seasonally adjusted to remove these bank float influences, which include "due from" biases. Only when there is a tremendous change in the level of the "due from" bias will there be an impact on seasonally adjusted M1 data. This is precisely what happened in late 1981 and early 1982.

The Monetary Control Act of 1980 had directed the Fed to charge member banks the full cost of clearing checks (previously a free service). Though the initial fees fell slightly short of covering check clearing costs, they nonetheless encouraged large banks to compete with the Fed for check clearing business by expanding their correspondent banking networks. When Fed check clearing fees were initiated in August 1981, many banks were still in the process of expanding their correspondent check clearing facilities. By October, however, the correspondent banking network had started to significantly reduce the volume of checks processed by the Fed. In some Reserve banks, the drop in volume ranged from 25 percent to 50 percent. Over the entire System, however, the Fed's share of total check processing fell quickly from 44 percent to 35 percent (according to Fed published reports). The Fed's loss of market share was equalled by a sudden and quantum increase in correspondent clearings.

The fourth quarter, 1981, upsurge in correspondent clearings produced a one-time jump in the level of non-reported bank float. Of course there are no data available to directly prove the sudden increase in the "due from" bias. During the fourth quarter, however, total net deposits of all banks increased by about $32 billion more than the combined deposit effect of bank credit growth and Fed open market operations. Bank credit growth and net deposit growth always display different growth rates, due partly to deposit shifts between domestic and offshore banks. But the discrepancy between bank credit and deposit growth during the fourth quarter was without precedent, and was not associated with any unusual deposit flows between domestic and offshore markets. Suspiciously, much of the fourth quarter deposit growth was in net demand deposits which, because of the shift of funds into newly introduced other checkable types of deposits, had been exhibiting very weak growth earlier in the year. Economists at Money Market Services, for example, estimated that M1 growth during the fourth quarter of 1981 was overstated by about $24 billion, due to increased correspondent clearings and the "due from" bias.

Rapid M1 growth during the fourth quarter was not accompanied by increasing economic activity. In fact, the economy was heading into the deepest recession since the thirties. Based on rapid M1 growth, monetarists predicted that the economy would expand briskly in 1982. Instead, the economy sank deeper into a depression during 1982.

Because M1 growth was much faster than that of nominal GNP growth during the fourth quarter of 1981 and during the first half of 1982, the calculated income velocity of M1 displayed a major decline never before seen. M1 velocity, measuring the number of times that M1 assets are used each year to finance GNP growth, is supposed to be relatively stable. The surprisingly unstable velocity of M1 during 1982 encouraged Fed officials to place less policy emphasis on M1. The M1 de-emphasis was also prompted by the Fed's discovery of the approximate size of the ''due from'' bias. This research discovery occurred late in April, prompted partly by several Wall Street economists, and was the triggering factor behind the May FOMC decision to ease reserve conditions in spite of continuing M1 growth in excess of its targeted range. A more obvious (though less important) contributing factor was continued economic weakness that began to weaken Fed expectations of renewed economic growth.

Fictitiously high rates of M1 growth reported by the Fed in late 1981 and early 1982 prompted Fed officials to maintain a restrictive monetary policy even though the economy had entered a deep recession. Policy was obviously pro-cyclical only because money supply growth could not be accurately measured. The subsequent drop in interest rates and the resultant economic recovery should be partly credited to the discovery of the large increase in the ''due from'' bias.

At the present time, Fed staffers try to adjust net demand deposit data for an estimated amount of ''due from'' bias. This adjustment is separately reported in the weekly H.6 statistical release. However, if there is a blackout in Chicago or New York, as there has been in the past, the resultant increase in bank float is hard to accurately estimate. In turn, net demand deposit data can increase far more than the estimated seasonal adjustment, producing a meaningless jump in the level of M1.

ERRORS IN ESTIMATING DEPOSIT DATA

Nonmember banks are not required to report their daily deposit levels to the Fed. Because the Fed does not receive deposit data from roughly two-thirds of all banks, it must estimate these levels (by type of deposit). These estimates have been based on a carefully constructed sample of small member banks which presumably have the same trends as small nonmember depositories. Almost all nonmember depositories are members of either the FDIC or FSLIC, and are therefore required to submit a complete accounting statement to these insurance authorities twice a year (on June 30 and December 31). The ongoing estimates of nonmember deposit levels are thus benchmarked against the semi-annual statements.

These statements do not, however, represent the condition of nonmember depositories throughout most of the year. June and December statement dates unfortunately coincide with statement dates used by many businesses. Just before business statement dates, most businesses pad their cash balances (demand deposits) and/or increase their short-term time deposits, to improve the appearance of corporate balance sheets. Deposits in nonmember institutions thus surge at these statement dates, which makes the benchmarking procedure subject to large errors. Fed revisions to historical money supply data based on the semi-annual benchmarking procedure have been generally in the upward direction.

The average revision of preliminary reported weekly M1 data has been about $800 million. In fairness to the estimating procedure, it should be noted that part of the reason for these substantial Fed revisions is the need to revise estimated seasonal adjustments. The seasonal adjustment process is a major measurement problem to which our attention now turns.

SEASONAL ADJUSTMENT PROBLEMS

By definition, seasonal variations are those variations that recur within a year. When viewing M1 data over time, one should take into account four types of variations. The first is a seasonal variation that, when eliminated from original data, leaves a rather smooth trend of data reflecting the second and third variations, cyclical changes and secular (long-term) trends. The fourth type is random variation, which cannot be predicted because of irregular recurrence.

For monthly data, 12-month moving averages smooth out all seasonal variations but do not affect cyclical or secular trends. By dividing averages into actual monthly data, one can produce an index of seasonality for each month under study. For M1, seasonal index numbers for a particular month are not the same from year to year. The change in monthly seasonals each year is generally in the same direction, and reflects a "moving seasonal." In most years during the 1970s, demand deposits increased by an increasing amount each subsequent April. These increases reflect a moving seasonal. When constructing a seasonal factor for the next April, as an example, one must forecast the extent to which April's seasonal variation might change once again.

A major reason why April's seasonal upsurge became greater each year during the 1970s was inflation, and the associated "bracket creep" that placed the average taxpayer into successively higher tax brackets. The rise in tax payments every April 15 was associated with more padding of household demand deposits in preparation for tax payments. At the same time, the Federal government experienced more frequent delays in processing individual tax returns, so the rise in the checking accounts of taxpayers receiving refunds (who tend to file early) came at the same time as the padding of accounts by those who owed taxes. The seasonal upsurge in demand deposit credit thus became greater and greater during each successive April. Fed staffers consistently underestimated this moving seasonal and, as a result, M1 growth during the 1970s displayed an upsurge every April on a seasonally adjusted basis. Another reason for the April deposit upsurge was the increased practice of government treasurers to pad their demand deposits to meet compensating balance requirements.

Obviously, if seasonality is defined as a variation recurring within a year's time, and if seasonally adjusted M1 data displayed a surge every April, then the seasonally adjusted M1 data have not been fully adjusted for seasonal variation. In revising and correcting historical seasonally adjusted data, Fed staffers have been suspected by some observers of avoiding the elimination of all of the April bulges, because they might confuse historians as to the reason for the Fed's tightening each April.

The inability to fully adjust for M1 seasonality during such months as April led to recurring monetary policy changes within each year. It was therefore cynically said that one might seasonally adjust monetary policy. Such a statement belied the importance given by Fed officials to M1 data at the time, and presented a very sad commentary on the state of monetary economics. Fortunately, moving seasonals have become somewhat less dynamic in recent years, and Fed staffers have been able to increase their accuracy in accounting for seasonality. At the same time, Fed officials have decreased their emphasis on short-term changes in the monetary aggregates because of the admittedly unreliable nature of weekly and monthly money supply estimates.

The discussion thus far has concerned problems in seasonally adjusting monthly data. The problems in seasonally adjusting weekly data are far more serious and difficult to solve. It is difficult to establish a moving average of weekly data for seasonal adjustment purposes because some years have 53 weeks instead of 52 weeks. An even greater problem arises from the fact that the relation of any given week to its respective month changes each year. For example, the first weekend in July next year may be one or two calendar days later than it was last year. And, for M1 data, seasonality varies by the calendar day of any month, not by the week. To overcome this problem, most weekly seasonal adjustments are made by adjusting daily data. Still, the weekly seasonals must be estimated and must be benchmarked with estimated monthly seasonals. The Fed has developed some very sophisticated techniques for eliminating reliance on weekly data in favor of summing daily seasonally adjusted data that take account of the fact that any given week will begin on different days from year to year. These techniques also attempt to take account of moving holidays and social security payments.

CONVERTING SHORT-TERM CHANGES INTO ANNUAL GROWTH RATES

Aberrant weekly surges in M1 are often dismissed by many analysts as not having much importance, because those surges will be offset by corresponding weekly declines. Most of the problems in money supply accounting, such as bank float and seasonal adjustments already mentioned, create short-term surges that are soon offset by large weekly declines. Contrary to popular opinion, however, each aberrant upsurge in M1 has more than a temporary effect. Fed officials and market analysts used to regularly take the latest weekly M1 level and average it with that of the three or four preceding weeks; this average is compared with a similar average ending four, or nine, or thirteen weeks ago, in order to determine M1's annual rate of growth over the past four, nine, and thirteen weeks. At one time during the 1970s, the FOMC regularly changed policy according to differences between the latest nine-week M1 growth and the targeted growth path. The averaging procedure creates a problem in accurately measuring annual growth rates because it enables extreme data to skew the averages.

Assume that M1, during each of the four weeks ended four weeks ago, had been reported to be a mere $2. During each of the first two weeks of the latest four-week period, M1 was again reported to be $2; no growth had occurred. During the third week of that four-week period, however, assume that bank float or faulty seasonal adjustments pushed the reported total of M1 up to $6. This aberrant change was offset in the latest week when M1 fell by $4 back to its actual level of $2. The average M1 level of that four-week period is $3 instead of the $2 average of the four-week period before it. Over the latest four-week period, M1 increased at 50 percent, representing an annual rate of growth of 600 percent. The foregoing example is obviously not realistic, but it demonstrates the skewing effects of unrealistic data. If the magnitude of the aberrant change were 100 times reduced, there would still be a 6 percent growth rate reported for M1 when, in fact, no such growth ever occurred.

DOES MONEY MATTER?

Federal Reserve objectives are often depicted by financial economists as "targets." Fed officials, however, have seemed to be cautious about using the term "targets," perhaps fearing that the public might hold policymakers accountable for precise achievement of objectives, which are more general in nature than the word "target" implies. Moreover, Fed officials often appear anxious to resort to language that weakens the standards of their accountability to Congress.

There are two types of Fed targets: operational targets and policy targets. Operational targets are assigned by the FOMC to the Open Market Desk. FOMC minutes, however, will not reveal any precise assignment of operational targets. Instead, Fed officials regard operational target assignments as strategies developed between Desk and FOMC staffs on the basis of related discussions and understandings developed at each FOMC meeting. Examples of operational targets are adjustment borrowings, net borrowed reserves, nonborrowed reserves, a funds rate target, and a funds rate peg. The differences between the latter two targets will be examined in detail in the next chapter.

As a general observation, net borrowed reserves were operationally targeted in the 1960s, and the funds rate was pegged during the 1970s. In the current decade, operational targets have included funds rate targeting, adjustment borrowing, and nonborrowed reserves. Reference to operational targets sometimes misleads the reader into the assumption that only one operational target is pursued at a given time, or that secondary targets of the Desk are always compatible with a primary objective. Neither assumption is correct, as the next chapter demonstrates, and neither holds true for policy targets.

Federal Reserve officials have declared for themselves three basic monetary policy objectives: stable prices, full utilization of national economic resources, and equilibrium in the international balance of payments. Though Congress delegated its Constitutional power of coinage to the Federal Reserve System, which it created, Congress has never fully taken the initiative to establish Federal Reserve monetary policy objectives and priorities among the sometimes conflicting objectives. With the enactment of the Federal Reserve Act, members of Congress assumed that the new central bank would not engage in the establishment of monetary policies; and when they discovered twenty years later that Fed officials were secretly establishing monetary policies, members of Congress merely endorsed the three broad objectives which Fed officials had developed. Since that time, Congress has not come to terms with policy priorities, nor has there been sufficient understanding of policy objectives for Congress to properly exercise oversight responsibility for the delegation of its power of coinage.

For example, the objective of full utilization of national economic resources includes full employment of labor, but is not limited to full employment (which is the standard assumption in Congress). Moreover, if the so-called "full employment" objective is regularly subordinated to the anti-inflation objective, as has generally occurred, then Congressionally enacted national policies of full employment appear incongruous with the reluctance of Congress to establish policy priorities for the Fed.

The Humphrey-Hawkins Full Employment and Balanced Growth Act of 1978 represented the first (though half-hearted) attempt by Congress to establish and monitor specific monetary growth targets set by the Fed. Due mainly to previous testimony of Fed Chairman Arthur Burns, Congress had become convinced that Federal Reserve control of money supply growth was a key link between Fed operations and the fulfillment of policy objectives. Money supply targeting by Fed officials was referred to as the establishment of intermediate policy objectives. Monetary policy changes at that time were not associated specifically with changes in the rate of inflation, economic growth, or growing balance of payments problems. Instead, policy changes were specifically timed to undesired variations of money supply growth from targeted ranges of growth.

According to disclosed policy doctrine, at the time of the Humphrey-Hawkins Bill monitoring of the three general Fed policy objectives constituted the basis upon which intermediate targets of money supply growth were established. Congress thus extended its "advise and consent" role to the establishment of money supply growth targets. Lacking understanding of money velocity and in want of more confident input from Congressional staffs, monetary targeting by the Fed was simply rubber-stamped by both House and Senate banking committees. Not too surprisingly, Fed officials fended off stricter standards of accountability by setting so wide the ranges of targeted monetary growth that probabilities of missing targets seemed nil. But overshoots did occur, and Congress found itself incapable of taking any corrective steps. In fact, members in both houses of Congress seemed gullible to any testimony rendered by Fed officials.

With the codification of money supply targets, financial analysts found it helpful to describe motives for monetary policy change in terms of policy targets. In order to forecast policy change, one obviously had to be aware of policy targets regardless of whether they were of an intermediate or long-term nature.

Due partly to the various structural, definitional, and measurement problems associated with monetary aggregates, the behavior of M1, M2, and M3 velocities became so bizarre and baffling during the 1980s that Fed officials gradually removed most policy emphasis from monetary aggregates, and made economic variables a primary policy target. When members of Congress belatedly awakened to the fact that policy targets no longer embraced the need to control money supply growth, some became upset that semi-annual Humphrey-Hawkins hearings had become (at the Fed's discretion) an exercise in futility, insofar as money supply targeting was concerned. But true to form, "paper tigers" never attempted to set their own agenda.

With the mid-'80s shift in policy targets towards such economic aggregates as real GNP growth and manufacturing employment, there was a corresponding shift in operational targets towards interest rate control. Interest rate effects on economic aggregates are well known, whereas their effects on monetary aggregates are not well-defined (as explained in the next chapter). The two principal operational targets were the discount rate and the funds rate spread over the discount rate. The Fed's policy had become economic rather than monetary in nature, a shift that was never authorized by a sleeping Congress.

While Congress and the Fed slept on money supply questions of the mid-1980s, monetary growth was permitted to exceed relatively high targeted growth ranges. To the cynic, it appeared that embarrassment avoidance was the principal guide used by Fed officials in setting ranges of growth for monetary aggregates. The 1983 upsurge in monetary growth, however, was probably void of long-range inflationary implication because much of the growth in money was direly

Graph 4.6

Annualized Growth Rates

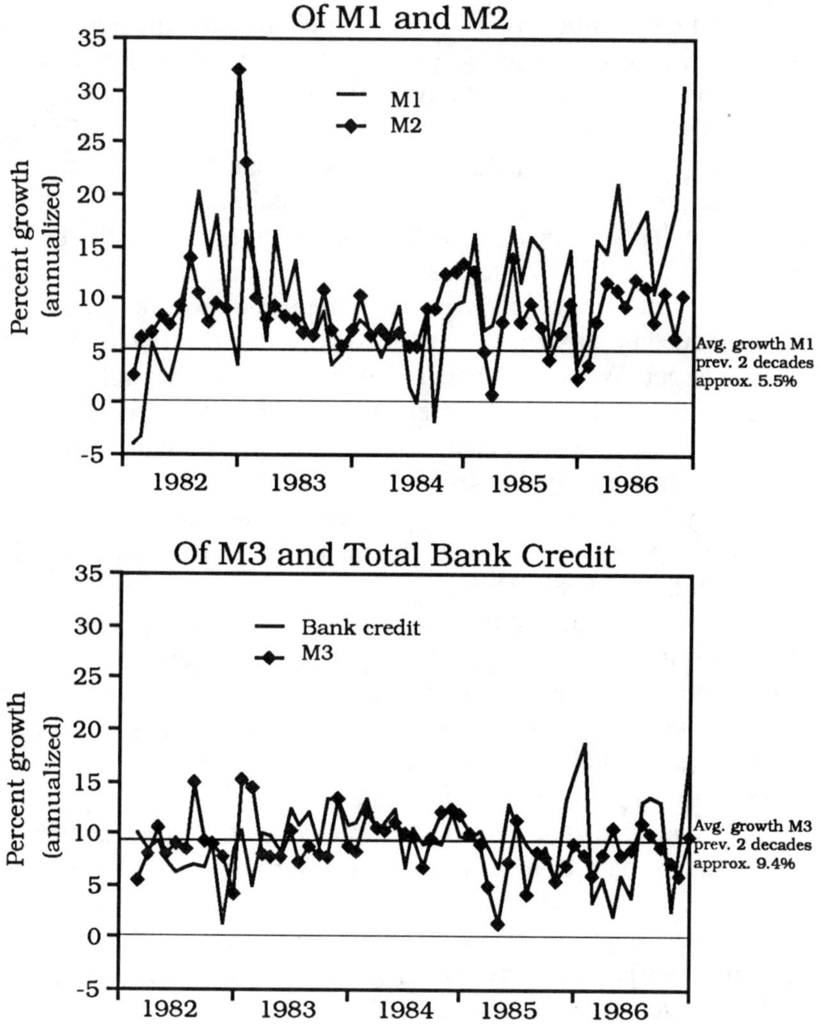

Monthly data of daily averages, 1982 through 1986. Source: Federal Reserve releases H.6 and G.7.

needed to address the 1982 liquidity crisis (to be examined later). The money supply growth from 1983 through 1986, however, remained excessive, particularly in relation to historical standards as opposed to liberally established upper limits of targeted ranges.

This extended period, in which excessive monetary growth was permitted, may have been the staging point for the return of inflationary pressures.

Though the linkage of money to economic activity and prices is blurred in the short-term picture, there is a clear relationship in the long-term picture. Whenever any nation has permitted excessive money supply growth for a number of years, rates of inflation have always risen as a result. The lag between this cause and its effect in the inflation picture varies considerably due to other important influences on price behavior, such as currency exchange rates and the strength of the economy. Whereas non-monetary causes of inflation do not always result in an appreciable rise in inflation rates because of other influences on price behavior, prolonged high rates of money supply growth do. Fed Chairman Paul Volcker once warned the public and Congress not to take their eyes off "the money supply ball." Ironically, Paul Volcker may have been the first to have done so.

Part of the Fed's problem in addressing money supply issues seemed related to an inability of Fed policymakers to look beyond short-term irregular behavior of money velocity. One is tempted to speculate that there must be secular velocity trends most relevant to the policy quest for stable prices, yet this author is not aware of any completed research on secular linkages of the economy to money supply (other than eyeball commentary such as this). Indeed, to arrive at secular observations, one must first be able to clearly grasp cyclical relationships in back of the velocity picture. This may be the hardest challenge of all.

Is the growth of monetary aggregates determined primarily by the demand for bank credit, or by the supply of reserve credit? Chapter 7 (Reserve Requirements) will help to make the following answer more convincing: In less than a 50 percent fractional reserve system, the demand for bank credit is theoretically a more important long-range determinant of money supply growth than the supply of reserve credit. With the current average reserve requirement ratio less than 4 percent (for reasons discussed in chapter 7), the demand for credit represents the driving force behind money supply growth, which is precisely why Fed policymakers decided to target credit demands (using a funds rate target) in late 1982.

If the demand function of money is so significant, then more research focus is needed on the demand side rather than on the supply side of money, consistent with the thrust of earlier chapters. It was previously described why liquidity of consumers, non-bank businesses, and banks lagged the business cycle, and why lagged changes in liquidity produced a lag in the cycle of credit demands (including government but excluding mortgage sectors) to the business cycle. The growth of money supply thus tends to lag cyclical changes in the economy. Unless the Fed exerts a very strong reserve supply influence on monetary growth, cyclical changes in such growth are more likely to lag, rather than lead, business cycles.

If secular trends in money velocity are to be observed with reasonable accuracy, the widely-held theoretical notion of money leading cyclical change must be eliminated (which historical data has already begun to encourage). This permits a more accurate lead-lag structure needed to identify and separate intermediate (cyclical) velocity behavior from secular behavior.

In other words, money velocities should be segmented by secular, cyclical, and short run (less than one year) tendencies. The latter is so irregular, because of measurement and definitional problems, that the task of accurately defining cyclical velocity behavior may be impossible. One is left with the rather obvious conclusion that the more misleading the short-term monetary variations, the harder the task of identifying intermediate and secular characteristics and, ultimately, defining the relationship of monetary growth to the three general Fed policy objectives.

Not only must money velocity analyses be statistically segmented by timeframes, they should also be differentiated between real and financial sectors. From 1983 through 1986, a significant portion of the huge growth in the dollar deposit base (money supply) flowed to offshore owners (deposits) because of escalating trade deficits. In particular, the Japanese market became flooded with dollar deposit credit which was initially used to purchase Treasury securities. In spite of record levels of new Treasury debt issues, the Treasury yield curve flattened significantly. The huge inflow of Japanese dollar credits to the long bond market produced a major bond market (price) rally. In addition to rising Japanese investment demands, American participants also found themselves in a highly liquid condition. Such liquidity arose not only from the rapid expansion of the dollar deposit base, but also from huge net worth gains stemming from the run-up in financial market values. As Japanese investors purchased marketable debt from American investors, the latter group "booked" their gains and, expecting more trading gains ahead, repositioned themselves on the long side of the market (purchased more securities). Because of the flood of incoming dollar credits (investment demand), no one wanted to prematurely leave the party (price rally). As a result, far too many dollars were chasing relatively scarce securities. Dr. Arthur Burns had previously warned that monetary neglect at the Fed would result in too many dollars chasing too few goods, and would result in inflation. No one ever seemed to take serious note of such an old adage. But it clearly erupted in the financial sector during the mid-'80s, inflating market values of financial assets.

The financial market rally was akin to the infamous "chain letter"; someone would at some time be left holding an over-valued piece of paper. When would this occur? It had to occur when bond investor returns from interest earnings and trading gains fell below returns in the real sector; and this is precisely what happened. Japanese investors first began diverting new dollar credits from bonds into equity markets, and soon thereafter into direct (real sector) investments. This pattern of behavior was not much different from that of OPEC members ten years earlier when dollar inflows were initially recycled back into financial markets before real sector investments could be implemented.

While the excited flows of new dollar credits were contained within the financial sector during the mid-'80s, continued money supply growth was not circulating as rapidly in the real sector (where dollar-sponsored trade deficit problems depressed returns on manufacturing investments). As a result, the money velocity picture became even more distorted. The easy projection to be made for 1987 to 1989 was one in which excessive liquidity would help slow the growth in demands for bank credit; money supply growth would moderate without much influence from Fed operations, and economic activity would gradually strengthen. Such developments should produce a resumption of normal long-term growth in the income velocity of money. The policy picture should have been a comfortable one in 1987—or should it?

The continued flows of excessive liquidity (money availability) from financial sectors to real sectors would help insulate the economy from the adversities of the trade deficit. Also, the dollar-related pressure for higher commodity prices would theoretically be accommodated (rather than mitigated) by flows of liquidity from financial to real sectors. Nominal GNP should thus have an inflation boost even though money supply growth seems to be (at least temporarily) in control.

The comforting picture is quite fraudulent, partly because money velocity measurements are not segmented between real and financial sectors. By the time the fraud is discovered at the Fed, it will be too late to prevent inflation; and by the time Congress awakens, high rates of unemployment and inflation will have already returned (which chapter 8 explores in some detail).

Even if economists can satisfactorily resolve all of the foregoing money supply issues, there still remains the age-old question of just what is money. While Fed Chairman Burns' policy target focused on money as a medium of exchange (M1), monetarists wanted a broader policy focus to include money as a store of value (M2 or M3). This debate was made moot by the fact that Dr. Burns had such difficulty in limiting the growth of monetary aggregates; so, monetarist criticisms focussed more on operational targets than on policy targets.

Broader monetary aggregates as policy targets pose a theoretical problem rarely seen in print; some components of broader aggregates do not serve as a medium of exchange though serving as a store of value. The classic definition of money requires that both characteristics of medium and value storing be present to distinguish money. M1 advocates generally fail to specifically point out that a CD certificate is not accepted at the supermarket as payment for purchases., Yet, the CD is such a near-money item that the distinction seems to be rather moot to monetarists.

If, however, the selection of a monetary aggregate for policy targeting is based on money velocities, then M1, M2, and M3 lose out to bank credit. When defining velocity in terms of a numerator including net imports as well as nominal GNP, bank credit exhibits the most stable velocity behavior, followed closely by M3 (as one might expect since its inclusion of currency is the major distinguishing factor from bank credit). M1 velocity is the least stable, as illustrated earlier. Such findings seem quite logical. The bulk of measurement and definitional problems apply to M1 components, not to those components exclusive to M2 or M3. One wonders just how much better M1 velocity could be if measurement and definitional problems could be resolved.

The theoretical beauty of bank credit is its simplicity; it measures additions to demand deposit credits (medium of exchange) and ignores how these dollar credits may be stored. This does not mean, however, that the M1 aggregate is without potential policy usefulness.

If M1 definition and measurement problems can be at least partly resolved, the resultant behavior of M1 data could be a useful proxy of transactional intentions of the public. Used in conjunction with bank credit growth, M1 data could help depict deposit composition dispositions of the public arising from deposit (interest) rate spreads and spending. If rate spread impacts can be econometrically isolated, then spending dispositions of the public could be derived from M1 data (particularly when using checkable deposits as a ratio to bank credit).

The author's recommendation is that, for policy-making purposes, Fed officials should focus on the source and composition of monetary growth. The source is bank credit, which is extended on the basis of demand for bank credit and reserve availability. M1, M2, and M3 aggregates provide useful information about the disposition of new money (particularly M1). In the final analysis, a balanced monetary view might be most appropriate for the FOMC, given priorities in the following order: Bank credit, M1, M2, and M3 (with the latter being a possible candidate for dismissal).

The final question involves the policy emphasis that bank credit and monetary aggregates should be given relative to real sector aggregates (such as GNP). Until monetary data become more meaningful and reliable, monetary aggregates should probably be subordinated to bank credit and real sector aggregates. Even so, monetary aggregates, in conjunction with bank credit growth, should command more policy respect than at present. Bank credit, in this context, should be targeted, and monetary aggregates should all be reduced to a ''monitored'' status at the FOMC. The bank credit target should be established partly on the basis of real sector aggregates, which embraces a so-called ''balanced'' policy approach. In short, money does matter; and, the suggested policy approach is intended to maintain the primary focus of monetary policy on the rate of money creation.

The degree of monetary emphasis at the Fed has gone to the extreme on either side of the balanced approach suggested. During most of the 1970s, monetary policy was almost exclusively focused on weekly M1 data. In recent years, however, Fed officials seem to have become so disillusioned by money velocity trends that they have placed almost all policy emphasis on real sector aggregates, with hardly any concern about monetary aggregates.

Fed officials are not alone in ascribing minimal importance to monetary growth in recent years. Debt market participants also tend to ignore incoming monetary data. However, if history tends to repeat itself, then excessive growth of bank credit and money supply since 1982 represents an inflationary risk to be realized in the absence of a money supply focus among Fed policymakers. The secular relationship of money growth and price behavior is easily hidden from a shorter term perspective. Like the man who accidentally fell from the top of a skyscraper without any visible concern while falling below the tenth floor, Fed officials seem oblivious to the monetary impact that is yet to come.

Congress once investigated why threats against Pearl Harbor were not properly heeded to establish a sound defense. Congress should also investigate why the monetary threats against stable prices are not being taken seriously at the Fed. This investigation would, in part, reveal that reactive rather than proactive policy making at the Fed is a contributing factor. Fed policy has historically reacted to adversity only after the problem is evident, not before.

Though Congress is willing to spend hundreds of billions of dollars on defense against communist threats, not even one percent of this amount will be authorized for research at the Fed. Yet to many observers, ongoing threats of inflation and economic slack could become a more serious national security factor than the communist threat. At a minimum, Congress should encourage and financially assist the Fed in resolving money supply definitional and measurement problems which will then help policymakers to determine just how important controlled monetary growth really is to this country and its partners abroad.

CHAPTER 5

Open Market Operations

INTRODUCTION

The next three chapters provide a detailed discussion of the tools of monetary control: open market operations, discount administration, and reserve requirements. Reserve management employs two sets of targets: policy targets (objectives) and operational targets (methods). In general, policy targets ranged from bank credit growth in the 1960s, to M1 growth in the 1970s, to GNP growth during the first half of the 1980s. Operational reserve targets used to meet policy objectives included net borrowed reserves targeting in the 1960s and after 1982, and nonborrowed reserves targeting from October 1979 to the fall of 1982. A policy of pegging the federal funds rate was pursued in the 1970s, and "de facto" funds rate targeting since 1982. Unlike funds rate pegging, funds rate targeting employs an intermediate reserve borrowing target to maintain general rather than specific control over the funds rate. The narrative of this chapter carries the story up to 1983, and focusses on reserve management. Reserve policies and funds rate targeting in the period of financial deregulation after 1982 will be examined in Chapter 7 in conjunction with the discussion of reserve requirement changes at that time.

OPEN MARKET PROCEDURES

At 11:15 a.m. EST on each business day, members of the FOMC staff at the Board of Governors hold a telephone conference with the Manager of the Open Market Desk at the Federal Reserve Bank of New York. A voting member of the FOMC, typically a Reserve Bank President, with his staff, also participates. The Desk Manager briefs participants on estimated reserve availability, including expected changes during the current reserve maintenance period, and on current developments in the financial markets, and then discloses his open market plans for the day and for upcoming days. After some questions and comments, the planned open market activity is either confirmed or (rarely) changed.

When the Fed enters the open market, Desk officials simultaneously contact all reporting dealers by direct telephone line, inviting bids or offers on securities to be purchased or sold. In turn, reporting dealers customarily notify newsmen of Fed operations through dedicated telephone lines to major wire services. Screen and wire services flash messages of Fed intervention, normally within 20 seconds of initial Fed contact with reporting dealers, to every major financial center of the world.

After each Fed entry, the debt market quotes displayed on screen services may become "subject" for several minutes; that is, previously established dealer bids and offers for debt securities no longer apply. Within a minute or two, traders must assess the policy importance (if any) of the Fed's open market operation and post new bids and offers. Debt market prices can change substantially after any given Fed operation. Often, however, open market operations have been anticipated in the marketplace, do not generate speculation about policy change, and have little impact on market conditions.

Almost all open market operations are designed to offset the reserve effects of changes in such operating factors as Federal Reserve float, Treasury deposits at the Fed, and currency in circulation. The day-to-day change in each of these factors can be quite large, requiring substantial operations to keep reserve availability unchanged. Such operations are described as "defensive operations." Dynamic operations, intended to *change* the availability of reserve credit in accordance with a change in the FOMC's reserve policy, are quite rare. Nonetheless, market participants must be on guard for any hint of policy change. Traders are apt to ascribe an operation to a policy change when, in fact, it was purely defensive in nature.

Careful to foster orderly market conditions, Fed officials seek to minimize the frequency of open market entry. If operating factors drain reserves in a reserve maintenance period, but are expected to supply more reserves the following period, Desk officials will not purchase securities the first week and sell them the second; they may execute repos during the first week, allowing them to mature (without replacement) during the second week. The outright purchase of securities by the Fed represents a permanent addition of reserve credit, whereas a temporary purchase of securities, under a repurchase agreement, represents a temporary addition of reserve credit.

Late in 1969, Desk officials surprised reporting dealers by requesting bids on a new type of operation: matched sale-purchase agreements. During the phone go-around, Desk officials explained to reporting dealers that matched sales were the reverse of repos: the Fed wanted to sell securities under an agreement to buy them back on the next business day. Market participants continue to use the term "reverse" rather than the official name. More recently, the word "matches" has often been used for the term "matched sales." With the creation of Fed reverses, Desk officials could temporarily drain reserve credit as easily as they had been able to temporarily increase reserve credit through repos.

ESTIMATING DEFENSIVE REQUIREMENTS

"Fed watchers" are highly skilled specialists capable of predicting daily open market operations. Market participants throughout the world employ Fed watchers to help them distinguish between defensive and dynamic open market operations, so that they can adjust their trading strategies to changes in monetary policy.

Both Fed staffers and their watchers base their forecasts of defensive requirements on the H.4.1 report, released weekly by the Board of Governors and entitled "Factors Affecting Reserves of

Member Depositories.'' The weekly report, released to the public, shows averages of daily data and Wednesday data. The staffs of the Board of Governors and of the New York Fed each prepare a similar report each day, showing the prior day's data, and making projections for the current day. Thus, the FOMC and Desk staffs are better equipped than outside observers to estimate the daily need for defensive open market requirements to offset the effects of market factors on the reserve aggregates.

The H.4.1 report shows all factors supplying reserves and factors draining reserves. The sum of factors draining reserves, subtracted from the sum of factors supplying reserves, must equal the amount of reserve balances of member banks on deposit at the Fed. These balances, plus vault cash held by member banks (which qualifies as legal reserves), equal total reserves. The H.4.1 report also shows the level of required reserves, from which excess reserves can be calculated by subtracting from total reserves.

Principal factors supplying reserves include securities held by the Fed (acquired through open market operations), reserve borrowings from the Fed by depository institutions, float credit, gold, and other assets (such as buildings and equipment). When these factors increase, reserve balances at the Fed increase. Factors draining reserves include currency in circulation, Treasury deposits at the Fed, foreign and other deposits, and other Fed liabilities. All of these factors are balance sheet items.

In forecasting defensive open market operations, all factors except security holdings and reserve borrowings must be separately forecast. As mentioned in Chapter 1, many of these factors display pronounced seasonal variations from week to week, and thus lend themselves to reasonably accurate forecasting. The outside Fed watcher can construct an operational forecast by constructing the H.4.1 report in reverse order:

1. Estimate the level of excess reserves. In recent years, excess reserves generally have averaged about $900 million per day; they previously averaged about $250 million per day. The reasons for this rise in average excess reserves will be discussed later. The daily average can be impacted by Fed operations,

but day to day variations tend to be large and difficult to predict. There are a few predictable deviations from the normal average, such as the tendency for excess reserves to be high in the last week of the year as banks strive to show extra levels of excess reserves in the year-end balance sheets they send to their stockholders.

2. Add to the estimated excess reserve level the estimated level of required reserves, to obtain the projected level of total reserves.
3. Subtract an estimate of vault cash to obtain the projected level of reserve balances to be held at the Fed.
4. Compare this projected level of reserves with the forecasted sum of all the operating factors (excluding open market operations and reserve borrowing) less the sum of all the factors draining reserves.
5. This comparison represents the projected total of reserve borrowings plus securities held by the Fed.
6. On the basis of an estimate of the Fed's current borrowed reserve target, subtract an estimate of the level of bank borrowings[1] at the discount window from the preceding total to obtain a projection of the level of Fed security holdings.
7. Compare this estimated total of security holdings with the daily average of the Fed's security holdings in the prior reserve maintenance period, to determine the increase or decrease in securities holdings that must occur during the upcoming period in order to keep net borrowed reserves unchanged.

Of course, a number of operating factors can exhibit aberrant changes from week to week, making the forecasting of defensive operations quite hazardous. Sometimes, Desk officials can take Fed watchers and market participants completely by surprise with the

---

[1]For illustrative purposes, no distinction is made here between different types of borrowings. In fact, only adjustment borrowings are influenced and thus targeted by Desk officials. Seasonal and extended credit borrowed through the discount facility must be forecasted separately, similar to operating factors. These borrowings should thus be treated as a component of "factors adding" reserves before inputting the borrowing assumption (adjustment borrowing target) into the forecasting equation.

execution of repos or reverses. When these surprises occur, it is tempting to ascribe them to a policy change instead of to a forecasting error. Yet staff forecasting errors constantly occur. Most staff forecasting errors are revealed by the Fed at a weekly (Thursday afternoon) press conference held at the New York Fed. Such information helps Fed watchers determine whether unexpected changes in net reserve availability (net borrowed or free reserves) occurred by accident or by design (as a result of a policy change). Because of the importance of such information from the Fed, major wire services regularly report on all information disclosed at weekly press conferences.

THE N.Y. METS AND THE N.Y. FED

The following personal experience helps to illustrate the occasional difficulties of projecting defensive requirements. At the end of October 1969 I was employed as a Fed watcher (and financial forecaster) at a large West Coast bank. Every Friday morning, I briefed senior executives on the current and prospective posture of monetary policy, examining in detail the meaning of the prior day's release of the weekly reserve and monetary data.

During the briefing on the third Friday in October, the vice president in charge of the bank's securities (and portfolio) division interrupted my Friday morning briefing by phoning to say that the Fed had just purchased bills in the open market, and the funds rate had quickly dropped from 10 percent to 5 percent. Bond prices had begun to increase significantly, as market participants concluded that the Fed had finally eased policy. But the vice president did not want to authorize his traders to take long positions in Treasury bonds before I could confirm his suspicion of Fed easing.

I immediately excused myself from the briefing and headed for the vice president's office. Three thoughts flashed through my mind. First, market participants had been predicting that the Fed would soon bow to increasing political pressures to ease its restrictive policy course, which had been designed to curb an excessive growth of bank credit.

Second, past easing of reserve positions had always been associated with a gradual decline in the funds rate, not a dramatic, one-day decline from 10 percent to 5 percent. Moreover, I had anticipated the bill purchase; a large month-end decline in float credit (consistent with intramonthly patterns) and a large seasonal outflow of currency from the banking system during the upcoming two months prior to Christmas had led me to project an outright purchase on the Friday in question.

Third, I thought of a photograph in the previous evening's newspaper of a celebration on Wall Street; the N.Y. Mets had unexpectedly won the World Series. Suddenly, I thought that clerks, processing cash items on the second floor of the N.Y. Fed, most likely had joined in Wednesday's celebration. If so, then Wednesday's holdover float would have soared upward, with related reserve credits being issued to banks on Thursday and Friday. The dramatic increase in float at a time when it was supposed to decline significantly, followed by further reserves supplied through the Fed's bill purchase, easily explained why the funds rate dropped so quickly from 10 percent to 5 percent.

By the time I reached the vice president's office, I had concluded that the Fed had not eased policy and that the open market purchase of bills was simply a bad mistake. When I initially summarized my conclusion for the vice president after he asked why the funds rate had dropped to 5 percent, I told him it was because the Mets had won the World Series. He laughed but, after hearing my explanation, reluctantly decided not to take on new long positions in Treasuries. It was a fortunate decision. After the weekend, Desk officials began mopping up the excess reserves they had mistakenly supplied through the bill purchase. Within several days, the funds rate started to climb back up to 10 percent, and many Wall Street dealers who had anticipated Fed easing ended up with substantial losses.

In my mind, however, this mysterious case was not closed. Desk officials are much closer to day-to-day developments than any Fed watcher can be; they should have been aware of the buildup in holdover float after the World Series. I could not imagine why they proceeded with the bill purchase. One year later, at a luncheon with the director of research (responsible for market factor forecasts) and other officials of the N. Y. Fed, I had my answer.

The luncheon conversation was proceeding normally on non-policy related matters, among people well trained in maintaining colorless talk and expressionless faces to prevent any disclosure or misrepresentation of policy leanings. At an early lull in the conversation, I posed my question. Without warning, my hosts broke into uncharacteristically hearty laughter, and I knew I had hit a nerve.

According to the director of research, the situation was worse than I had deduced. Concerned about clerks celebrating the Mets' victory, Desk officials had gone to the second floor processing area to investigate. Not only were clerks off the job celebrating, but, to the officials' horror, some had been tearing up 1401 punch cards (used at that time to process cash items) and throwing them onto the street below. The processing of cash items had been dealt a most severe blow!

Why, then, did Fed officials proceed with the bill purchase on Friday morning? The research director explained that he, along with most Desk officials, worked throughout most of Wednesday night, Thursday, and Thursday night, to sort out the cash items and put check processing back together again. By Friday morning, with this task completed, most of these officials had collapsed for some well-earned sleep, leaving junior officials in charge to carry out the open market plan previously established. "If you think I was physically able to think about open market projections by Friday morning," the director concluded, "you're completely wrong."

My mystery was now solved, case closed. But this incident demonstrates the human element behind market changes and surprises, an element transcending the sophisticated methods and structure of the marketplace. The incident also illustrates the unpredictability of market factors, the hazards of projecting defensive requirements, and the potential value of Fed watching services.

CUSTOMER REPOS

No discussion of open market procedures would be complete without an examination of *customer repos*. Desk officials execute customer repos chiefly on behalf of foreign central bank accounts at the Fed, distinguishing them from System repos by announcing their size during the open market go-around.[2] Historically, the size of a customer repo has ranged from $700 million to a maximum of about $2.5 billion. System repo volumes generally exceed $3 billion and sometimes $4.5 billion. The Fed also announces the size of outright purchases of securities on behalf of customers, which usually range from $100 million to $300 million. Customer sales of securities also occur, though infrequently.

When a foreign central bank wires dollar drafts (perhaps acquired through sale of its currency for dollars in foreign exchange markets) to the N.Y. Fed, the Fed debits the reserve accounts of banks on which drafts are drawn and credits the central bank deposit accounts. On the H.4.1 report, then, foreign deposits will rise after receipt of these wires, and bank reserves will decline accordingly.

Because deposits at the Fed do not earn interest, foreign governments and central banks prefer to use their deposit credit to purchase interest-bearing securities (almost always Treasury securities), either outright or under repurchase agreements. Foreign depositors need to hold deposit balances at the Fed to clear financial and trade-related transactions, but keep these balances at the minimum clearing levels. Thus, changes in foreign holdings of dollars are mostly reflected in their holdings of interest bearing securities, so that foreign deposits at the Fed usually remain quite stable from week to week and produce only small changes in reserve availability.

When the Fed purchases securities for a foreign central bank in the open market, reserves in the banking system increase, thus offsetting the decrease in reserves that occurs when foreign deposits rise. The customer's wire to the Fed specifies whether securities are to be purchased outright or under repurchase agreements, depending on how long the dollar credit is to be left under Fed management. If clearing balances at the Fed will require replenishment within several

---

[2]The volume of System operations is never announced, but the size of a specific transaction can sometimes be calculated from H.4.1. data, providing that there was only one transaction during a reporting week, or that a System repo or reverse occurred on a Wednesday (shown separately in the H.4.1 report). The competitive bidding procedure used in executing customer repos is identical to that used in executing System repos.

weeks, the customer will probably opt for repos. At present, the Fed holds more than $100 billion of securities purchased outright and executes about $3 billion of repos daily for customer accounts.

Desk officials can execute customer repos either in the open market or, more commonly, directly with the System's account. The latter option, being executed internally through matched-sales, has no effect on bank reserves and thus does not serve to offset the effect on bank reserves of increases in foreign deposits.

In computing the volume of defensive operations required on a given day, the Desk staff, by convention, assumes that all customer repos will be arranged internally with the System account. If there is a need to add reserves, some of these repos in fact may be executed in the open market. The Desk frequently employs this option when the need for defensive additions to reserve credit is small. During such periods, one round of System repos would probably add more reserve credit than needed, while the more limited size of customer repos will enable Desk officials to fine-tune their supply of needed reserve credit.

When the Desk executes customer repos in the market, it is merely adding reserve credit back into the banking system originally drained through wire transfers from foreign central banks. But when the Fed employs foreign customer funds by executing internal matches, there is no reserve offset to wire-related debits to bank reserve accounts, and nonborrowed reserves decline. On the Fed's balance sheet, the latter transaction creates a decline in bank reserves deposited at the Fed (on the liability side of the balance sheet), and also produces a decline in Fed security holdings (on the asset side). When the Fed executes customer repos in the open market, member bank reserve accounts are credited for the purchase, and Fed security holdings, on behalf of customer accounts, increase.

Desk officials execute customer repos at about the same time every day (11:40 a.m. to 11:55 a.m. EST) in order to divorce the operation from speculation on reserve needs, market conditions, or monetary policy. In recent years, customer repos have, on rare occasion, been used to signal a change in policy. Whenever there is a clearly recognized large adding requirement during a given week,

Desk execution of customer repos can signal a turn to tighter reserve policy, even though customer repos are not supposed to be policy-related. In this rare situation, the use of customer repos by the Fed signals a reluctance to supply all of the reserve credit needed to prevent net borrowed reserves from increasing.

PRO-CYCLICAL OPEN MARKET PROCEDURES

Until 1983, the reserve maintenance period, during which member banks must maintain required reserves, was defined as one week, commencing on Thursday and ending on Wednesday. These reserve requirements were based on deposit liabilities occurring two weeks previous. For years, monetarists criticized this system of lagged reserve requirements (LRR). Then, in 1984, a system of contemporaneous reserve requirements (CRR) was adopted, shortening the time elapsed between the reserve maintenance period and the computation period to two days. The reserve maintenance period was extended to two weeks, still ending on a Wednesday.

Despite relatively tight monetary policies, the growth of bank credit during 1969 often exceeded modest growth rates desired by the FOMC. Monetarists concluded that net borrowed reserve targeting was pro-cyclical under LRR. If the Desk were following a net borrowed reserves target, and banks increased their loans and investments in a given week, the resulting expansion in deposit liabilities (and money supply) would not affect system-wide reserves until two weeks later, at which time the Desk would be forced to increase the supply of nonborrowed reserve credit to offset the increase in required reserves and leave net borrowed reserves unchanged. Thus, bankers had little incentive to curtail loans and investments during a given week, since their reserve requirements would not change until two weeks later, at which time the Fed would be forced to satisfy the increase in required reserves.

Monetarists argued that the Desk added reserve credit to the banking system at precisely the wrong time, fueling monetary growth when such growth was already rapid. When monetary growth was weak as deposit liabilities and the level of required reserves contracted, Desk officials absorbed reserve credit, again at the wrong time. To correct this problem, monetarists advocated targeting nonborrowed reserves.

Swayed by these arguments, Dr. Arthur Burns, who became Fed Chairman early in 1970, directed his staff to provide for a constant growth rate in nonborrowed reserves, regardless of changes in weekly required reserve levels. By April, nonborrowed reserve targeting had replaced net borrowed reserve targeting in daily open market operations. The change in Desk procedures could not have been more poorly timed.

Required reserve levels normally surge upward in April. At the end of March, corporations liquidate repos and other investments and reduce time deposits, in order to increase demand deposit totals and record a large amount of cash in their quarterly statements. Under LRR, this shift of funds from low reservable time accounts (accounts with low reserve requirements, such as CDs) to high reservable demand deposits regularly produced an upward surge in reserve requirements two weeks later. By mid-April, the second installments of property taxes are due to local governments, and income taxes to the IRS. Individuals and businesses pad their demand deposits in preparation for taxes, increasing required reserve levels still further. In most years since the 1960s, inadequate facilities have delayed Federal government processing of tax payments in April. Demand balances thus sit idle, awaiting tardy debiting, and required reserve levels surge further upward.

In April 1970 required reserves rose appreciably each week, but Desk officials ignored the increases and provided for a moderate increase in nonborrowed reserves. As a result, net borrowed reserves increased significantly, reflecting substantial tightening of reserve policy, and the funds rate soared upward. Because recent growth of M1 (which Dr. Burns was beginning to stress) had not been far above desired rates, market participants were puzzled by the dramatic tightening of reserve conditions.

In the midst of this uncertainty in the marketplace, the Treasury announced terms of its regular quarterly refunding package. The May coupon auctions attracted very little dealer or retail interest, raising the possibility that the Treasury would not be able to sell enough coupons to redeem maturing coupons, and might be forced to issue involuntary notes of indebtedness to holders of maturing coupons. Any publicity concerning the possibility of a Treasury default might prevent the Treasury from selling an additional amount of short-term bills over the short run to refinance maturing debt. The Treasury did manage to avoid default, but only amidst extraordinary rumors that officials invited and accepted large dealer bids submitted after the auction deadline.

In the final analysis, pursuit of a nonborrowed reserve target disrupted the debt market and nearly prevented the Treasury from meeting its financing requirements. Stunned by the enormous failure of nonborrowed reserve targeting, Dr. Burns and his staff immediately looked for another operational target alternative to nonborrowed reserves. After a brief experiment with RPD (reserves to support private, non-bank deposits) targets, the Fed abandoned (until almost ten years later) the attempt to control deposit creation through nonborrowed reserve targeting.

FUNDS RATE PEGGING

By adding or draining reserve credit, the Fed can lower or raise the funds rate toward a given target level. Having failed to find an adequate alternative to the net borrowed reserve target, Dr. Burns instituted funds rate pegging as a means to control money supply growth indirectly by influencing the demand for money. Because the prime rate and other bank lending rates are linked with the funds rate, as explained in chapter 3, Desk operations can control the general level of lending rates by controlling the funds rate level.

Assuming that higher interest rates will curtail the demand for credit while lower interest rates will stimulate such demands, Dr. Burns reasoned that if the Fed could control money rates through funds rate pegging, then it could also control the demand for credit and the growth of the money supply. However, by the end of the 1970s, after years of funds rate pegging, Fed officials concluded that such control of money rate levels was not capable of controlling money supply growth. Money supply growth exceeded target throughout most of the funds rate pegging era. In October 1979, funds rate pegging was abandoned in favor of re-instituting reserve targeting. But at the end of 1982 Fed officials again adopted a funds rate target as a means of controlling money supply growth. Not too surprisingly, monetary growth has been beyond Fed control since the switch back to funds rate targeting.

Flow of funds data show that aggregate credit demand does vary according to interest rate levels, and that credit demand curves slope downward to the right (displaying interest rate elasticity). However, money supply growth is not linked with *total* credit demands. It is linked with *bank* credit demand. If a corporation borrows funds from the bond market, it taps existing liquidity. But when it borrows from a bank, new deposit credit is manufactured.

When interest rates are low, a corporation prefers to finance its working capital requirements through the bond market as opposed to a bank. The corporate treasurer naturally assumes that interest rate cyclical patterns will continue, and that low bond yields represents an opportunity to lock in low long term borrowing costs. Bank prime rates may also be low, but can be expected to rise in the future. Conversely, when interest rates are high, corporate treasurers prefer to avoid long-term bond financing in favor of shorter-term bank financing, whose interest cost will decline as interest rates later begin a cyclical downturn.

The concept of high or low interest rates is relative, and each corporate treasurer will have a different assessment about current rates being high or low relative to an expected cyclical rate pattern. As a result, as interest rates rise, an increasing number of treasurers will conclude that they will not go higher, and that current long-term bond financing costs are high in relation to prospective bond yield levels. Conversely, when bond rates are declining, an increasing number of treasurers will conclude that rates are not going to decline further and that long-term bond financing is an attractive alternative to bank financing.

Accordingly, when money rates are rising, there is a gradual (though somewhat irregular) shifting of corporate financing away from bond markets toward bank loans. Conversely, when money rates are declining, bond financing totals tend to rise while business loan totals display weak growth. In other words, strong growth in business loans made by banks is accompanied by rising interest rates, while weaker growth of business loans is accompanied by declining interest rates—precisely the opposite relationship one would envision under the concept of interest elastic bank credit demands.

Some economists have scoffed at the above notion because, they assert, it is only natural to expect interest rates to rise in response to strong business loan demands. Similarly, they assert that weaker loan demands must be followed by lower interest rates, as one would expect under the laws of supply and demand. These economists fail to realize that the Fed, not loan demand, controls the level of money rates. And when the Fed increases money rate levels to slow the demand for credit, the business demand for *bank* loans rises instead. Business loan demands are the swing factor in bank credit growth, one reason why debt market participants used to pay such close attention to weekly business loan data when the Fed targeted bank credit instead of money supply. Consumer credit demands are well noted for their inelastic response to interest rate changes. Mortgage extensions are, of course, highly sensitive to interest rate changes. But their magnitude of change is frequently overshadowed in the business cycle by changes in business loan totals.

The aggregate demand for bank credit extensions is inelastic to interest rate changes, a conclusion already underscored and in need of future repetition. However, the demand for bank credit displays an income elasticity. A Fed-induced rise in interest rates will, with variable and lengthy lags, weaken national income growth. Such income weakness has previously been accompanied by a slower pace of bank credit extensions, and by reduced growth in total nonfinancial credit raised (total domestic nonfinancial debt). In other words, increased interest rates will moderate the demand for bank credit, but only after a lengthy process of weakening national income (and employment).

It should be noted that the frequent pro-cyclical supply of reserve credit under funds rate pegging could have been, but was not, partly offset by more aggressive use of the funds rate peg. The Fed made insufficient upward adjustments to the funds rate peg in response to excessive M1 growth. Most often, inflation rates rose faster than the

Graph 5.1

Relationship of Interest Rates, Corporate Bonds, and Business Loans

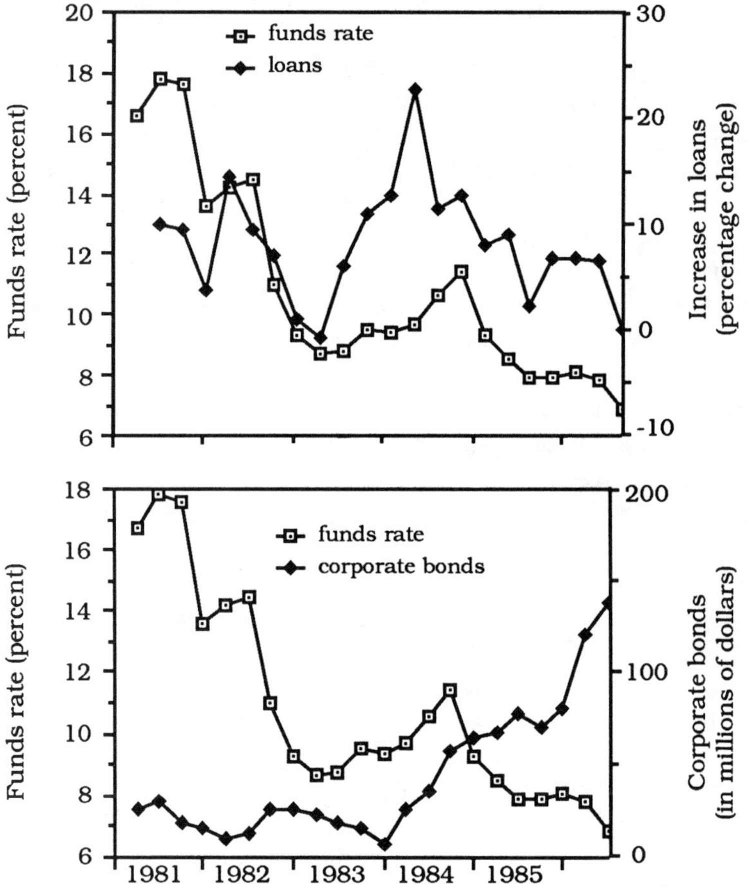

When money rates decline, corporate bond totals tend to rise. In contrast, changes in money rates and increases in business loan totals are positively related. The rate of change in loan totals is shown because loan totals are constantly increasing.

Source: Federal Reserve H.15 and G.7 releases and the National Income and Product Accounts.

funds rate peg, which kept the funds rate below the inflation rate. Negative real money rates helped to stimulate the economy which, in turn, fostered strong demands for bank credit.

Bank credit extensions (money supply growth) are far more responsive, over the intermediate term, to changes in reserve availability than to changes in interest rates. Accordingly, the most important pro-cyclical feature of funds rate pegging of the 1970s was reserve availability and not negative levels of real money rates. The pro-cyclical provision of bank reserves should have been quickly detected by persistent growth of M1 above targeted ranges, but was not. Today's funds rate targeting has also been accompanied by excessive monetary growth, but this too has failed to raise concerns about potentially pro-cyclical monetary policy.

MECHANICS OF PEGGING THE FUNDS RATE

Under funds rate pegging, the FOMC allowed the funds rate to vary only within a narrow range. Typically, whenever the funds rate rose (fell) to more than ⅛ percent above (below) target, Desk officials executed overnight System repos (reverses) to restore the funds rate to its target level, regardless of reserve needs or defensive requirements. Market participants recognized that overnight System repos and reverses were rate-related, unlike *term* System repos and reverses, and customer repos.

Consider, for example, a 6 percent funds rate peg. If the funds rate rose to 6¼ percent and Desk officials executed overnight System repos, funds traders would recognize the Fed's intention to lower the funds rate and would revise their bid and offer rates accordingly. If Desk officials executed overnight reverses when the funds rate was at 6 percent, funds traders would know immediately that the funds rate target had been raised. By increasing their quoted rates until the Fed executed overnight repos, traders could ascertain the new rate peg, which was usually ⅛ percent (sometimes ¼ percent) less than the rate at which repos were executed.

Desk officials often signalled tighter policy through customer repos, which were not supposed to be rate-related. Assume that market factors have drained reserve credit and pushed the funds rate up from its targeted 6 percent to 6¼ percent. Suppose that, instead of executing overnight System repos, Desk officials execute $1.5 billion customer repos. Because customer repos are reserve related and not rate-related, the Fed's actions cannot be attributed to the higher funds rate. In light of the Fed's failure to respond to the new rate (with overnight System repos), market participants can assume that the Federal Reserve has lifted the upper limit of the funds rate range (and, hence, the peg). Thus, in addition to meeting the Fed's defensive adding requirement, customer repos also signalled a higher funds rate peg because Desk officials were displaying indifference to the higher funds rate.

Immediately, traders would quote the funds rate at 6⅜ percent, then wait for about five minutes to see if this higher rate would prompt rate-related repos. If not, traders would start quoting funds at 6½ percent, and wait to see if Desk officials executed O/N System repos at this higher funds rate. Normally, rate-related repos would be executed at 6½ percent because the Fed generally did not raise the funds rate peg by more than ⅜ percent at any one time, and the upper limit to a 6⅜ percent peg would be 6½ percent.

In the foregoing example, market factors could have started to push the funds rate upward, followed by customer repos to signal an increase in the funds rate peg. But during the funds rate pegging era, market factors rarely pushed the funds rate upward, whereas bad M1 news always did. Under Dr. Burns' leadership, Fed officials became preoccupied with weekly M1 data. Whenever a weekly M1 increase pushed a 9-week M1 growth rate (seasonally adjusted annual rate) above the 9-week FOMC targeted growth range, the funds rate peg was usually lifted within one week. Market participants thus began to focus on weekly M1 data.[3]

Whenever weekly M1 data exhibited an increase to push its growth rate above target, funds traders immediately raised their quoted rates above the previously known upper limit. If Desk officials

---

[3]During the sixties, when bank credit growth (and, hence, bank loan growth) represented a policy target (not an operational target), debt prices reacted to weekly releases of bank loan data. During the funds rate pegging era of the seventies, when short term M1 growth became a policy target, debt prices reacted to weekly M1 data. Had the Fed's policy target been apple pies, then debt prices would have responded to news about apple pie production.

quickly executed O/N System repos, then traders would lower quoted rates. If a firmer policy dictated a higher funds rate peg, Desk officials would not immediately execute repos, and quoted funds rates would increase until repos were executed. Accordingly, every time M1 exhibited excessive growth, the Fed was forced to supply more reserve credit in a pro-cyclical fashion. Hence, excessive reserve supplies also contributed to excessive rates of monetary growth through most of the seventies. Ironically, Dr. Burns' criticism of net borrowed reserve targeting as a pro-cyclical influence led to a much greater degree of pro-cyclical influences under funds rate pegging.

Sluggish monetary growth should have theoretically prompted expectations of a lower funds rate peg, which in turn would have prompted execution of overnight reverses. Sluggish monetary growth, however, was not a persistent problem during the funds rate pegging era.

EVEN KEEL POLICIES

An even keel policy implies that Fed officials will neither change nor hint at changing monetary policy. During the sixties, Fed officials observed even keel policy just prior to and during the Treasury's quarterly refunding operations. Any policy change during the auctions could create market confusion and so limit auction bidding.

For example, if the Fed were to *tighten* policy *after* a refunding auction but prior to settlement of the new issues about ten days later, dealers could incur large losses and so might be reluctant to bid for future Treasury issues. On the other hand, if monetary policy were *eased after* refunding auctions, then dealers would make large profits at the expense of the taxpayer. Similarly, signs of *easier* policy just *prior* to a Treasury auction ran the risk of discouraging institutional investors from participating in coupon auctions for fear that the easier policy signals might be false and that coupon prices might therefore decline during the when-issue trading period.

Even keel policies were nearly abandoned during the seventies for two reasons. First, growing deficits had prompted the Treasury to increase the frequency of its financing operations. Fed officials felt that strict observance of even keel policy at each Treasury auction would unacceptably reduce Fed policy flexibility. Second, weekly M1 growth was regarded as too important a policy target to forsake in the pursuit of even keel policy.

Initially, Chairman Burns limited the observance of even keel to a few days after major Treasury auctions. Later in the 1970s, he abandoned even keel altogether. For example, immediately following Halloween in 1978, an unexpected upsurge in weekly M1 data prompted a special FOMC telephone conference in which officials decided to raise the funds rate peg during the November refunding auctions. Dealers incurred heavy losses, termed the policy change "Burns' trick or treat," and became very reluctant bidders in future auctions. Chairman Burns was later forced to return to some even keel observance.

THE POLICY OF GRADUALISM

Monetarists should have directed their criticism of monetary policy in the 1960s not at net borrowed reserve targeting but at the policy of gradualism, under which policymakers did not allow the net borrowed target to rise or fall significantly over the short run. The purpose of this policy was to allow financial markets the opportunity to make orderly adjustments to changes in monetary policy, but its effect was to enhance the cyclical behavior of the economy.

Had the FOMC changed its net borrowed target more aggressively during the 1960s, Desk officials could have mitigated high growth tendencies of bank credit and money supply by allowing net borrowed reserves to increase. Monetary policy was pro-cyclical only because Desk officials fully funded every (lagged) increase in required reserves.[4] Thus, when Fed officials in the 1970s grafted the policy of gradualism to funds rate pegging, pro-cyclical tendencies were strengthened.[5]

---

[4]In October 1979, Fed Chairman Paul Volcker reintroduced net borrowed reserve targeting, but without limiting funds rate variations. Under very high net borrowed targets, the funds rate rose appreciably over a short period of time, taming money supply growth. From October 1979 until 1983, when funds rate targeting was re-employed, monetary growth remained within the FOMC's annual targeted ranges.

[5]Funds rate changes during the 1970s averaged ¼ percent with each policy change, compared to funds rate changes of 3 to 4 percent with some policy changes in the early 1980s.

Pro-cyclical reserve policy encouraged excessive money supply growth throughout most of the decade, aggravating the effects of OPEC's increase in energy prices, to drive inflation upward. The rising rate of inflation outpaced the Fed's gradual increases in the funds rate peg, and the rate of inflation soon came to exceed the level of short-term interest rates. Negative real interest rates strengthened aggregate credit demands rather than weakening them.

Late in the 1970s, the dollar came under severe attack in foreign exchange markets. The declining exchange value of the dollar increased inflationary pressures in the U.S. In 1978 and 1979, in a series of so-called "dollar rescue packages," the Fed tried to halt the dollar's plunge by increasing both the discount rate and funds rate peg, but the dollar continued to sink to new lows.

Currency exchange rates respond to many influences, and are therefore difficult to analyze or predict. One of the principal determinants of exchange rates is the real interest relationship of one currency to another. The dollar rescue packages of 1979 sought to create a real interest rate advantage for the dollar over other major currencies. This objective was indeed reached during the summer of 1979, yet the dollar continued to tumble. Such unexpected dollar behavior was ascribed by currency traders to a lack of dollar credibility. Specifically, the funds rate pegging policy of the Fed was not considered to be a credible means of limiting monetary growth and inflationary pressures. With the declining dollar, traders could only expect more U.S. inflation. Central bankers abroad also felt that Fed policies lacked credibility, and had exhibited reluctance to help the Fed support the dollar through intervention in exchange markets.

Early in October 1979, newly appointed Fed Chairman Paul Volcker attempted to arrange a coordinated central bank intervention in foreign exchange (FX) markets to rescue the dollar, but he was unable to secure the cooperation of foreign central banks. Mr. Volcker called an emergency weekend meeting of the FOMC, on 24 hours' notice, to convince FOMC members to abandon funds rate pegging in favor of reserve targeting, with which he had previous experience at the N.Y. Fed. He realized that reserve targeting would increase dramatically the trading ranges of the funds rate, but he reasoned that a broad funds rate band could be employed to soothe market concerns during the transition to reserve targeting.

The funds rate band initially adopted by the FOMC had a range of four percentage points. The Fed tried to assure market participants that Desk officials would conduct rate-related operations whenever the funds rate strayed outside the established band. Market participants, many of whom had not experienced net borrowed reserve targeting during the sixties,[6] were concerned that it might lead to very volatile funds rate behavior.

Fed officials realized that traders would be tempted to ascribe every Desk operation to changes in policy, just as they had done over the past decade. To discourage speculation about funds rate motives behind purely defensive operations, Fed officials decided to execute all System repos and reverses between 11:35 a.m. and 11:45 a.m., and keep customer repos executions between 11:45 a.m. and 11:55 a.m. Occasional exceptions to these operational times have not been significant. Outright operations for customer and System accounts continued to occur between 1:00 p.m. and 1:45 p.m. The standardization of Fed intervention times helped to underscore the defensive nature of System operations, partly because previously the established regular time for executing customer repos had successfully demonstrated the defensive intent behind all customer operations. Though customer repos had occasionally been used to signal policy change, their execution was always consistent with defensive requirements.

The October 1979 Mystery

Just what the Fed started doing in October of 1979 is still debated among economists (including some at the Fed). Fed announcements implied that nonborrowed reserve growth would become a primary

---

[6]Due to the stress associated with their position, traders tend to retire early, and most traders are relatively young.

operational target, replacing funds rate pegging. They disclosed that new research was attempting to predict the money multiplier which, in turn, would enable Desk officials to translate monetary targets (FOMC policy targets) into targeted nonborrowed reserve growth paths. Because these nonborrowed paths were to be followed between FOMC meetings, they were no different than M1 or M2 growth paths targeted on an inter-meeting basis. As a result, the nonborrowed targets were really policy as well as operational targets.

To illustrate, operational targets can be modified from one settlement period to the next as a means of compliance with a policy target. An M1 policy target might be sought through use of a net borrowed or nonborrowed operational target. Or, a nonborrowed policy target might be pursued through either a net borrowed or nonborrowed operational target. Bear in mind that one distinction between a policy and an operational target is the source of authority; the FOMC sets policy targets which guide Desk officials in setting short-term operational targets.

Confusion surrounding the October 1979 Fed announcement was generated, in part, by Fed assurances that a money multiplier could be predicted with reasonable accuracy. Earlier chapters in the book should suffice to make it obvious that Fed promises of multiplier forecasts could not be kept, and were not. Precise multiplier forecasts could automate desk operations, and the inter-meeting policy target of nonborrowed reserve growth could be rather blindly followed on a week-to-week basis without concern about creating disruptive reserve or market conditions.

If the deposit multiplier is stable, which, of course, is far from the truth, then total reserves will precisely determine growth of deposit liabilities and their required reserve levels (falsely assuming that deposit shifts can be predicted). A reserve borrowing "assumption" can be made, which is really a borrowing target, based on the amount of reserve restraint desired. Or, restraint can be dictated by lowering nonborrowed reserve growth which, relative to required reserve growth, determines the borrowing assumption. A prescribed nonborrowed growth path can therefore automatically adjust reserve (borrowing) conditions based on unexpected variations of bank credit and required reserve behavior (which is basically the source of total reserve behavior).

If, however, the multiplier linkage is more imagined than real, then large discrepancies will develop between nonborrowed reserves targeted and required reserves (regardless of whether lagged or contemporaneous reserve requirements are used). Reserve borrowing pressures will thus gyrate from one settlement period to another, producing extreme funds rate variations. This, of course, is precisely what the Fed wanted to avoid in the transition period, and even afterward. Accordingly, Desk officials had to have some leeway in setting weekly reserve borrowing assumptions and short-term nonborrowed targets. From a technical standpoint, therefore, the nonborrowed objective had to be regarded as both a policy and an operational target.

Without accurate multiplier forecasts, nonborrowed policy targets were in fact subordinated to their parent set of monetary targets. If, between FOMC meetings, money growth was significantly exceeding target, the nonborrowed path would have to be significantly adjusted, thus rendering the operational nonborrowed target of questionable value. Desk officials were aiming at an elusive nonborrowed target which would have to be regularly re-set relative to monetary growth targets. To summarize, the value of a nonborrowed target, either as a policy or operational target, seemed to be discredited by structural realities.

Reserve data following the October 1979 announcement show that weekly net borrowed reserve levels stabilized for the first time since their targeting was abandoned in 1970. One would normally assume that the aggregate, being subject to operational targeting, will exhibit more stability than non-targeted aggregates. As just discussed, for example, a borrowings target leads to nonborrowed variations; or, a nonborrowed target leads to more variations in reserve borrowing aggregates (adjustment or net borrowed). Following the October 1979 announcement, the funds rate displayed far more variation than when it was pegged. Net borrowed reserves stabilized. There was no perceptible change in the variable behavior of nonborrowed reserves (except for April 1980). So, what aggregate was really targeted?

Fed officials still maintain the targeted aggregate to have been nonborrowed reserves. However, they do not comment on whether there was also net borrowed targeting (which they often refer to as a "free reserve" target). Indeed, several "off-the-record" comments by Fed staffers with FOMC clearance have admitted that post-October 1979 operations were targeting net borrowed reserves. Bear in mind that, as discussed, a net borrowed target cannot be followed by Desk officials until it is translated into a nonborrowed target for daily operations. There had to be a nonborrowed target accompanying the 1979 change. At issue is the veracity of the term "assumption" versus "target" or "objective" used by Fed officials to preface reserve borrowings. The Fed cannot be accused of presenting false information, but data support the accusation that Fed officials wanted to hide behind a veil of secrecy in 1979. Why?

The answer is that monetarists had misdirected their policy criticisms of the 1960s to net borrowed targeting instead of the policy of gradualism. Chairman Volcker knew that the Fed's credibility was under close scrutiny in currency exchange markets, and that he could ill-afford to give monetarists an easy target for their criticism; domestic ankle-biting could hurt the dollar's credibility. The Fed's announcement caused confusion and created market fears, which helped to boost the dollar's exchange rate.

The shift to reserve targeting was not merely aimed at restoring international credibility. Mr. Volcker shared the inflation concerns of monetarists about persistently high rates of money supply growth. Mr. Volcker had just arrived at the Board from the N.Y. Fed, where "traditionalist" policy doctrine had been deeply rooted. In fact, the monetarist leaning of the Board, under Dr. Burns, tended to strengthen traditionalist doctrine at the N.Y. Fed, where Mr. Volcker had been thoroughly exposed to net borrowed targeting. The nonborrowed targeting experiment in April 1970 deepened the doctrinal rift between the N.Y. Fed and the Board. It seems fair to speculate that Mr. Volcker brought to the Board in 1979 a deeply-rooted disposition toward targeting net borrowed reserves, as opposed to nonborrowed reserves, as the primary operational objective.

The veil of secrecy also seems to partly apply to Fed staffers, as well as to Congress and the public. Three Fed staffers just might provide five different operational accounts (according to a worn-out joke). One gets the impression, in dealing with staff, that internal information dissemination strictly observes the ''need to know'' principle.

This discourse of the October 1979 argument should now be laid to rest, with the help of a footnote that most Fed watchers had concluded early in 1980 that the return of reserve targeting keyed off the ''borrowing assumption''—net borrowed reserves. A prime reason for covering the argument in depth is the probability of yet another return to net borrowed targeting (expected by the author) in 1988, guised once again as a nonborrowed targeting scheme. In order for an operational nonborrowed target to be credible, it must be closely linked with a nonborrowed policy (inter-meeting) target confidently linked with a broader policy objective. This is a structural impossibility, which challenges Fed officials to develop more interesting language in the future, if they dare try another ''nonborrowed hoax.''

Another Nonborrowed Experiment

When the Fed initially set the net borrowed reserve target at $2.5 billion in October 1979 (a record level), the funds rate rose appreciably to 20 percent. Given the discount rate at the time (it was raised from 11 percent to 12 percent on October 8 immediately after the FOMC special weekend meeting on October 6), and the net borrowed target level, the 20 percent funds rate was predictable given the relation between adjustment borrowing and the spread between the discount rate and the funds rate.

The high funds rate not only scared market participants, but troubled Fed officials as well. The Fed's resolve to target reserves instead of the funds rate faltered. Even before the funds rate began to exceed the specified (and wide) funds rate band, the Fed started to execute rate-related operations in December 1979, continuing through the following January and early February. A mid-February hike in the discount rate (to 13 percent) signalled a return to reserve-related operations and to reserve targeting.

President Carter actually sealed the doom of the new procedure when, in February 1980, he prevailed on Congress to enact credit controls, in the hope that such controls could supplement Fed efforts to slow the growth of money and credit and permit the Fed to relax its policy restraint. Congress enacted the credit control program, however, without Fed concurrence, and the private sector overreacted (as Fed officials had feared). Bank loans to businesses and individuals contracted in March, when they normally expand significantly. Deposit credit, manufactured through bank loans, declined instead of exhibiting normal growth. Required reserve levels thus declined in April when they had exhibited large weekly gains in previous Aprils.

Fed staffers were still designing a method for inter-meeting targeting of nonborrowed reserve growth. Paul Volcker was nonetheless willing to experiment with any new nonborrowed targeting procedure. By April 1980, exactly ten years after the first fiasco with nonborrowed reserve operational targets, the Fed had already launched a poorly timed effort to target nonborrowed reserves.

Desk officials provided for steady nonborrowed reserve growth during April 1980, ignoring the unusual decline in required reserve levels. The previously high level of net borrowed reserves vanished during April, and the funds rate plunged accordingly. In fact, the April-May drop in the funds rate was the largest two-month decline in the funds rate ever recorded. By midyear, money supply was again growing at an excessive rate, and market participants were already calling the Fed's experiment "the great policy error of April 1980." FOMC members agreed with the market assessment and directed Desk officials to create an 8 percent funds rate floor through the use of rate-related operations.

The Fed did not abandon the establishment of inter-meeting nonborrowed growth paths in 1980 (though they finally did so at the end of 1982). However, the imposition of more narrowly defined funds rate levels on a reserve targeting operation rendered the policy targeting of nonborrowed reserves a rather meaningless exercise.

Under the operational doctrine emerging by mid-1980, adjustment borrowings rather than nonborrowed reserves became the targeted reserve aggregate. A year later, rate-related operations (narrow funds rate constraints) nearly vanished from the open market scene, which probably left the "borrowing assumption" as the most significant determinant of conditions in the reserve (funds) market.

Graph 5.2

Reserve Targeting

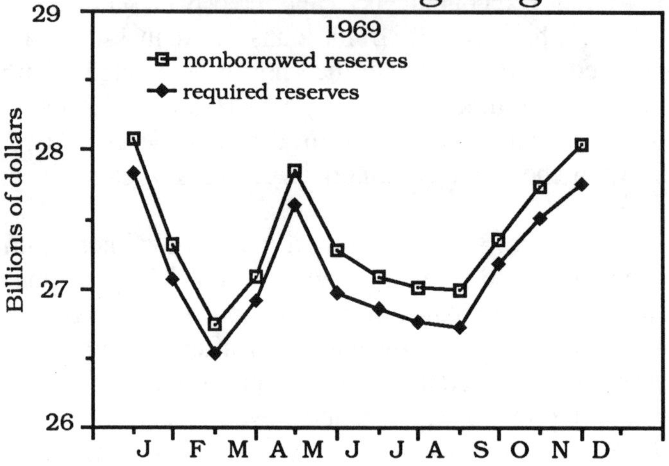

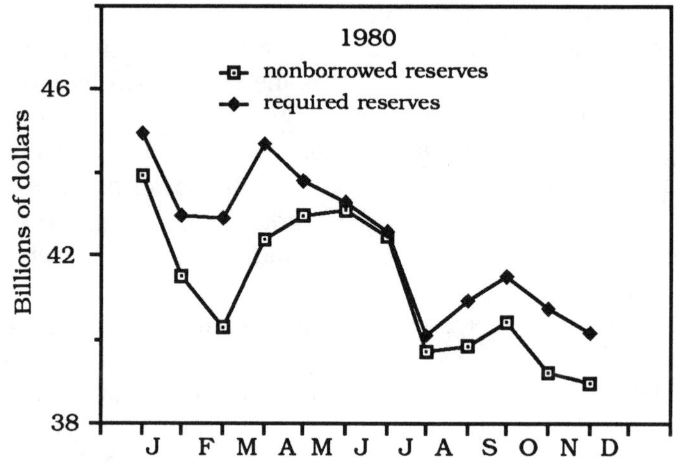

Net borrowed reserves is equal to required reserves minus nonborrowed reserves (the space between the lines). During 1969, a period of required reserve targeting, the net borrowed reserves remained fairly constant. However, during April 1980, a period of nonborrowed reserve targeting, net borrowed reserves dropped precipitously, which constituted the "great policy error of April 1980" (see Graph 5.3 on the next page). Source: Federal Reserve release H.3

Graph 5.3

Funds Rate and Net Borrowed Reserves

(monthly averages of daily data)

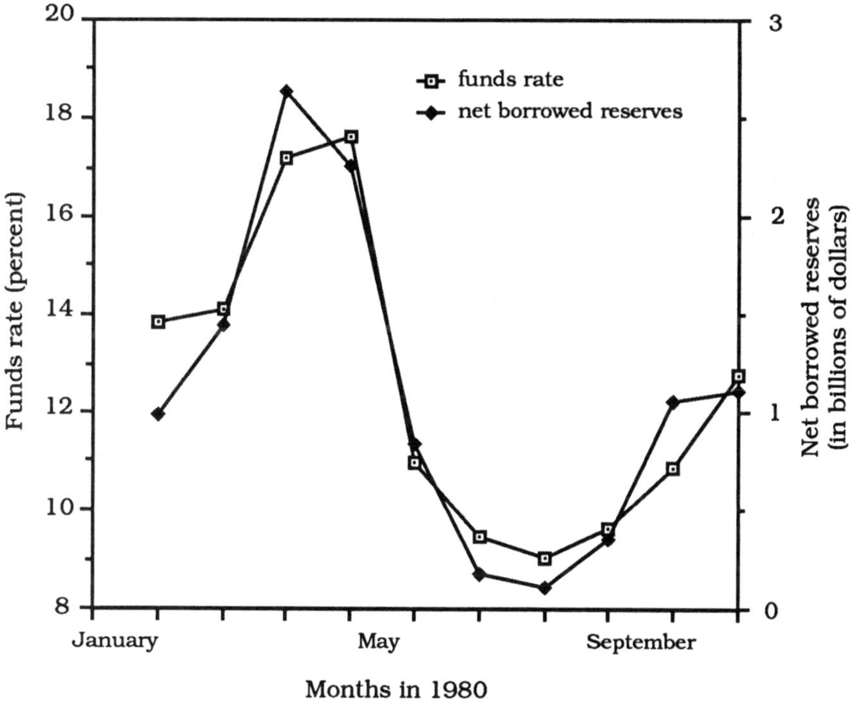

Federal Reserve Board efforts to target nonborrowed reserves resulted in "the great policy error of April 1980." Net borrowed reserve levels fell and the funds rate plummeted.

Source: Federal Reserve release H.3 and H.15.

When investigating a new structure of reserve requirements in chapter 7, the historical narrative on operational targets will resume.

A LEGACY

In spite of the horrible results of funds rate pegging, its use left Desk officials and market participants with a valuable legacy. The methods used by Desk officials to signal a change in policy during the 1970s basically apply to current operational tactics. Though overnight System repos or reverses may now be strictly reserve-related, they are used at times to forewarn market participants of a change in reserve policy. For example, if the Fed executes overnight System repos instead of customer repos to fulfill a moderate defensive requirement, the operation may signal an error disposition toward ease rather than toward firmness; this might hint at policy leanings toward ease or underscore FOMC resistance to any reserve firming. If the Fed executes customer repos instead of System repos when a large adding requirement exists, officials may be signalling firmer policy intentions or resistance to erring on the side of ease.[7]

Desk officials encourage analysts to ignore traditional signals, hoping to flexibly pursue reserve goals without arousing policy suspicions. Yet when policy shifts have occurred without much recognition, the Desk has re-employed the traditional signals cited above.

No attempt is being made to discredit Desk officials. Instead, it is always prudent to beware of dogmatic assertions, which normally reflect noble aspirations better than reality.

Perhaps the best legacy of the funds rate pegging era has been the Fed's reluctance ever again to employ a direct control over the funds rate. Upcoming chapters will disclose why the Fed has once again abandoned reserve management as a tool of monetary control. Officials now establish a reserve target to create a general level of the funds rate believed to be consistent with moderate growth of

---

[7]Term repos continue to be regarded as strictly reserve-related and have not been used as a policy signal.

credit demands (and money supply). Unfortunately, Fed officials have yet to learn that lending rates do not have desired effects on bank credit demands.

CHAPTER 6

Discount Administration

INTRODUCTION TO A HEATED DEBATE

Open market operations serve as the leading edge of restraint when the Fed uses reserve management to control monetary growth; administrative discipline at the discount window serves as the cutting edge of restraint. However, when the Fed uses the funds rate to control monetary growth, the cutting edge is the funds rate-induced rise in interest rates. The most important factor influencing the funds rate under reserve targeting is the level of the discount rate set by the Federal Reserve Board.

In chapter 3 it was explained why the funds rate normally will be above the discount rate. Under lagged reserve requirements (LRR), the funds rate tended to be about 25 basis points above the discount rate when net borrowed reserves were zero. It tended to rise an additional 25 basis points for every $100 million of net borrowed reserves. Under contemporaneous reserve requirements (CRR), which have been in effect since February 1984, reserve utilization has been far less efficient; around $500 million of free reserves are needed to keep the funds rate within 25 basis points of the discount rate. In other words, given levels of reserve borrowings and the funds rate have been associated with higher levels of excess reserves. To most economists, the greater availability of excess reserve credit in recent years belies the need for reserve borrowing gains occurring with temporary increases in the funds rate spread over the discount rate.

It is commonly perceived that reserve borrowings ("assumed" or targeted) are increasingly determined by a positive funds rate spread that invites borrowing abuse.

During 1982, when net borrowed reserves remained largely unchanged (and close to zero), the discount rate was cut from 14 percent to 8½ percent, and the funds rate declined from 14¼ percent to 8¾ percent. There were no reserve pressures either before or after reductions in the discount rate, yet the funds rate changed dramatically. Fed officials subsequently recognized the importance of the discount rate as the major determinant of the funds rate.[1] As a result, discount rate policies (established by the Board) have become a more dynamic part of monetary policy.[2]

With an apologetic warning of a small amount of redundant narrative, an over-simplified generalization about member bank borrowing behavior has to be corrected before this chapter effectively communicates. Most economic analyses in print either directly assert or imply that the level of reserve borrowings is determined primarily by the spread of the funds rate over the discount rate. This would mean that most reserve borrowings are in fact an abuse of the borrowing privilege, motivated mainly by arbitrage opportunities. Surely most bankers want to exploit arbitrage opportunities, yet most discount officers are presumably diligent in fulfilling their responsibility to administer reserve loans in accordance with Regulation A.

If all bankers were free to arbitrage borrowed reserves, the funds rate would almost never rise above the discount rate. It is crucial to bear in mind the reason why a funds rate spread over the discount rate develops: reserve deficient banks are not allowed to regularly

---

[1]In fact, the discount rate accounted for 100 percent of the decline in the funds rate. However, when net borrowed reserves increase, the discount rate rarely accounts for 100 percent of changes in the funds rate. In postwar interest rate cycles, Fed discount rates accounted for roughly 85 percent of funds rate levels.

[2]Indeed, in early 1983, the funds rate replaced reserve management as a tool of monetary control. In 1985, when GNP growth objectives became more important than money supply targeting, Fed officials began to emphasize funds rate targeting (and discount rate policy) as the principal method of controlling GNP growth. Product demands are indeed interest rate sensitive, unlike many credit demands. Thus, perceived economic trends, rather than perceived monetary trends, came to govern interest rate changes. Without Congressional consent or recognition, monetary policy became GNP policy.

use the discount facility to meet reserve requirements, and must therefore bid more aggressively for reserve funds in the market. This bidding pressure will predictably raise the funds rate over the discount rate, inviting other banks to abuse (arbitrage) the borrowing privilege.

The maintenance of a positive funds rate means that (under the laws of supply and demand) the bid-volume of reserve deficient banks in the funds market exceeds the volume of total reserve borrowings from the discount window, plus available excess reserve credit. The funds market has never been depicted by any known analyst as being perfectly efficient; there are always excess reserves which never find their way to reserve deficient banks, and at the end of a reserve settlement period, remain as excess reserves. The restrictions of Regulation A cannot prevent borrowing abuses, only limit them. Discount administration cannot be expected to be uniform among all District banks, or uniformly imposed over time. Because of a necessarily imperfect borrowing structure, arbitrage borrowings from the Fed vary considerably each week as a percentage of total borrowings.

One method of estimating the relative proportion of arbitrage to total reserve borrowings is to assume that small bank borrowings (reported weekly by the N.Y. Fed) need not have occurred because of the large reserve surplus position of nearly each bank. If a small bank aggressively reduces its reserve position in the funds market at a rate higher than the discount rate, and if it can show a one-day deficiency of reserves as a result, this bank is entitled to borrow from the Fed even though the relatively low discount rate constituted the motivating factor. Carrying relatively large surplus reserve positions, small bank managers need not worry about their ability to keep away from the discount window for the required number of weeks before another arbitrage borrowing (abuse) can slip through the administrative barrier of discipline. Persistently reserve-deficient money center banks have no such assurance of being able to keep a safe distance from administrative discipline. This does not mean that large banks avoid arbitrage. They do indeed abuse the borrowing facility, but do so much more cautiously than small banks, particularly when the "big boys" are such easy targets for administrative snipers.

In recent years, the percentage of small bank borrowers (presumably most of the abusers) to total borrowings has significantly declined because of a rise in excess reserves. Due to a dramatic decline in reserve requirement ratios stemming from financial deregulation and the Monetary Control Act, and because of deposit shifts in small banks toward relatively low reservable consumer accounts, reserve requirement levels for almost all small banks declined for several years until mid-1986 (according to Fed surveys released by the N.Y. Fed).

While required reserves dropped, vault cash levels maintained by consumer-oriented small banks rose significantly as a percentage of total deposits. Not only did transaction needs of consumers continue a brisk upward trend, but bank competition for consumer deposits encouraged widespread installation of automatic teller machines (ATMs). Though consumers love ATMs, bankers do not. ATMs have produced a less efficient management of vault cash by necessarily increasing vault cash required relative to each deposit dollar. Small banks thus find that vault cash held exceeds required reserves each business day. It has become impossible for most small banks to qualify for reserve borrowings because they cannot demonstrate need (a one-day reserve deficiency).

The borrowing need requirement has become even harder to meet among small banks because they must continue holding balances at Fed District banks for check clearing purposes. In fact, most of these deposit (clearing) balances represent excess reserves that cannot be loaned to money center banks. There has therefore been a substantial rise in excess reserve levels in recent years which are generally unavailable to the rest of the banking system because they are in fact clearing balances, not reserve balances.

Fed officials have tried to improve on the realism of reported excess reserves by excluding from the reported total that portion of small bank vault cash which exceeds reserve requirements. There remain, however, small bank clearing deposits at the Fed which do not serve a reserve purpose, and thus continue to inflate excess reserves. Desk officials receive daily internal estimates of bound and unbound member bank reserves. The unbound total represents clearing rather than reserve mandated reserve deposits of those depositories with vault cash exceeding required reserves.

The clearing balance portion of excess reserves varies significantly (and seasonally) at certain times of the year, producing meaningless and confusing changes in excess reserve levels. Because the "noise" portion of excess reserves is kept secret by Fed officials, it is not possible for econometricians to update the new relationship between reported reserve conditions and the funds rate spread over the discount rate. More important to the discount administration issue at hand, much higher levels of reported excess reserves will continue to persist at times when total reserve borrowings rise. Of course, the borrowing rise will be associated with a rise in the positive funds rate spread. You can bet that many economists will seize upon this evidence as proof that the funds rate spread determines the level of reserve borrowings. To be sure, a reserve borrowing will boost total reserves which, relative to a fixed average of required reserves, adds further to the excess reserve total. It will surely be argued that the borrowing was never needed because of relatively high (often higher) excess reserve levels. These analysts will probably never ask or understand just why the funds rate spread developed in the first place.

Ironically, the reduced percentage of small borrowers (locked out of the borrowing facility) means that (with all other things being unchanged) the funds rate spread and high excess reserves are accompanied by *less*, *not more*, abuse of the borrowing privilege.

It is imperative that analysts finally rid themselves of the false notion that the funds rate spread is the primary determinant of reserve borrowing levels; it does encourage borrowing abuses, but of a recently diminished volume. Of course, if discount administration were to tear down all perceived borrowing restraints, the funds rate would almost always equal the discount rate.

COST VERSUS NON-COST RESTRAINT

These observations permit making a distinction between cost and non-cost means of restraining bank credit. Because the discount rate almost always acts as a funds rate floor, as previously documented, it is not necessary for a high funds rate to be accompanied by any reserve restraint. An 18 percent discount rate with no reserve restraint will set the cost of money at 18 percent, quite high considering the absence of reserve restraint. Such a tactic would be consistent with a Fed objective of restraining the demand for bank credit (and hence monetary growth) by controlling and maintaining high interest rates. This cost method of restraint has yet to succeed without first weakening national income and employment.

Alternatively, a non-cost approach can be employed by keeping the discount rate low (such as 4 percent), accompanied by substantial net borrowed reserve pressures (over $2 billion). People have forgotten what a ''credit crunch'' felt like; no matter how willingly borrowers might incur higher interest costs, bank credit was simply not available. $2 billion net borrowed reserves can shut down bank credit growth and monetary growth, and for the relatively cheap price of about 9¼ percent funds rate (based on the above example, using the original funds rate spread estimating equation). The $2 billion net borrowed reserve restraint will limit bank credit extensions, not the 9¼ percent funds rate.

Chairman Paul Volcker had misgivings about non-cost methods of restraint because of the seemingly arbitrary nature of allocating relatively scarce credit resources through bank loan officers. A free market approach advocated by Mr. Volcker had to rely on high interest rationing of scarce credit resources, which is one reason why the discount rate plus penalty was pushed up to 18 percent in 1981. Did Congress ever question the adverse effects of cost restraint on low income families, or the higher income bias it had on the distribution of national income? The rich subsequently became richer relative to the poor; families below the poverty line rose in total. Just think, a Democratic President and a Democratic Congress directly enriched the rich. Were they conscious of Fed doctrine? No, it seemed that Washington politicians remained asleep in spite of rather loud grumbling.

This chapter now examines the history of discount administration, the experiment with a penalty discount rate, and the controversy associated with various methods of administering discount rate policy. The chapter ends with a proposal to create a dynamic role for discount rate policy by pegging the discount rate to the inflation rate.

PASSIVE VERSUS DYNAMIC DISCOUNT RATE POLICIES

During the 1960s, discount rate changes were lagged to changes in open market policy. The Fed used reserve management as its main tool of monetary control; strict administrative discipline at the discount window was the cutting edge of restraining monetary policy. A discount rate change could provide a highly visible confirmation of policy change.

In the latter part of the decade, the funds rate rose significantly above the discount rate. Political pressures prevented Fed officials from raising the discount rate each time they tightened reserve policy. Meanwhile, Fed officials repeatedly insisted that monetary policies followed, rather than led, debt market trends; free market forces initiated increases in the funds rate. Accordingly, whenever they did raise the discount rate, Fed officials depicted the action merely as an adjustment needed to better align the discount rate with prevailing money rates. During the next decade, because the discount rate had no effect on the pegged funds rate, Fed officials' passive attitude toward discount rate policy continued.

In 1969, Fed officials assured Congressional banking committee members that they would not tighten monetary policy to offset an increasingly stimulative fiscal policy. By the end of the 1970s, however, Fed officials were openly threatening Congress with tighter policies if mounting fiscal deficits were not trimmed. Dr. Burns deserves credit for engineering the Fed's political escape from passive policies. He convinced gullible banking committee members that the Fed was not targeting interest rates (when in fact the Fed was pegging the funds rate), only money supply growth. If the Fed pumped more money into the economy, Burns assured them, interest rates would fall only in the short run; in the longer run, excess money supply would push inflation rates upward, and interest rates would subsequently rise to new highs. Thus, little Congressional criticism accompanied the more dynamic management of the discount rate by which, by the end of the 1970s, Fed officials hoped to boost the weakening dollar's value in foreign exchange markets.

PENALTY DISCOUNT RATE

The move toward dynamic discount rate management in the late 1970s set the stage for the disastrous experiment with a penalty discount rate in the early 1980s. A discount rate set well above the funds rate is called a penalty discount because it imposes a large cost penalty for borrowing reserves from the Fed.

The roots of the penalty discount rate go back to the late 1960s, when the Fed released a comprehensive study on the discount mechanism. Part of this study focused on whether restraint at the discount window should be qualitative or quantitative in nature. The study noted that administrative discipline could not be uniformly applied throughout the System and, as a result, created inequities among member banks. As an alternative means of restraint, the study recommended the use of a penalty discount rate. The higher the cost penalty for borrowing from the Fed, the greater the restraint against using the discount facility. This penalty, the report concluded, would represent a more uniform and quantitative means of applying restraint at the discount window.

At its release, the Fed's report generated some academic interest in the penalty discount rate concept. After mid-1979, however, the concept gained the active support of monetarists. Monetarists applauded the Fed's discontinuance of funds rate pegging in favor of what they thought was nonborrowed reserve targeting.[3] However, they were dismayed that money supply growth had escalated after April 1980 and, during the second half of 1980, blamed the failure to control monetary growth on the passive management of the discount rate.[4] Monetarists claimed that tighter policies failed to control monetary growth because, when the funds rate increased above the discount rate, banks merely resorted to profitable borrowings from the discount window. As nonborrowed restraint was applied, banks simply obtained more reserves from the discount window, and the accelerated growth of total reserves sustained excessive monetary growth.

---

[3]It took several years for monetarists to realize that the Fed had instead returned to net borrowed reserve targeting.

[4]Monetarists did not fully understand the effects of the Fed's nonborrowed targeting error of April 1980, and so sought an alternative explanation for why monetary growth should continue to be excessive.

Some monetarists were more realistic in wanting the supply curve of reserves at the discount window to be steeper so that the increase in the funds rate would be much greater.

There were proposals to make the discount rate rise in response to a rise in total adjustment borrowing. Thus the cost, to an individual bank, of accommodation at the window would rise as more banks tried to borrow. This would have the effect of causing the funds rate response to reserve shortages to be larger and quicker. Under a nonborrowed reserves targeting procedure advocated by monetarists, this would cause the response of interest rates to excessive money growth to be quicker, hence excess money growth might be quickly reversed.

Because monetarism had been associated with a strong devotion to laissez-faire principles, President Reagan staffed some Treasury positions with monetarists, and the White House staff took monetarist recommendations quite seriously. Accordingly, the Administration started to pressure the Fed to establish a penalty discount rate.

Chairman Volcker capitulated to Adminstration demands, and the Fed began raising the discount rate in 1981 with the suspected goal of creating a penalty discount rate. Each time the discount rate was raised, however, the funds rate rose by an equal amount. It soon became obvious that the discount rate could not be raised without having the funds rate rise also. Indeed, the funds rate spread over the discount rate continued to correlate perfectly with the then stable level of net borrowed reserves. It was noted in FOMC minutes at the time that most members expressed surprise over the funds rate "leapfrogging" around the increase in the discount rate. Had these Fed officials possessed an elementary understanding of the funds market, they would not have been surprised, nor would have the Fed experimented aggressively with a penalty discount rate.

To comply with Administration demands, the Fed developed its own version of a penalty discount rate: the surcharge. Under the new plan, banks that borrowed more than once each month would pay a surcharge on top of the discount rate. Fed officials initially set the surcharge at two percentage points, then raised it to four percentage points when the discount rate reached 14 percent (these levels persisted throughout most of the penalty rate era). Accordingly, frequent borrowers paid an 18 percent rate, and less frequent borrowers paid the 14 percent discount rate. Concurrent reserve restraint varied between $1.0 billion and $1.8 billion net borrowed reserves, averaging about $1.5 billion. This moderate restraint kept the funds rate about three percentage points above the 18 percent discount rate applied to frequent borrowers, and also allowed well-managed banks to avoid frequent borrowings even while trying to expand their shares of the bank loan market. Most banks took advantage of the opportunity to borrow at 14 percent whenever they had avoided reserve borrowings for more than a month. At such times, a bank was said to have a "free pass" to the discount window, underscoring the strong arbitrage motive to sell 14 percent reserve credit (borrowed from the Fed) in a 20 percent-plus funds market. Far from restraining reserve borrowings, the penalty discount rate plan actually invited widespread abuses of the borrowing privilege.

PRICING FED FUNDS UNDER THE PENALTY DISCOUNT RATE PROGRAM

Banks do not want to hold excess reserves, because reserve balances do not earn interest. The opportunity cost of holding excess reserves has risen steadily during the post-war period, commensurate with the rise in the funds rate. However, weekly excess reserve credit is not completely wasted. Member banks can carry forward into the new reserve maintenance period excess reserves held in the last period, provided the excess reserve carry does not exceed two percent of their daily average reserve requirements. During the subsequent reserve maintenance period, actual reserve holdings can be less than required reserves to the extent of the positive reserve carry (of excess reserves). Successive positive reserve carryovers are permitted. Similarly, member banks can carry a reserve deficiency forward, provided the deficiency does not exceed two percent of required reserves. A reserve deficiency carried forward must be made up in the next settlement period; consecutive deficient reserve carries are not permitted.

Banks tried not to accumulate significantly more excess reserve credit than they were permitted to carry forward, despite the ease with which they could acquire reserves under the penalty discount plan. Nonetheless, during many statement weeks, accumulated excess reserve credit pushed the funds rate down on the last day of funds trading for the week. It was hard to sell excess reserves to another bank with excess reserves, no matter how low the funds rate might be at the close of a reserve maintenance period. Borrowing abuses thus created an excess reserve bias for a slightly lower funds rate. The spread of the funds rate over the 18 percent surcharged discount rate was not quite as large, relative to net borrowed reserves, as spreads had been previous to the penalty rate scheme.

Why was the funds rate based on the 18 percent surcharge rate rather than on the 14 percent discount rate, particularly when banks borrowed more reserves at 14 percent? The answer is that the 18 percent rate represented the marginal cost of borrowing. The average cost of reserve credit to member banks was certainly not as high as 18 percent, or even 14 percent. In fact, for banks with large branch networks attracting huge sums of 5 percent passbook savings funds, the average cost of reserve credit was probably less than 10 percent. But if such a large bank had a persistent reserve deficiency, and if it had been to the discount window within the past month, the bank would gladly pay more than the 18 percent penalty rate to stay away from the discount window in order to gain a "free pass" to 14 percent money during an upcoming reserve maintenance period. In this case, the marginal benefit of borrowing from the Fed would actually exceed 18 percent, considering potential costs of disciplinary actions.

DEATH OF THE PENALTY DISCOUNT RATE

Moderate reserve restraint accompanying the penalty discount rate had a negligible effect on money supply growth, partly because the "due from" bias substantially overstated monetary growth (as previously explained). While monetary growth and interest rates soared upward during 1981, the economy was sinking into "the great recession.'' By early 1982, the Fed (and the marketplace) expected the recession to be rather serious. Nonetheless, Fed officials kept the penalty discount rate and monetary policy unchanged. Based on inaccurate money supply data, noted monetarists and some Fed officials were predicting a major upsurge in the economy with renewed inflationary pressures. Such forecasts were dead wrong!

The 20 percent funds rate era marked the biggest policy mistake of the century, creating economic misery for people throughout the world. The record level of nominal and real interest rates in the U.S. prevented central bankers overseas from lowering their administered rates (to protect their currency value), in spite of the economic slump that the U.S. had exported to Asian and European economies.

On Wall Street, meanwhile, large dealer and broker firms were going out of business. The interest rate-related drop in the market value of securities held by dealers and by other large financial institutions had produced a substantial drop in net worth and borrowing capacities. Market firms, as well as other large businesses, became illiquid; debt market conditions became disorderly. By May 1982, amidst rising threats of financial dislocations, Fed research discovered the extent of the ''due from'' bias magnitudes. It was quickly realized that high interest rate policies of the Fed were needlessly pushing the economy into recession. In fact, had the Fed not begun to lower the discount rate by the end of July, a major financial dislocation would probably have occurred.

At the May FOMC meeting, Fed officials decided to eliminate net borrowed reserve pressures. As the funds rate declined toward the 18 percent surcharge rate, the Fed reduced and subsequently eliminated the surcharge. Simultaneously, net borrowed reserve pressures were eliminated, so the funds rate declined to a level approaching the 14 percent discount rate. Then the Fed began to cut the discount rate (by 50 basis points) every other week during the summer months. By the end of 1982, the discount rate was at 8½ percent, and the funds rate at 8¾ percent.

Discount rate reductions during the latter half of 1982 clearly led (and created) the downward trend in interest rates. Yet, just prior to the reductions in the discount rate, Chairman Volcker had assured a concerned Congress that ''the Fed has no magic wand to wave'' to

Graph 6.1

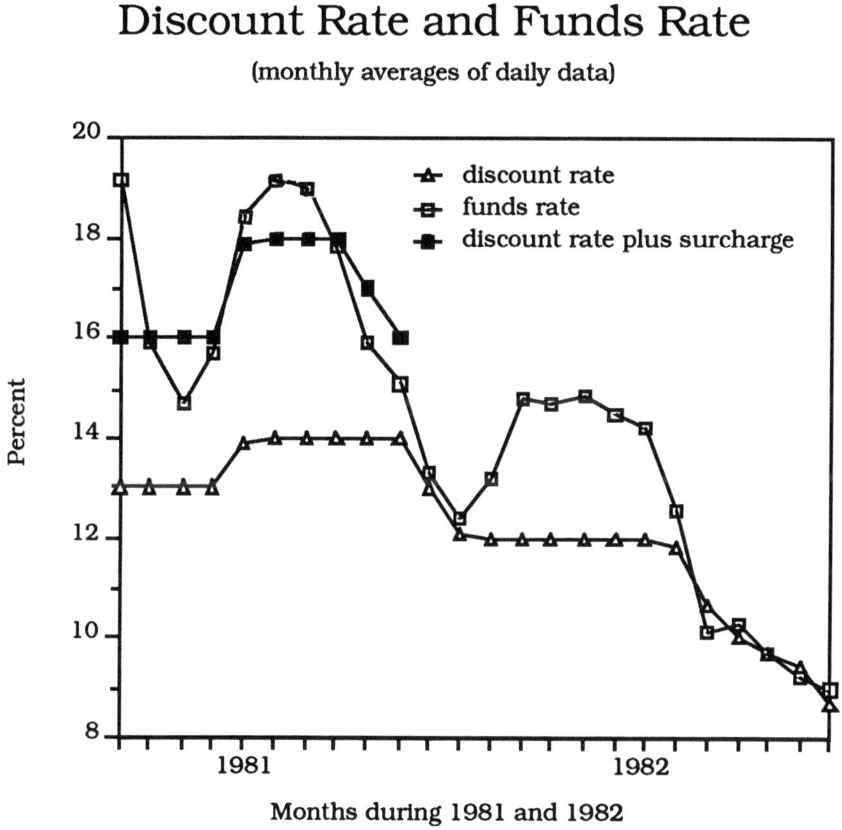

During 1981 the high funds rate resulted mainly from the high discount rate, including the discount rate surcharge. During the beginning of 1982, the spread of the funds rate over the discount rate was caused by net borrowed reserve pressure which, when eliminated by mid-year, allowed the funds rate to closely track reductions in the discount rate.

Source: Federal Reserve H.15 releases and March 1982 Federal Reserve Bulletin.

lower interest rates. Mr. Volcker was wrong. The discount rate was indeed a magic wand, and Fed officials were forced to wave it, to use the discount rate more dynamically to address the economic and financial crisis created by ill-conceived Fed policies. As President Reagan later noted, the 1982 plunge in interest rates occurred in spite of rising fiscal deficits, which Chairman Volcker had previously cited as a principal cause of high interest rates.

It is tempting for historians to credit Fed policymakers for aggressively lowering nominal interest rates in 1982, commensurate with the drop in inflation rates. Certainly Board members were encouraged by indications of less intense inflationary pressures, but their discount rate actions were only partly motivated by incoming inflation news. Based on Board member statements and FOMC minutes at the time, progress in the ongoing "battle against inflation" was regarded on Wall Street as "justification" rather than motivation behind discount rate reductions. Historians seem to forget that the ex-post picture is so much clearer than the ex-ante implications of current trends. In fact, Mr. Volcker occasionally dampened expectations of further discount rate easing by warning of a premature let-up in the inflation battle. Were it possible for anyone to confidently assess current and future rates of inflation, then Fed officials would probably have avoided pushing real interest rate levels so far above previous record levels.

A PROPOSAL

Though the non-cost method of restraint through administrative discipline at the discount window should be the principal tool used to restrain monetary growth, there is an important dynamic role for discount rate policy. The discount rate should always be set close to the perceived underlying rate of inflation. Accordingly, the funds rate should never drift below the inflation rate to a negative real interest rate level. As the need for monetary restraint increases, net borrowed reserves and the funds rate should increase accordingly. The funds rate thus rises commensurately above the rate of inflation, creating higher real interest rate levels.

In using a cost method of restraint, higher discount rates and money rates must first weaken the aggregate growth of national income before a predictable easing of bank credit demand occurs. The Fed can push interest rates high enough to weaken money supply growth. The question is how high? How long? And at what economic price? By requiring the Fed to link its discount rate to any guesstimated underlying rate of inflation, Congress can assure that its constituency will never be forced to answer these questions. Why?

On the basis of the funds rate spread in relation to net borrowed restraint, if the discount rate is at the rate of inflation, money rate (funds rate) increases above the rate of inflation (to positive real levels) cannot exceed 500 basis points (5 percentage-point spread) without first creating a credit crunch (by sustaining net borrowed reserves at $2 billion). Of course, a credit crunch should be avoided as an overkill to excessive monetary growth, and can be avoided inasmuch as reduced monetary growth is quite likely to emerge prior to crunch conditions. But, if crunch conditions accidentally occur, the *real* money rate limit should theoretically not exceed 5 percent, roughly half the real money rate record accidentally achieved in 1982. An accidental credit crunch obviously risks undesired economic weakness, but surely not to the extent of the high-cost discount rate policy of 1981 and 1982.

In short, the economic risks inherent with non-cost oriented reserve restraint seem to be far less than those associated with cost-related restraint made possible through high discount rate policies.

In addition, if Congress mandated a floating discount rate, political pressures against discretionary discount rate hikes should be obviated, helping to insure against a recurrence of the negative real money rates that previously weakened the dollar, and against renewed inflationary pressures.

As chapter 8 will examine, a Congressionally mandated discount rate peg to inflation rates does not destroy Fed independence; it helps to fulfill Congressional responsibilities to the electorate that arose from delegating the Congressional power of coinage to the Federal Reserve. Such Congressional oversight responsibility was recently complicated by structural changes affecting reserve requirements, to which informed attention must now turn.

CHAPTER 7

Reserve Requirements

RESERVE REQUIREMENT CHANGES AS A TOOL OF MONETARY CONTROL

Required reserves represented 9.7 percent of all member bank deposit liabilities at the beginning of 1970. Correspondingly, the maximum deposit multiplier (calculated as the reciprocal of the required reserve ratio) was about 10. With this multiplier, if Desk officials increase total bank reserves permanently by $100 million, the eventual expansion of bank deposits could amount to nearly $1.0 billion. If credit demands are weak, however, as they were during the Depression, deposit expansion could fall far short of $1.0 billion, leaving a significant portion of the increase in reserves as excess reserves in the System.

Prior to the Monetary Control Act (MCA) of 1980,[1] Congress granted the Federal Reserve Board broad discretion in setting the ratio of required reserves for various types of deposit liabilities. By

[1]The Depository Institutions and Monetary Control Act of 1980, or the MCA, specified the required reserve ratio the Fed could impose on transaction deposits and nonpersonal time deposits in order to affect monetary policy. For transaction accounts totalling more than $36.7 million (this cut-off is raised annually) the reserve ratio was initially set at 12 percent. For transaction accounts totalling less than $36.7 million and for nonpersonal time and savings deposits maturing in less than 18 months, the initial reserve ratio was set at 3 percent. The MCA empowers the Federal Reserve to vary these requirements within specified ranges. Reserve requirements for depository institutions that are not Federal Reserve members are to be phased in gradually. The phase-in will be complete in September 1987, at which time there will be no distinction between members and nonmembers so far as reserve requirements are concerned.

changing required reserve ratios, the Federal Reserve Board could also change the maximum deposit multiplier. Consequently, Board members could significantly influence the rate of deposit expansion and money supply growth. To slow money supply growth, for example, the Board might raise reserve requirements on demand and time deposits.

Prior to the 1980s, increases in reserve requirement ratios were not accompanied by a change in net borrowed reserves. Accordingly, increases in the level of required reserves, stemming from the hike in reserve requirement ratios, were fully funded by the Fed (in terms of an increased supply of nonborrowed reserves). As a result, the funds rate spread over the discount rate was not measurably affected.

With almost all reserve requirement ratio increases, market analysts had expected that the Desk would not fund the increase in reserve requirement levels, and net borrowed reserves and the funds rate would therefore increase. Each time the Fed failed to fulfill these market expectations, analysts would question the purpose of increasing reserve requirement ratios. Analysts apparently forgot that higher ratios would soon reduce the deposit multiplier, and thus slow the expansion of bank credit and money supply.

Bank liability managers, however, increasingly shifted the structure of their deposit liabilities to lower reservable deposits, as a defensive response to firmer Fed policy. Accordingly, the average reserve requirement applicable to total deposits did not rise commensurately with each increase in reserve requirement ratios, and the hoped-for reduction in the deposit multiplier was often not measurable. This might encourage one to question the effectiveness of reserve requirement management when surrounded by highly creative liability managers.

While phasing-in greater monetary restraint, the leading edge of restraint is imposed through Desk operations (as previously discussed). Reserve requirement ratio increases have lagged rising levels of net borrowed reserves. Bank liability managers are quick to take defensive actions against illiquidity at the first signs of reduced availability of reserve credit. As tighter reserve conditions are phased-in, liability management continues its effort to circumvent the Fed policy objective of slowing bank credit growth. Liability management has never been able to fully circumvent the restraining aim of restrictive policy, regardless of whether reserve requirement ratios are raised. But if the latter course of action is taken periodically throughout any period of policy restraint, the marginal capabilities of liability managers are increasingly impaired.

More importantly, any increase in average reserve requirement ratios achieved by the Fed will directly lower the future growth potential of deposit liabilities, relative to a given level of net borrowed reserves. In this context, required reserve policies of the Fed can be an important tool of monetary control which does not always create *measurable* impacts on the funds rate.

OPTIMAL RESERVE REQUIREMENT AVERAGE

Rarely has the concept of optimal reserve requirements been analyzed in print. While it is theoretically obvious that zero reserve requirement ratios can be too low, it may not be so obvious that 100 percent requirements may be too high. Taking, for the moment, the extreme case of having all deposits fully reservable (100 percent average reserve requirement ratio), the Fed can achieve near-full control of monetary growth. However, the initial move toward 100 percent requirements would require an enormous increase in non-borrowed reserves, financed by a commensurate upsurge in Fed holdings of treasury debt. Fed purchases of bills and coupons of the required volume could not be readily accommodated by reporting dealers, and could temporarily create a high degree of instability of debt market conditions. Non-bank dealer selling of Treasuries to the Fed would also create a surge in demand deposit credit which, under a 100 percent reserve requirement system, would require potentially damaging deposit reduction adjustments elsewhere in the banking system.

Some leading monetarists have advanced the notion of establishing 100 percent requirements on checkable deposits to significantly strengthen the linkage between Fed open market operations and M1 growth. Requirements on non-checkable accounts would be left unchanged, which implies that a much greater policy emphasis should be placed on money as a medium of exchange (M1) as opposed to money as a store of value (M2). One major disadvantage of the proposed change is that defensive open market operations could become too large to sustain orderly debt market conditions.

The distribution of deposit credit between checkable and non-checkable accounts can be significantly impacted by such exogenous factors as tax payment dates. Consumers typically shift non-checkable credit to checkable accounts in advance of tax dates, producing a seasonal upsurge in the checkable deposit component of M1. Assuming that monetarists do not seek to prevent deposit shifts arising from exogenous factors, the open market desk would be required to temporarily raise nonborrowed reserves through a substantial volume of Treasury debt purchases, disrupting market conditions.

Alternatively, bank access to the discount window could be temporarily eased. Repeated occurrences such as this to seasonal deposit shifts complicates discount administration, however. Total reserve control is essential, but it is compromised when discount officers cannot easily screen out borrowings unrelated to deposit shifts and required reserve changes.

The fractional reserve system has the advantage of elasticity, allowing banks to accommodate pressing credit needs at the time of need and at the point of need. However, reserve requirement ratios can be too low, with a correspondingly high deposit multiplier. The higher the multiplier, the greater the undesired money supply consequence of reserve management errors (arising from aberrant behavior of H.4.1 factors affecting reserve availability). In other words, the higher the deposit multiplier, the greater the difficulty of controlling monetary growth.

Graph 7.1 plots various reserve requirement ratios in relation to their corresponding maximum deposit multiplier. The purpose of the graph is to illustrate the trade-off between minimizing deposit multipliers and minimizing the volume of reserves required. To approximate an optimal trade-off, it is assumed that there will be equal disadvantages on either side of the optimal trade-off. True relative cost of errors might differ from the assumption, but for a wide range

Graph 7.1

Deposit Multiplier and Reserve Requirement Ratios

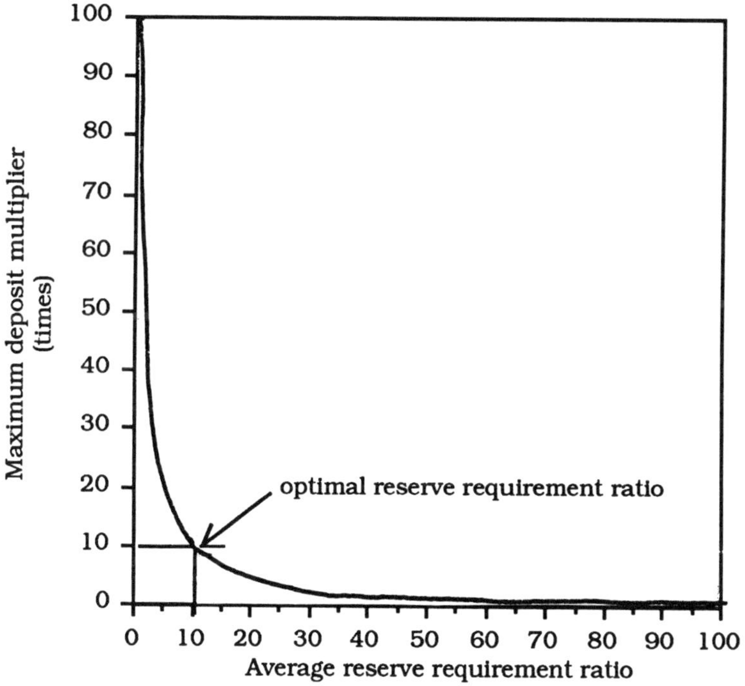

of relative assumptions the optimal reserve requirement ratio (average) seems to fall close to 10 percent. A one-dollar marginal reduction in the deposit multiplier will create more than a one-dollar increase in required reserves when the average requirement ratio exceeds 10 percent. Similarly, marginal dollar increases in the deposit multiplier will exceed dollar reductions in required reserves when reserve requirement ratios are lowered below 10 percent.

FED LOSES RESERVE REQUIREMENTS AS A TOOL OF MONETARY CONTROL

Unfortunately, the Fed does not release detailed data which, for the member banking system only, enables computation of an average required reserve ratio. When such measurement was possible at the beginning of 1970 the calculated average was 9.7 percent, close to optimal. Currently available data suggest that this average ratio has since declined below 4 percent, an estimate which one Board staff member in 1986 confidentially stated to be "close." If the average reserve requirement ratio, for example, falls from 10 percent to 4 percent, the deposit multiplier maximum rises from 10 times to 25 times. Such a quantum change weakens the Fed's ability to precisely control the growth of money supply through reserve targeting, particularly with increased dynamics of bank liability management.

Demise of reserve requirement management by the Board, as a tool of monetary control, occurred in conjunction with Congressional passage of the Monetary Control Act of 1980 (MCA). MCA provided for a uniform extension of reserve requirements to all depositories. Previously, reserve requirements set by state governments for state-chartered (non-member) banks were significantly lower than those set by the Federal Reserve Board for member banks. Until the late 1960s the higher reserve requirements observed by member banks did not significantly affect their earnings because the funds rate was relatively low. As the funds rate rose during the 1970s, however, the opportunity cost of holding more non-interest earning balances at the Fed rose commensurately. Many state-chartered member banks began to leave the System in favor of lower reserve requirements.

The attrition of System membership initially involved small member banks, but, within several years, banks with several hundred million dollars of deposits began to withdraw from the System. During the

1970s, Fed Chairman Burns tried to limit attrition by offering smaller member banks seasonal access to low-cost reserve funds from the discount window. Although the seasonal borrowing program helped to slow membership withdrawals, they continued at an alarming pace. By 1980, member bank deposits, which had once represented more than two-thirds of all bank deposits, comprised less than half of all deposits.

MCA proponents in 1980 argued that proportionate decreases each year of the member bank deposit base were slowly eroding the Fed's ability to control monetary growth. Under a fractional reserve system, an inter-bank deposit, qualifying as reserve credit for non-members, does not fully create the reserve asset in another depository that it would if held by a central depository such as the Fed. Pyramiding of non-member reserves enables a non-member deposit expansion of a very high multiple of Federal Reserve credit. Risks inherent to the non-member system would be far more obvious and serious if small banks had the widespread opportunity to capitalize on strong demand for bank credit, as opposed to selling reserve credit (or losing it) to larger member banks through the funds market (or through deposit markets). MCA proponents perceived that the Fed's ability to control monetary growth was partly dependent on maintaining a proportionally large member bank deposit base whose growth was significantly influenced by reserve operations.

If it is believed that Fed control of money rates can be effectively used as a tool to control the demand for bank credit, and hence the growth of money supply, then the need for uniform extension of reserve requirements, as an act of monetary control, would probably have received less emphasis than it did from Fed officials in 1980. It could be argued that the Fed's ability to control money rates was also threatened by attrition of system membership. But this issue was not raised, primarily because the focus of monetary control by Fed officials, at the time, was on reserve targeting. The funds rate targeting concept was adopted by the Board later in October 1982. Also, the structural picture surrounding funds rate targeting strongly suggests that the attrition problem would have to become extreme prior to weakening money rate control by the Fed.

It is important to remember that the policy doctrine surrounding MCA legislation envisioned reserve management as the principal tool to be used in achieving monetary control. Such reserve emphasis was consistent with the subsequent 1981 effort to tighten monetary control through cost restraint applied to reserve borrowings (penalty discount rate) and consistent with contemporaneous reserve requirements implemented in 1984.

By legislating a uniform extension of reserve requirements, Congress also closed the parameters of reserve requirement ratio management by the Fed. In addition, state banking political pressures prevented raising relatively low non-member requirements sufficiently to match member reserve requirements. The latter were thus lowered (on average) as a compromise for some increases in non-member requirements needed to legislate uniformity.

To mitigate impacts of MCA-mandated change, reserve requirement changes were phased-in through September 1987. In addition, all non-member depositories (including thrifts) were permitted access to the Federal Reserve's discount facility.

Though MCA contributed to an undesired lowering of member bank reserve requirements, it had a greater negative effect of replacing most of the Fed's authority to manage reserve requirements with Congressional management of reserve requirements. Fed officials were not in a position to object because of the MCA's big advantage of preserving the Fed's base of reserve influence. The new precedent of Congressional reserve requirement management nonetheless set the stage for further reserve requirement actions by Congress, which also helped to further lower average reserve requirements of member banks.

Congressionally authorized creation of new bank deposit offerings to consumers in most instances involved an extension of the checkable feature of demand deposits to various types of consumer savings accounts on which interest was earned. From a political point of view, the "small guy" was being given a chance to earn interest on transactions accounts, in keeping with business access to repo and Eurodollar markets, which also resemble interest bearing demand deposits. The Congressional liberalization of consumer deposit restrictions was a part of a political move towards financial de-regulation, initiated by the Reagan Administration.

Because of the checkable features associated with new consumer deposits, Fed officials successfully argued for Congressionally authorized reserve requirements on these deposits, which would be the same as the 12 percent requirements required on other transaction accounts under MCA. As a result, average reserve requirements on consumer deposits would have increased were it not for a Congressional desire to protect "the little guy" by abolishing reserve requirements on *non* transactions consumer accounts.

Reserve requirements were retained only on non-personal time and savings accounts. Because non-transaction deposits held by households were subject to no federally-mandated reserve requirements, households were exempted from the reserve requirement "tax" on their holding of non-checkable deposits. The abolition of reserve requirements on non-transaction accounts also accorded with the then-prevailing Federal Reserve view that monetary policy should focus on controlling the stock of transactions money (M1). On balance, such financial de-regulation contributed to a lowering of the average reserve requirement of member banks.

IMPORTANCE OF REQUIRED RESERVE POLICIES

The decline in average reserve requirement ratios was noted with some public concern by Fed officials. Yet, to avoid political confrontations on financial deregulation and MCA, related Congressional testimony by Chairman Volcker mentioned without much emphasis his concern about reduced reserve requirements of the banking system. By October 1982 Fed officials had concluded that reserve requirement ratios, which had largely been excluded from their jurisdiction, were sufficiently low to prevent reserve targeting from having much effect on the growth of bank credit and money supply. Attendant high multiples of deposit expansion became almost impossible to reasonably project because of the increased dynamics of liability management among money center banks. With the perceived breakdown of the linkage between reserve operations and monetary growth, Fed officials felt obligated to resurrect operational control of money rates as a means of controlling money demand and monetary growth. Such consequence of reserve requirement policy is potentially tragic, and warrants closer examination of rate targeting impacts.

Several Wall Street economists, regularly surveyed by Money Market Services, have periodically tried to measure the interest elasticity of the demand curve applicable to bank credit. Fed staffers were concurrently investigating the interest elasticity of aggregate credit demand. When assessing changing interest rate impacts on money demands, the relevant focus is bank credit demand, not aggregate credit demand. Credit demands accommodated in non-bank markets utilize existing monetary assets. Such distinction between these credit aggregates is critically important to the issue of interest rate targeting because of different credit demand elasticities manifest over the intermediate term.

Wall Street studies on bank credit demand characteristics, only one of which is known to have been made publicly available as a position paper, reach the conclusion that, in the aggregate, the demand for bank credit is almost completely interest inelastic. Interest rate changes simply do not correlate with the growth behavior of bank credit, even when accounting for changes in reserve availability. Of course, these studies readily acknowledge the existence of interest-elastic demand for total non-financial credit. One might expect that, as a subset of total non-financial domestic credit, bank credit growth should correlate with total credit raised. Over the short run, as previously explained, the ratio of bank credit to total (non-financial) credit varies significantly. One major reason for such variation is the shift in corporate credit demands between bond and bank markets, which is based on current and prospective interest rate trends. The magnitude of this corporate finance factor often seems to create an upward sloping business loan demand curve, as opposed to downward sloping. Graph 5.1 illustrates this tendency (as opposed to a tight correlation), from which one can reasonably anticipate some rise in business loans (monetization) resulting from any Fed-induced rise in interest rates.

Though interest rate increases will rarely be associated with an intermediate term reduction in bank credit demand, over the long run bank credit demand exhibits an income elasticity which establishes the parameters of its co-variance with aggregate credit demand.

High levels of real interest rates will predictably reduce aggregate (non-financial) credit demand growth. Such demand response has been so significant that credit flows were perceived to be dislocated. Credit dislocations mirror attendant disruption to product flows, which result in weaker growth in national income. Over the longer run, income effects on total and bank credit demands are presumably equal and, at the very least, reduced income growth negatively affects bank and total credit demand. In the short run, negative income influences give rise to personal and corporate illiquidity, which is more readily accommodated in bank rather than in non-bank markets (the latter being illiquid also) because banks can manufacture new liquidity.

In the longer run, Fed-induced high levels of real interest rates undeniably weaken the demand for bank credit (money) and the growth of money supply. However, the interest rate effect had to be transmitted through national income weakness. Because the long range linkage of Fed-controlled interest rates and bank credit demand is not direct, any interest rate target attempting to restrain monetary growth will tend to first weaken the economy before slowing monetary growth. Over the shorter run, there is evidence that higher rates may pro-cyclically stimulate monetary growth.

The last statement may seem contradictory because, on the one hand, high real rates slow the economy before slowing money growth, consistent with the previous thesis that money supply growth (being driven mainly by demand factors) will cyclically lag GNP growth. On the other hand, the potential for high interest rate stimulation of monetary growth over the short run may have a pro-cyclical influence, implying that money growth can lead the business cycle.

Chapter 4 made a distinction between cyclical and secular relationships of money growth and the economy. It was explained that secular trends in money led those in the economy, particularly inflation trends. The cyclical pattern of inflation has certainly not been co-terminal with the cycle of real GNP growth. This is why periods of stagflation must be acknowledged, when stagnating real growth is accompanied by persistent inflationary pressures. Stagflation is not a predictable cyclical recurrence, and it arises from variations in cyclical lengths between real GNP growth and inflation. Both endogenous as well as exogenous factors are assumed to cause such differences in cyclical lengths.

If it is assumed that stable prices are the primary objective (not full employment) of monetary policy, as has generally been the accepted priority in the past, then the previous pro-cyclical monetary reference made is focused more on the inflation cycle, which in recent decades appears to be occurring at larger intervals than the real GNP cycle. On a secular basis, influences on monetary growth seem to be more closely linked with the inflation cycle than with real GNP. Admittedly, enormous amounts of econometric research are needed to translate such a casual observation into predictable economic behavior.

A summary of four hypotheses will help underscore the monetary consequences of recent reserve requirement changes. First, excessive monetary growth can, if allowed to persist, have pro-secular inflationary consequences, which may be thought of as pro-cyclical if one is willing to divorce the real GNP cycle from the longer-spawned inflation cycle.

Second, the cyclical behavior of monetary growth is largely derived from demand factors which lag the real GNP cycle. If monetary policy is reactive to incoming data rather than proactively creating appropriate monetary circumstances for the future, policy actions will also lag the GNP cycle in a pro-cyclical fashion.

The third hypothesis is that the so-called ''non-cost'' operational approach of targeting reserve credit availability has some (though limited) capability of counteracting GNP cyclical effects on bank credit (money) demand. Even if such capability were strengthened, however, the associated operating target(s) would have to be established proactively rather than reactively in order to avoid pro-cyclical policy actions.

The final hypothesis is that if policy actions of the Fed can counter cyclical demand impacts on money growth, then the secular influence of monetary growth on inflation can be regulated to achieve the policy objective of stable prices.

Congressional policy fostered lowering of average reserve requirements of member banks, which was marginally offset by raising and extending reserve requirement ratio uniformity among all depositories. As previously discussed, Federal Reserve monetary influences are operative mainly on the member depository system, less so among non-members. MCA, however, did stem membership attrition and attendant loss of Fed leverage. Yet Congress, directly and indirectly, left Fed officials with a non-discretionary low reserve requirement policy, which Fed officials quietly concluded would negate effectiveness of reserve targeting. They felt they had no choice but to return to interest rate targeting, which has far more economic than monetary impacts.

The return of rate targeting occurred at a time when Fed officials were reluctantly replacing lagged reserve requirements with contemporaneous reserve requirements (which will be examined shortly). The stated purpose of such change was to strengthen the monetary growth response to reserve targeting. The obvious irony of the situation was that an expensive structural change in reserve requirements was being made at the time when Fed officials had concluded that pre-ordained reserve requirements had become inconsequential to the restraint of monetary growth. The shift to funds rate targeting was also prompted by a shift in policy emphasis from monetary growth to GNP growth.

In a diplomatic and partial attempt to hide the structural incongruity of implementing interest rate targeting simultaneously with contemporaneous reserve requirements (CRR), Fed officials emphasized the difference of the new funds rate target from the previously employed funds rate peg; and the use of a reserve borrowing target, as a means of controlling the funds rate, was heralded more as an operational target than the funds rate. Conveniently, the reserve borrowing target was couched in terms of reserve targeting to create impressions of consistency with the start of CRR. Diplomatic historians were later to add further explanation that CRR strengthened the Fed's control over money rates as well as tightening the reserve linkage to monetary growth.

The foregoing semantics seem to border on "mumbo-jumbo," but they were carefully used by apologists in and out of the Fed to create a misleading image of credibility. Yet Governor Wallich, in April 1983, gave a speech which represented a rather detailed description of the new operating procedure.

The Governor described relationships between the funds rate, reserve availability, and the discount rate. These relationships, examined in previous chapters, had never previously been connected with policy doctrine at the Fed, as far as anyone can recall. Fed officials had previously insisted, for example, that the funds rate was an accurate barometer of the total amount of reserve pressure brought to bear on the banking system, regardless of the discount rate level which had previously been viewed as a lagging rate (adjusted only to discourage borrowing abuses).

Governor Wallich described new relationships in which the discount rate served as a floor for the funds rate, above which the funds rate rose in response to the level of reserve borrowings. Whereas a number of monetarists (including some Fed staffers) had previously depicted reserve borrowing levels as arbitrage abuses sponsored by the funds rate spread (over the discount rate), Governor Wallich depicted precisely the opposite: borrowing levels determined the funds rate spread.

Mr. Wallich explained that Desk officials would henceforth employ a reserve borrowings target which, in conjunction with a given discount rate, would create a predictable funds rate average (allowing, of course, for some variations based on market factors described in the first chapter). Under funds rate pegging, Desk operations were triggered more by undesired rate variations than by short-term surprises in reserve availability. As previously explained, funds market psychology played a more important daily role in determining funds rate changes than did changes in reserve availability. The missing link between reserve availability and the funds rate spread, however, has always emerged in conjunction with some sort of reserve targeting.

Consideration must temporarily be given to describing the new Fed operational plan disclosed by Governor Wallich. One could describe the new operation as the targeting of reserve borrowings, as the Governor did. Of course, the targeting of reserve borrowings requires a good forecast of excess reserves (which became difficult under CRR—to be discussed). A net borrowed target must then be calculated to arrive at a targeted level of nonborrowed reserves (relative to required reserves). One might therefore insist that the Fed was going to target nonborrowed reserves. But such claim could not easily be made because inter-meeting nonborrowed growth paths ceased being targeted in October 1982. One final description did emerge: funds rate targeting.

The funds rate target description, as opposed to a reserve borrowing target, seemed more accurate to Wall Street economists because, as Mr. Wallich explained, the primary purpose of the reserve borrowing target was to meet a funds rate objective (target). By controlling the funds rate, and hence other money rates, Mr. Wallich explained that the Fed could control the demand for money. Not only was this contention wrong, but it was not documented by Fed staffers, who had researched the interest elasticity of domestic non-financial credit (debt) instead of bank credit. The domestic non-financial debt aggregate became a ''monitored'' aggregate. Presumably, this aggregate would have graduated to a targeted status had its change in growth statistically led to better monetary forecasts. But this did not occur insofar as private economists are aware.

Under the new plan, one or several monetary targets represented the principal policy target(s), with nonfinancial debt (credit) and the funds rate serving as derived policy targets of a second order (monitored status or ''intermediate target''). No such uncertainty existed with respect to operational targets which, in order of priority, were the funds rate and reserve borrowings.

It was assumed that reserve borrowings specifically meant adjustment borrowings, but Fed public relations officials insisted on reporting reserve borrowing data to include seasonal borrowings as well. This implies that Desk officials do not treat seasonal borrowings as factors affecting reserve credit, similar to extended credit. At times, Fed accountants would (for legal reasons) temporarily treat emergency borrowings as adjustment borrowings rather than as extended credit. So-called ''reserve borrowings'' thus soared upward without a commensurate rise in the funds rate spread. Though temporary, these problems can play havoc with econometric research.

The funds rate relationship to the discount rate presented in this book differs from the one used by Fed staffers. In the Fed's forecast model, the coefficient of the discount rate is somewhat less than one (which is implicitly assumed with the author's use of a funds rate *spread* as the dependent variable). Also, reserve borrowing effects on the funds rate are claimed by Fed staffers to vary incrementally according to magnitude of reserve borrowings. While such difference in perception may be of significance from a forecasting view (which doesn't appear to be significant), there is no difference in the basic concept of funds rate determinants.

The funds rate target of the Fed also differed from the funds rate peg in terms of daily Desk operations being reserve-related rather than rate-related. Such observation made it more credible for Fed officials to insist on describing the new operational target as a reserve borrowing target instead of a funds rate target. Wall Streeters, however, did not buy the Fed's claim, and have consistently referred to the new operating procedure as funds rate targeting.

Apart from the irony of commencing funds rate targeting with the new CRR, real sector aggregates (such as GNP and manufacturing employment) began to establish themselves as more reliable policy targets than monetary aggregates. Sluggish economic growth was accompanied by rather baffling high rates of M1, M2, and M3 growth from 1984 to 1987. This seemed to be a repeat of late-1981 and 1982. The more recent monetary upsurge, however, was not fictitious, as was the "due from" bias cause of the previous monetary upsurge. Yet the 1984-86 monetary surge was viewed with far more suspicion at the Fed than the 1981-82 growth excess.

Accepted policy doctrine is based partly on the false notion that monetary cycles are supposed to closely fit economic cycles, with variable lead-times. Accordingly, when money supply data failed to conform to the false notion, the monetary targets were discarded in 1984 from the policy making arena, and accompanying secular relationships of money to inflation were obscured from policy examination.

This conveniently reinforced the importance of funds rate targeting. Because interest rate changes have a far more predictable effect on economic aggregates than on monetary aggregates, the increased importance of economic variables as policy targets blended perfectly with the new operational funds rate target. Technically speaking, there was no monetary policy; there was a GNP policy. However, such distinction could be more fundamental than technical. Since when did Congress ever authorize the Fed to implement economic growth policy? Why did congress allow the Fed to essentially abandon monetary targeting as a key policy objective, in direct conflict with the monetary aims of the Humphrey-Hawkins Act?

The reason why our time-capsule journey toward progressive understanding of theoretical issues is rested within reserve requirements is that Congressional usurping of the Fed's reserve requirement authority also reduced the effectiveness of reserve management as a tool of monetary control. A few Fed staffers have privately used this argument to explain why the Fed's only recourse was back to interest rate controls. Even if rate targets do not control money demands, they certainly control economic demands. And if money does lag the business cycle because of demand and liquidity forces (which is a growing perception in financial markets), then GNP targeting under current operating procedure should not give rise to money-induced inflation on a longer-term basis. Therefore, the Fed is not violating any Congressional authority; it is simply making the best of a weakened financial structure inherited by the Fed from Congress.

The Fed defense argument sets the stage for the introduction of contemporaneous reserve requirements (CRR). It seems rather incongruous to attempt strengthening the role of reserve management and monetary control at the time when these noble objectives were being put back on the history shelf. In defense of the Fed and Congress, the CRR initiative came from the White House.

Incorrectly believing that free market conservatism necessarily embraces monetarism, as opposed to more "traditional" monetary doctrine, President Reagan was disposed toward appointments of monetarist-leaning economists to important positions in his administration. In 1983 when Paul Volcker's four-year term as Fed Chairman was to expire, the President reportedly conditioned the reappointment of Mr. Volcker to another Chairmanship term on the agreement that the Board replace lagged reserve requirements (LRR) with CRR. An undocumented (though believable) story depicts Mr. Volcker as an opponent of CRR, but having to nonetheless compromise his position in order to continue applying his valuable experience and capabilities to defusing of the world debt crisis. As a result, CRR entered the Fed picture largely at the urging of influential monetarists.

CONTEMPORANEOUS RESERVE REQUIREMENTS (CRR)

Under strictly contemporaneous reserve requirements, the reserve computation period would be the same as the reserve maintenance period. In other words, a bank's deposit liabilities during a particular reserve computation period would determine the level of required reserves during that same period. In fact, the reserve requirements rules in effect since 1984 are not strictly contemporaneous in this sense. The reserve maintenance period lags the reserve computation period by two days.

The contemporaneous determination of reserve requirements was suspected to be too much of a task for many banks, particularly smaller ones, who were unable to determine their deposit levels promptly to meet the requirements. As a result, these banks might opt to maintain reserve positions significantly above required levels as insurance against unexpected reserve deficiencies. Such sloppy reserve management would increase excess reserves, particularly when softer funds rate conditions reduced the opportunity cost of holding excess reserves. If, however, there was to be any tightening of the linkage between open market operations and the growth of bank credit, it was felt that unnecessarily high (and unpredictable) excess reserve levels should be minimized.

The Board's staff did their best to design a CRR system which would mitigate problems inherent with CRR. In order to reduce reserve management uncertainties among bankers, the Fed decided to lag the maintenance period two days from the computational period. Accordingly, bankers would have a reasonably good idea of their reserve settlement requirements toward the end of each maintenance period. In addition, the Fed extended both the reserve maintenance and computational periods from one week to two weeks. The reasoning behind such change was that daily changes in required and total reserves have much less effect on two-week averages of daily data than on weekly averages of daily data. The two-week period would thus make it easier to make needed reserve adjustments towards the close of each reserve maintenance period.

Another exception to a theoretically pure CRR system was the exclusion of non-transactional deposits from contemporaneous reserve requirements. Mr. Volcker wanted to avoid CRR as much as possible, and realized that monetarists in the White House were at the time concerned more about M1 growth than the growth of broader monetary aggregates. Because transactional deposits are excluded from the broader aggregates, Volcker correctly suspected that he could exempt non-transactional deposits from contemporaneous requirements without objection from White House advisors. This exemption, of course, made it easier for bankers to cope with CRR.

Reserve management practices among smaller bankers nonetheless became less efficient, and excess reserve levels rose under CRR. It appears that the frictional level of excess reserves rose from about $150 million to $450 million because of reserve uncertainties inherent under CRR. With the ongoing decline in required reserve levels among small banks, previously discussed, growing vault cash levels subsequently raised excess reserves up closer to a billion dollar daily average.

EXCESS RESERVES BELIE DEFINITION

The rise in excess reserve levels will make more difficult the targeting of a reserve borrowing "assumption." Fed staffers believe that a stable behavior of excess reserves will emerge after a full transition is made to MCA and to CRR. Perhaps a more accurate expectation might be that excess reserve changes will be more varied because of sharp swings in clearing balances at the Fed, and because of reserve management difficulties inherent with CRR.

Precise control of reserve borrowings depends, of course, on the accuracy of the excess reserve assumption used to calculate a nonborrowed target. Such control could encourage Desk officials to modify defensive estimates more on the basis of hourly funds rate behavior than on subsequent incoming daily data. Such an option, however, could easily be construed by market participants as being rate-related rather than reserve-related. The specter of funds rate pegging would return instantly. The current option being followed places primary emphasis on available reserve data rather than on the funds rate. Though this option keeps the Fed at a safe distance from funds rate pegging, it leads to somewhat greater funds rate and reserve borrowing variations. This makes it somewhat more difficult for Fed watchers to quickly identify any change in the reserve borrowing target and the associated change in the central tendency of weekly funds rate averages (of daily data).

LOW RESERVE REQUIREMENTS HAVE NOT DESTROYED RESERVE LINKAGES TO MONEY SUPPLY GROWTH

The objective of this chapter has been, apart from looking at the many facets of reserve requirement policy, to examine just how critically important reserve requirements can be as a tool of monetary control. If monetary growth policy swings away from the extreme of benign neglect towards the other extreme of nine-week M1 targeting, hopefully the policy perspective will stop moving somewhere in the middle of two extremes. In addition, it is hoped that related velocity analyses will differentiate between real and financial sectors, and between intermediate and longer-term segments. An associated refocusing on the bank credit aggregate should also be extremely helpful (as explained in chapter 4).

The foregoing dream, nonetheless, is made more distant by inappropriate reserve requirement policy. Several points must be stressed in this regard. First, the focus of restraining policy is clearly the money center banks (and other large regional banks) where bank loan demands are usually intense. Second, the path towards controlling large bank extensions of credit is reserve availability; the alternative round-about path of interest rates economically damages most of the bank constituency before restraining influences arrive at bank offices.

Third, and the most important point, reserve pressures can affect loan extension policies of large banks even though reserve requirement ratios are admittedly too low. Of course, the deposit multiplier is potentially high, particularly with the dynamics of large bank liability management. The reserve linkage has been weakened, but not destroyed.

The basic strategy of restraining policy, and the only one that works, is aimed at forcing large banks to the discount window through aggressively managed shortages in the supply of nonborrowed reserves. Repeated exposure to the threat of administrative discipline can within nine months probably exhaust most liability management options. Prior to such inevitability, bank asset management policies begin to become more restrictive (almost immediately with mortgage credit, making it hard for federal agencies to insulate the housing sector from any type of Fed restraint). The lower reserve requirement ratios are, the higher adjustment (or net) borrowing targets must become to reduce the portion of aggregate credit demands monetized through bank credit extensions. This, of course, means that funds rate spreads will be higher during periods of restraint, a negative outcome of not using reserve requirements as a tool of monetary control. Yet, as previously examined, the interest rate cost implication of such non-cost (reserve) restraint is far less than a discount rate method of cost restraint. The victims of the non-cost approach are mainly bankers and home buyers, not the entire constituency of Congress.

Before concluding this argument, it is helpful to return to CRR and explain how restraint does *not* work. Some monetarists still claim that two-week contemporaneous reserve requirements on transactions deposits create incentives for bankers to concurrently liquidate bank credit, thus obtaining new reserve credit that will make reserve borrowings unnecessary. At the same time, bank credit liquidations (achieved through security sales or through non-replacement of maturing loans) will lower deposit liabilities, and concurrently lower required reserve levels of the banking system. Required reserves can thus adjust to targeted growth of nonborrowed reserves, under CRR, rather than having an LRR structure force Desk officials to adjust nonborrowed reserves according to changes in the level of required reserves. Reserve borrowings and the funds rate spread should not exhibit much change to a constant nonborrowed growth path inasmuch as deposit liabilities and required reserve levels adjust to (interact with) the nonborrowed target.

The validity of the CRR picture painted by monetarists depends on what bankers do in defense of illiquidity. At the outset of the manuscript, it was explained why large banks buy deposits (and Fed funds) rather than liquidate loan or investment assets as the first line of defense against Fed-imposed illiquidity. Such actions do not affect reserve availability, only the efficiency with which existing reserve credit is utilized. Econometric proof for academicians is unfortunately lacking because of the impossibility thus far of statistically isolating all short-term determinants of liability management actions. Yet there seems to be a very simple way to find out just what bankers do in defense of illiquidity: ask them! And this is precisely what Money Market Services has done over the years.

Without known exception, officials of large banks make reserve adjustments through the funds market, the discount facility, and the depo market long before any appreciable portfolio adjustment is made by allowing short-term investments to mature without replacement. Forced liquidation of portfolio holdings (selling into secondary markets) does occur as a short-term adjustment, but only on rare occasions among large banks, and only as a second line of liquidity defense. Within six months, reserve adjustments increasingly require security and loan portfolio adjustments to tighter reserve conditions.

Reserve position surprises at large banks rarely provoke contemporaneous adjustments outside of the Fed funds and Eurodollar markets. Asset management adjustments to changing reserve conditions are based on reserve trends extending well beyond any two-week reserve maintenance period. Liquidity adjustments used by large banks do not vary from LRR to CRR.

Not one monetarist has ever publicly produced one witness from large bank management to verify the crux of the CRR claim. The monetarist theory is so convincing that its proof has never been widely sought. Yet a more traditional view is challenged for empirical proof, as large bank surveys fail to impress the highly sophisticated mindset of academicians. An appeal is made to the reader to at least consider that the weight of evidence is clearly on the side of the traditionalist claim that CRR represents no value added.

A traditional view might, moreover, be used to suggest that CRR actually further weakened the Fed's influence on monetary growth. Recalling the game of musical chairs depicted in the second chapter (and described again in different terms above), it can be seen that the time over which reserve borrowing pressures invade asset management policies depends on the frequency of exposure to potential administrative discipline at the discount window. This, in turn, depends more on the periodicity of settlement periods than on the number of business days. Taking, for example, a reserve maintenance period of one year, nonborrowed reserve shortages would obviously force repeated bank reserve borrowings within the settlement period, which immediately incurs administrative discipline (including possible denial of borrowing access). However, a given shortage of nonborrowed reserves to required reserves (under CRR or LRR) will not necessarily prompt a borrowing exposure to discipline within 45 business days, though such is easily triggered by a settlement date after only 5 or 10 days. No empirical evidence exists for an imagined statistical reverse; in-depth banking experience and logic are unfortunately required to understand how a settlement date (day) hastens the time of reconciliation with the Fed.

A periodicity of weekly settlements rather than bi-weekly settlements increases the frequency of disciplinary risks associated with reserve restraint by a multiple of two. It follows, then, that weekly settlement periods have twice the time efficiency of restraining bank credit extensions compared with bi-weekly settlements. The issue of settlement periodicity is not indigenous to the issue of CRR, but the bi-weekly settlement unfortunately accompanied CRR's installation in 1984, which is another reason why it can be argued that the CRR program weakened the reserve linkage to bank credit growth.

Congressional "oversight" means overseeing delegated authority, but is more aptly defined as impaired vision insofar as the importance of reserve requirements and reserve accountability are concerned.

A final note may seem too obvious to mention, but it is important to appreciate the potential synergism derived from proper coordination of the three tools of monetary control: open market operations, discount administration, and reserve requirements.

CHAPTER 8

Fed Independence

INTRODUCTION

Everyone respects the power of money, but some do not respect the way in which the Federal government uses its power of coinage. Money creation is under the jurisdiction of people who are, in part, distinguished by the law degrees they possess as senators and members of Congress, particularly those assigned to Senate and House banking committees. Some of these committee members do possess economic degrees, and a few have gained considerable financial and monetary experience by virtue of their committee tenure.

To many voters, the power of coinage is too awesome to entrust to politicians, a view not fully shared by the authors of the Constitution, which entrusted the power of coinage to Congress. The fact that this power was delegated by Congress to the Federal Reserve, which Congress established, does not displace the Congressional power of coinage; only a change in the Constitution can accomplish this. Yet any time Congress meddles too deeply into the delegated monetary affairs of the Fed, there is often a publicly expressed concern that the Fed's independence is being compromised. What independence?

In most countries, the central bank reports directly to a Treasury department or finance minister. In the United States, however, legislative founders of the Federal Reserve System sought to insulate the central bank from political pressures by allowing for autonomy in the System's operations. The Fed is a quasi-independent agency in that its actions need not be ratified by the executive branch of the government, though the President retains the power of appointing the members of the Board of Governors. Appointments are subject to approval by the Senate, and the Board also must report its policy decisions to Congress.

Constitutionally, the Congress is entitled to delegate its power of coinage and to oversee the performance of the agency that receives this power. Though equipped with the authority to change the structure of the agency that it has created for this purpose, historically Congress has been reluctant to interfere with central bank policy but at the same time has been unwilling to make the Board directly accountable to the Administration. The belief persists that policy decisions of the Federal Reserve should be independent of the political ambitions of the President and members of Congress.

The Constitutional principle of separating executive and legislative powers is being upheld, but there is growing concern that the Board of Governors does not report to anyone, despite its influence over financial and economic conditions. Some ''conservatives'' continue to protect the Fed's independence, but some ''liberals'' are questioning the propriety of the present accountability structure.

The purpose of this chapter is to examine the current debate on Fed accountability. What are the issues of the debate and what is the actual relationship between the Fed and the Administration?

THE PRESIDENT AND HIS APPOINTEES

Despite the President's power to appoint Federal Reserve Board members, executive influence over Federal Reserve policies has been minimal. Although initially sympathetic to Administration views, nominees have often changed their policy perspective after in-service indoctrination by Fed staffers and peer group interaction. Within a year, new Board members may well vote for policy actions which their nominating President deplores. Some Presidents have met frequently with the Federal Reserve Chairman and requested changes in policy. However, the influence of such requests is limited by the fact that members of the Board, including the Chairman, are not accountable to nor removable by the President. Other types of Presidential appointments may also experience a change in policy dispositions, depending partly on the depth of relevant experience they are able to apply in appointed positions.

The President's nominating strategy is partly to blame for this lack of loyalty. Unlike Presidential appointments to the Supreme Court, where nominees are experienced jurists, appointees to the Federal Reserve Board sometimes lack expertise in monetary and financial market economics. There are notable exceptions, of course. Though President Carter had scant familiarity with the Fed and with monetary policy, his nominee for Fed Chairman, Paul Volcker, had years of Fed staff experience. Nevertheless, Volcker's background did not insure Carter against the Chairman's subsequent actions that raised the prime rate above 20 percent, depressed the economy, and contributed significantly to President Carter's defeat at the polls in 1980. In this example, Presidential influence on policy was weakened by his lack of relevant experience. Suffice it to say that harmony between the White House and the Fed depends partly on the depth of understanding of monetary principles by the President and his nominees. Such observation does not have much bearing on how well each will ultimately serve in their government posts.

There is a Wall Street bias, however, in favor of those Board nominees having monetary experience. And there seems to be a public misconception that the President has considerable monetary policy influence by virtue of his power to nominate Board members.

CONGRESS AND THE FED

It is somewhat surprising to the average voter that Congress, not the President, has the greatest amount of potential influence on Fed policies. The voter misunderstanding probably evolves from an impression that Congress has not done much to impose restraint upon the Fed with regard to general policy objectives and methods. In other words, Congress seems to have delegated its power of coinage without many strings attached. If Fed independence is to be preserved, just what discretionary authority do the people want Fed officials to have?

The crux of the Fed independence issue, and the associated relationship of Congress with the Fed, seems to be limited to policy making that determines how monetary tools of control are to be used. For the moment, however, it may be helpful to "back into" the crux of independence by first considering what is *not* part of the independence issue.

Congress has created and defined parameters of monetary tools of control. Of course, open market operations were developed at the Fed, but later had to be sanctioned by Congress. There seemed to be no argument that direct Congressional involvement was required for establishing monetary tools, because this was linked with Congressional structuring of the central banking system.

Congressional establishment of monetary goals seems to approach a sensitive area in which the Congressional role of "advise and consent" has been used. Whereas Congress was proactive in regards to monetary tools, it was essentially reactive in matters of monetary objectives (not to include Fed regulatory objectives). From a theoretical viewpoint, however, it is hard to comprehend how Congress can delegate the enormous power of coinage to Fed officials without telling them precisely what goals the Fed must pursue in using such power. It should, in theory, be the Fed's role to "advise and consent" and the role of Congress to dictate monetary goals. The only delegation thus involves how monetary tools are to be used to achieve well-defined goals (and related priorities). Such use is derived from monetary policy decisions which the public seems to insist on keeping independent of political ambitions.

One suspected reason why Congress has taken a reactive stance on the question of monetary goals is a lack of monetary understanding. Such required understanding of monetary issues is restricted because of language barriers created partly by the Fed's veil of secrecy.

THE FED'S VEIL OF SECRECY

Every central bank operates behind some veil of secrecy. Immediate public knowledge of every policy discussion and decision would unnecessarily disrupt the financial markets. The Fed is far more secretive than other central banks. Fed officials are evasive when asked about their policy strategies. For example, Congress is currently told that the Fed targets reserve levels for open market operations. Such targeting occurs, but only for the purpose of controlling the funds rate and other money rates. Fed officials have sometimes told Congress that policies remained essentially unchanged when, in fact, policy changes had been accurately detected by financial market participants.

Congress can oversee Fed policies by reviewing Federal Open Market Committee (FOMC) minutes. These summary minutes were released with a 90-day delay until the Freedom of Information Act forced a quicker release. Nonetheless, the FOMC continues to insist that the minutes of each meeting not be released until *after* the subsequent meeting. This means that the markets, the Congress, and the public *never* have full information available on the FOMC policy that is *currently* in effect.

Congress urged an immediate release, but Fed officials insisted that summary minutes could not be prepared for public release within 30 days of each meeting and that a quicker release might disrupt debt markets. Debt market participants have long suspected that Fed officials correct (rewrite) summary minutes of one meeting at the subsequent meeting, in order to hide inter-meeting policy reversals, and thus portray a consistent policy image. This would mean that not all inter-meeting phone conferences are duly reported (another strong suspicion on Wall Street).

Congressmen complained that the summary minutes were too poorly written and too general to provide any meaningful information. Fed officials insisted these minutes represented their best and most candid effort, a claim that market participants found debatable but which Congressmen did not challenge.

The secrecy examples cited thus far are a bit trite, yet have been of concern to Congressional banking committees. A major concern should be that of cunning deception by Fed officials, an accusation which the reader can judge.

When the Fed was pegging the funds rate, Fed officials told Congress that only money supply relative to money demand determines interest rate levels; and the only Fed target employed was a money supply target (principally M1). Did the Fed have a right to hide behind its veil of secrecy, to keep from Congressional view the fact that interest rate control was indeed sought to regulate money demand? Fed officials accurately presented their policy beliefs, but were they deceptive?

Fed officials have a responsibility to counsel Congress on fiscal deficit effects. Their advocation of reduced deficits has been realistically laced with promises of lower interest rates. This advocation, however, enters into deception when trying to deny most of the Fed policy impacts on interest rate levels, leaving fiscal policy as the dominant culprit. Repeating a previous example, Chairman Volcker assured Congress in the summer of 1982 that there was no "magic wand" the Fed could wave to reduce high interest rates created by rising fiscal deficits. Surely he knew that the discount rate was a "magic wand" because the Fed within weeks began lowering the discount rate, and within five months interest rates fell dramatically in spite of rising fiscal deficits.

At the present time, it would be safe to assume that banking committee members believe the Fed to be targeting reserve borrowings instead of the funds rate. This bit of deception, however, may expire if Fed officials replace the funds rate with reserve borrowings as the primary operational target, a welcomed change which a few Fed watchers expect to occur prior to the end of 1987.

Turning to policy targets, examples of deception are fewer and a bit less meaningful. After warning Congress to keep an eye on the "money supply ball," Chairman Volcker did not subsequently inform Congress that Fed officials began to look away from money. The truth later shocked some banking committee members.

Former Fed Chairman Burns became rather well-known for his elusive maneuvering behind the veil of secrecy. After stressing the importance of M1-targeting to Congress, above-target M1 growth pushed Congress towards raising an issue of Fed accountability. Dr. Burns side-stepped the issue by calling banking committee attention to more moderate M2 growth and the greater economic importance of M2 growth. The funds rate peg, meanwhile, continued to be adjusted on the basis of M1 rather than M2 growth. Later, when

Congress sought Fed clarification on the M1 versus M2 issue, Dr. Burns held out the importance of both aggregates, with reported Fed policy leanings toward M1 at the time (which had temporarily dipped back within targeted range while M2 rose slightly above target).

When Congress more recently sought information on intermediate policy goals and their priorities, Chairman Volcker rather accurately described the policy arena as a mixing bowl of economic, financial, international, and monetary variables; he called it a ''balanced'' policy approach, and subsequently cited specific variables in an order of presumed priority. There was no substantive interaction of Congress with the Fed on these policy targets; Fed information was rather passively received.

FOMC minutes might represent one of the few coded languages yet to be understood in Washington, D.C. De-coding begins with a proper mindset. As previously mentioned, Fed officials have tried to disavow most responsibility for interest rate changes which, following Governor Wallich's 1983 disclosure of a funds rate target, seemed a bit incongruous. Any defense or insurance against political attack was nonetheless desired. The discount rate, being the most important determinant of interest rate levels, was shielded from public concern by repeated characterizations of this rate as lagging money market trends. Discount rate changes were depicted as merely routine operational adjustments to keep the rate in line with other money rates. Such rate alignments presumably sought to mitigate reserve borrowing abuses, though market participants perceived other motives behind discount rate policy.

To foster public misconceptions about the role of the discount rate, anticipated reductions were commonly preceded by FOMC policy desires to reduce the funds rate to the discount rate level. During 1985 and 1986 there was a sustained disposition of the Board to lower the discount rate in response to sluggish economic growth. The FOMC was also disposed toward easier money rate conditions in spite of persistently rapid monetary growth. FOMC policy was directed towards minimizing the funds rate spread which, apart from economic reasons, kept open the discount rate policy options of the Board.

Because of the FOMC's policy to minimize the funds rate spread, Desk officials were required to keep adjustment borrowings down at minimal levels (about $150 million each day). Such a low reserve borrowing level, against the backdrop of rising excess reserves caused by CRR and clearing balance requirements, required Desk officials to supply nonborrowed reserve credit in significantly greater volume than required reserve levels. Free reserve averages were therefore sustained at relatively high levels.

Such FOMC policy was, in fact, mandating a liberal availability of reserve credit. It was a policy which no one could honestly claim had any degree of reserve restraint whatsoever. Mr. Volcker later reflected back on the 1986 reserve posture of the FOMC, and characterized policy as being quite accommodative. Nonetheless, FOMC minutes during 1985 and 1986 repeatedly characterized FOMC policy as a policy of reserve restraint. Minutes claimed that undesired variations in monetary growth (in light of changing economic conditions) could warrant an inter-meeting change in policy toward somewhat greater or lesser reserve restraint. Not only was reserve restraint absent, but the importance of monetary growth as a policy target was misrepresented. Worse yet, the primary operating target was incorrectly claimed to be reserve conditions (presumably the reserve borrowing target) as opposed to the funds rate target.

The veil of secrecy draped over FOMC minutes during 1985 and 1986 blurred public vision to an extreme. The policy target picture was not very clear, and the picture of the primary operating target and that of policy stance were obtained from the wrong negative. This is one important reason why members of Congress have difficulty making much sense out of Fed information submitted. During legislative hearings, these members of Congress are often forced to give a "thank you" acknowledgement of the Fed chairman's answer to a direct question, when the answer completely side-stepped the question with mind-boggling jargon and not-so-relevant platitudes. The veil of secrecy, in sum, has gone to an extreme of reducing the Fed's accountability to Congress.

If Congress took appropriate initiative to establish and monitor policy goals and targets (intermediate objectives), the Fed's veil of secrecy would be shredded in the very critical area of Congressional oversight responsibility. FOMC minutes should specifically cover any shifting of policy targeting emphasis. Minutes should also accurately reveal changes in operational target priorities so that Congress and the public can better monitor Fed methods used to meet intermediate objectives (and thus long term goals).

The operational directive issued to the Desk by the FOMC should continue to be vaguely worded, which appropriately shields the exact nature of policy adjustments already in effect. These adjustments slowly become clear to market participants, thus fostering orderly market adjustments to policy changes. Such is both the suggested purpose and use of the Fed's veil of secrecy.

DELEGATING THE POWER OF COINAGE

The topic of this section should constantly be reviewed by Congress and the Fed. As a starting point, it is suggested that Congress legislate Federal Reserve broad goals and general priorities of monetary policy. There is no apparent need to change the three generally accepted goals and priorities. The mere act of Congress in this matter helps to develop the proper public recognition that delegation of authority must be accompanied by general orders.

Congress should determine parameters of intermediate objective (policy target) decision-making delegated to the Fed, with the advice and consent of the latter.

The Fed should be required to periodically assess the appropriate use of monetary tools, and publicly present detailed findings to Congressional banking committees for their advice and consent.

Finally, one objective of monetary policy has to be the regulation of money supply growth. But such a target of policy actions has to be well defined and measured. Congress must be assured that the funding of Fed and Congressional staff research is sufficient to begin resolving the definitional and measurement problems of money. It is further suggested that the bank credit aggregate be included in the national monetary picture because it plays a central role in creating and storing our medium of exchange. The bank credit (deposit base) linkage to policy goals is easier to observe than its various monetary subsets, and measurement problems are relatively minor.

THE CALL FOR CONGRESSIONAL ACTION

Apart from problems of confidently including money growth among policy targets, Congress should be carefully examining structured weaknesses caused by its reserve requirement policy and CRR. Higher requirements and broader Fed authority should be authorized as soon as possible. Reserve accountability must be improved. At the same time, however, constraints should be placed on Federal Reserve discount rate authority.

The issue of cost versus non-cost methods by monetary restraint has not been considered by Congress. Decisions or de-facto policies on the method of restraint have enormous economic consequences. The history of errors made by the Fed in this particular policy arena has had brutal economic consequences unknown to Congress. This is why the cost versus non-cost issue probably warrants immediate Congressional attention.

An equal priority item on the Congressional agenda is to bring money back into the policy picture, and keep it there. It increasingly appears that the excessive monetary growth of recent years will foster a renewal of inflation in future years that once again compromises our national quest for full utilization of economic resources. Quite likely, a student in the next century, looking back at this century's monetary binges in such countries as Germany and Israel, will find it difficult to understand how Americans could ignore the inevitable inflationary consequence of prolonged high rates of monetary growth. Congress also has hindsight. A glance at the rear-view mirror should reveal oncoming forces that could overtake us without some steady steering control over money supply growth in the future.

Index

The Author

Robert A. Jones is highly regarded as one of the most successful Fed Watchers of his time. He pioneered the on-line financial analysis industry, and founded the well-known firm of Money Market Services (MMS). Through a worldwide economics staff, MMS serves 7,000 institutional clients including governments and central banks.

Mr. Jones also founded Market News Service, and the International Institute for Economic Advancement.

Mr. Jones is perhaps the only economist to accurately predict the dramatic rise in interest rates during the late seventies, and their record decline in 1982. Since 1985, he has been warning of a renewal of inflationary pressures, for a number of reasons explained in this book.

Power of Coinage contains an abundance of new information regarding the functioning of financial markets and the Federal Reserve. The historical perspective used in much of the book enables less knowledgeable readers to quickly grasp important monetary concepts. Startling conclusions reached are used to criticize Congressional monitoring of its delegation of the power of coinage to the Federal Reserve.